Female Domination

An exploration of the male desire for Loving Female Authority

By

Elise Sutton

Female Domination
An exploration of the male desire for Loving Female Authority

ISBN 1-4116-0325-7

Dedications

To my Mother: Although you will never read this dedication, it was you who first taught me the true meaning of Loving Female Authority.

To my Husband: Thank you for teaching me that real masculinity is expressed through genuine submission. Your life is a living testimony that man is exalted only when he is willing to be humbled. You are the 24/7 love of my life.

To Kathy and James: Thank you for your support and diligence. This book would not have been possible without your help.

To all the people who are mentioned in this book: Thank you for being willing to share the private and intimate details of your life so that others may benefit.

To the female readers of this book: Thank you for having the courage to explore this subject. It is my hope that this book will motivate you to dream big dreams in life and it is my hope that you will find romance with a man who will strive with you to make those dreams come true.

To the male readers of this book: It is my hope that this book will speak to you and answer some of the questions you have struggled with. Thank you for not giving up on your desires, even though they may go against what society has taught you. It is my prayer that every man will experience loving female authority at some point in his life.

Disclaimer:

This book explores controversial sexual activities. Neither the author of the book nor its publisher assumes any responsibility for the exercise or misuse of the practices described in this book.

The sexual lifestyles discussed in this book are between consenting adults who are experienced and educated about their lifestyle choices. Although the author is open about her sexuality and lifestyle choice, she by no means is encouraging the readers of this book to engage in any activity that is discussed within this book. She encourages those who are interested in these lifestyle choices to become educated so they can take all care and precautions to reduce risk, anticipate problems and when necessary, to avoid risky activities.

The author's opinions and commentaries are just that, her opinion based on her years of experience with alternative lifestyles. Her advice and observations are not professional advice based on her career field. Likewise, the people quoted within this book are only giving their observations based on personal experience. It is the responsibility of the reader to become educated about the risks involved in these lifestyle choices.

Those who practice D&S make a real and explicit distinction between consenting acts between adults for mutual pleasure and any and all acts of violence against non-consenting partners. Imposing any sexual act on a reluctant partner is immoral and offensive. Imposing it on an unwilling partner is a criminal offense. Additionally, the law varies from state to state so each person needs to know what is legal and what is illegal in their state when it comes to sexual practices and activities.

This purpose of this book is to explore and promote loving female authority between consenting partners.

Contents

Preface

The purpose of this book is to examine the Female Domination lifestyle. What is Female Domination? Why do men desire Female Domination? How do couples practice Female Domination in today's society? We will discover that Female Domination is a large tent with many forms, expressions and lifestyles contained therein. I will share the personal and intimate experiences of forty different couples who have incorporated Female Domination into their relationships. Some couples like Female Domination to be soft and sensual, some like it hard and rough, some like it wild and trend setting, some like it romantic, some like it untraditional, some like it primarily in the bedroom, and some like it both inside and outside the bedroom. Regardless of the flavor, most claim to have better marriages and relationships thanks in large part to the Female Domination lifestyle.

We will witness how Female Domination can build the bond of intimacy and trust between couples. We will discover how Female Domination can defuse arguments, relieve stress, transport sex to a higher level than just the physical, empower women in society, and inject excitement into the mundane tasks of life like household chores. We will see how Female Domination can satisfy the inner male child, build up a woman's self-esteem, add spice to the bedroom, re-ignite romance, and cause a power exchange within the female/male relationship. We will discover how society is evolving toward Female rule, one relationship at a time.

We will also examine the why from a psychological perspective. For if we understand why men have submissive desires toward the female gender, where these desires originate from, and how common these desires are within men, we will see that what some have considered to be perversion or anti-social behavior, is in fact normal and natural. I believe society is changing and a power exchange is occurring and I hope that the readers of this book will better understand that power exchange.

My personal experience with Female Domination began in the early 1980's while I was attending college. I frequented a pansexual support and educational group that dealt with Dominance and Submission (D&S) within personal relationships. My original purpose for attending a meeting of this D&S group was to do research for a paper on human sexuality. I will never forget how nervous I was and how uneasy I felt when I walked into that room for the first time. There were about thirty people present, of which twenty-five were men. I could feel every eye upon me, looking me over and checking me out. I persevered and by the time the night was over, I was beginning to feel comfortable. Since it was an introduction meeting for first-timers, nothing strange or out of the ordinary occurred. It was basically people of this D&S group explaining who they were and what they were about. My curiosity was peaked that night and I found this subject of D&S to be most fascinating.

There was a social time after the meeting and I mingled with some of the people, asking many questions. What I discovered was that the majority of these first-timers were men who wanted to be in the submissive role to a woman. Basically, they were in search of a woman who would dominate them sexually. Since it was a pan-sexual group, there were some self-proclaimed dominant men but most of the males present at this meeting wanted to be in the submissive role. I found this to be quite interesting. I was a so-called feminist and while I was hearing lectures in college on how women were struggling to gain equality in our society, here was a room full of men that did not want women to be their equals but rather their superiors.

I grew up in a traditional, male-dominated household, therefore I struggled with my upbringing and the patriarchal societal programming that had indoctrinated me since I was a little girl. I have always been a spiritual person, a Christian, who loves God and Jesus. While I am thankful for my religious upbringing in that it made me a God-conscience individual, the Catholic Church and its male dominated hierarchy force-fed me a theology that made me view my gender in an unflattering light. This was a major stumbling block for me as I tried to succeed in a so-called man's world. Feminism appealed to me but I never did buy into the male hating dogma that so many of my female professors and some of my girlfriends preached. I liked men and I actually hung around more with boys than with girls. This was true in my childhood and this was true in college. I developed a love and a respect for the male gender but I also began to realize the male gender's many weaknesses. I discovered that women possessed the superior intellect and a much higher moral character.

I kept most of my thoughts and evolving philosophy to myself, trying my best to fit within this male dominated society. I was always an out-going woman but I never considered myself to be dominant. I certainly had never heard of Female Domination or Female Supremacy but this D&S group had opened the door to a whole new world. It was a safe-haven, away from societal expectations, where men could express their true natures and women could experiment with a whole new side of their personality, a side that was frowned upon in society and in religion. Here, men could be submissive and women could be dominant.

I was invited back by this group and while I convinced myself that I was attending purely for educational and research purposes, the fact was that I had become curious and interested in this alternative lifestyle. The next week I met more of the regulars and while there were an increased number of women, it was apparent that the submissive men were the driving force behind this group. The men far outnumbered the women and that would be the case week in and week out. Needless to say, being a female, I became quite popular in a hurry.

As I socialized and conversed with the members of this D&S group, I met a woman who invited me to a luncheon made up of exclusively dominant women. I accepted her invitation and attend this luncheon. There I met some of the most fascinating women I had ever encountered. Most of them were employed in the field of professional Domination. They had male clients who paid them a healthy sum of money to be sexually dominated. The woman who invited me to this luncheon was a professional Dominatrix and I formed a very close friendship with her. I learned much from her about D&S and Female Domination. I even worked with her for a short time, agreeing to do professional Domination when one of her clients requested a session with two dominant women.

The money was great for part-time work and the education I received about D&S was invaluable.

I continued to research D&S and in particular, Female Domination. I evolved in my own personal growth and I became a self-described Female Supremacist. By my definition, a Female Supremacist is a woman who believes that women are the superior sex over men. She is a woman who has come to believe that society would be better served if it were governed by women instead of men. A Female Supremacist believes that women should be in positions of authority, from government clear down to marriage, where the wife should rule over the husband. A Female Supremacist believes that women and men are not equal but rather different. She believes that they both have strengths and weaknesses, but that the woman has more strengths than the man and that she contains the traits that is best fitted to be in a position of authority.

I majored in Psychology and minored in Sociology in college. I wanted to use my education, so when my friend encouraged me to become a professional Dominatrix like her, I declined. However, I remained an active member in the D&S community and I eventually decided to combine my two loves in life, Female Domination and Psychology. I offered more than just a D&S session, I also offered counseling if a male client wanted to better understand why he desired to be sexually dominated by a woman. I placed an ad in the City paper as well as in a few of the publications where my Dominatrix friend advertised, and before I knew it, I had myself a small but loyal clientele. Over the next decade, I developed a rather large clientele, offering a combination of professional Female Domination, counseling and practical advice.

I start with each person that I counsel from the basis that they are special and a valuable creation made by God. I don't believe that God makes mistakes and thus I don't feel a person is perverted or a mistake of nature. With that as the foundation, I am then able to be non-judgmental. I believe that God is the judge, not us. I don't believe we were put here on this Earth to criticize, judge, or condemn other human beings. We are not to judge others unless we want to be judged ourselves. Who am I to say that another person's sexual desires or core nature is wrong? I have my own desires that others may feel are unusual. Each of us has our own unique nature, personality and temperament. With that in mind, I can be open minded and understanding as I listen to others bare their soul to me.

I have my core beliefs and I am a person of Faith. I believe in right and wrong and I believe in morality. I don't think that all behavior is acceptable and I don't believe that society should tolerate or ignore destructive or dangerous behavior in human beings. However, when it comes to the subjects of human sexuality, domination and submission, and male submissive desires, I feel that I am a bit of an expert based on years of study, observation and participation. What I have learned is that there are reasons why men have these desires and a person's core nature expresses itself in the sexual realm through different sexual desires. It is important to understand why people do what they do but it is more important to care for the person who is struggling with life or with themselves. Most people do not need to hear that they are wrong but rather that they are special. That has always been my approach.

I have researched Female Domination and male submission for over twenty years. I have counseled with submissive men and female dominant couples and I have interviewed many couples that practice this lifestyle in varying degrees. I have personally lived this lifestyle and I still actively practice this lifestyle. This book is based on my many years of searching, seeking, asking, learning and living Female Domination.

I realize that the D&S community encompasses many different lifestyles and that Female Domination is only one of the flavors of the D&S community. This book is not about the D&S community in totality but is solely about Female Domination and male submission. There have been a number of excellent books written about D&S and BDSM. This book is different because it separates Female Domination from the other flavors of D&S and strictly focuses on Female Domination and its societal impact; past, present and future. Female Domination is unique because most of our institutions are patriarchal. Society is evolving and the empowerment of women is not isolated from the desire of men wanting to submit to women both sexually and socially. This book will examine the correlation between the two and the current trend in societal evolution.

I must forewarn the readers that this book will talk about some very intense and controversial sexual practices. I will be sharing the lifestyles of real people who are not unlike your family members, the people you work with or the people you socialize with. I want this book to be both educational and entertaining. I will try my best to be descriptive without being too graphic but in some cases, being descriptive will strike some as being graphic. This book will no doubt arouse, titillate, shock and challenge. However, it is my hope that above all it will enlighten and educate.

Introduction

So what is Female Domination? The entire term seems to be a contradiction to our male dominated society. Female Domination (or FemDom as some refer to it) did not originate from dominant women or feminists. It was men who coined the phrase Female Domination to categorize their sexual and social desires to submit themselves to the female gender. So is Female Domination merely a sexual fantasy that some men harbor or is it a reflection of a societal evolution?

A little over twenty years ago, I was first introduced to the concept of Female Domination when I attended a meeting of a pansexual organization that dealt with Dominance and submission (D&S) within personal relationships. What was most telling about this group (that welcomed anyone who desired to be sexually dominant or submissive) was the majority of the members were submissive men in search of a dominant woman. There were self-proclaimed dominant women in attendance but the submissive men outnumbered them at least twenty to one. Since I was present at this group for the purpose of educating myself further in my studies of Human Sexuality, I interviewed some of the dominant women and submissive men in an informal manner. Being a rather outgoing and aggressive female myself, I found myself attracted to this world of Female Domination.

My curiosity in Female Domination has developed into twenty plus years of studying and practicing this alternative lifestyle. I have educated myself about the subjects of Female Domination and male submissive desires. Based on my years of study, observation and participation, I have learned that there are sexual and social reasons why men have submissive desires toward women. I have discovered that a person's core nature expresses itself in the sexual realm through different sexual desires. To the novice, a man that desires to be on the bottom during intercourse is normal but a man who desires to be spanked or whipped by a woman is perverted. However, I have come to understand that both of these fore mentioned desires stem from the same core desire. That desire is to be sexually dominated by a woman. It is expressed differently but it is the same deep-rooted motivation. Not only that, but this deep-rooted nature can evolve and the man that desires to be on the bottom during intercourse today may very well develop a desire to be spanked or whipped by a woman tomorrow.

From studying the practice of Female Domination, I learned about the core natures of both men and women. As a woman who was raised in a so-called male dominant traditional family, it was a revelation to me to discover the natural dominance and supremacy of the female gender over the male gender. This revelation became the key to unlocking and understanding all submissive desires within men. It matters not how these desires are expressed through different fantasies. The root and the core of these are all the same. Namely, the desire of the male gender is to be dominated and ruled by the female gender. Therefore, no expression of this submissive nature surprises me or shocks me. I have heard it all from the males I have interviewed and counseled and I have seen it all through my own participation in the Female Domination lifestyle.

Men desire corporal punishment (being spanked or whipped by a woman), forced feminization (being emasculated by a woman), humiliation, strap-on sex (being the receiver of a woman's rubber phallus), water sports (such as forced enemas or golden showers), and other D&S activities. Men want to worship the female by tending to her physical and sexual needs (body worship) and men want to be made into a domesticated servant to their wives. But the common thread to all these sexual and submissive desires is the longing for loving female authority. To me, that is the true definition of Female Domination. Female Domination is Loving Female Authority. That is what most men are seeking from the female gender. All of these specific fetishes or desires are the outward expressions of a man's need and hunger for loving female authority.

I have been able to help a number of males to come to terms with their desires and their natural submissive nature. Likewise, my knowledge of female domination and its social and sexual importance helps me to share with women why men have these desires and how exploring these desires with them in a safe and sane environment can develop a strong bond of intimacy between the female and the submissive male. I share with women how Domination and submission and more specifically, Female Domination, can be liberating for the woman. It can cause a power exchange within her marriage and that power exchange can be beneficial for both parties.

Before I began counseling with submissive men and before I embraced the female domination lifestyle, I was of the opinion that only a man with a low self-image or a man that was sexually dysfunctional would desire to be dominated in such extreme ways by a woman. However, after over twenty years of studying and practicing this lifestyle, I have discovered that these desires are very common within men. I have concluded that the number one sexual fantasy and desire among men is to be dominated by a woman. Furthermore, I now understand the dynamics about why men desire these things, where these desires originate from, and how they can fit within one's sexuality and personal relationships in a healthy way.

There is a natural born desire within men that causes them to desire to be dominated by a woman. I believe that males are born with this desire and I also believe that this desire is enhanced through a man's childhood experiences with his female authority figures. A male is carried in the womb of a woman, he is birthed into this world by a woman, he is nurtured at the breasts of a woman, he is disciplined by the loving hands of a woman, and he is loved and comforted by a woman. There is a special bond between a young boy and his mother or female guardian. Part of this is sexual. Most of the time, a young boy is bathed, caressed, nurtured and spanked by adult female authority figures and this stirs submissive desires within young boys. When they reach adolescence, a lot of boys begin to experiment with their sexuality, as they are curious and drawn to the female, her beauty and her mysterious ways.

There is usually a form of the desire to submit mixed in with the sexuality. A young boy grows accustomed to being bossed around and dominated by the adult female authority figures in his life. Then when he begins to enter puberty, his sexual fantasies often involve being the helpless sexual victim to one of his adult female authority figures like a teacher or a babysitter. I believe that is when B&D (Bondage and Domination) desires are birthed within men. Not all boys start out their sexual exploration with these types of fantasies but many boys do.

When these boys grow up to be men with submissive desires, they often still maintain the fantasy of being an innocent and helpless boy that is being dominated or sexually used by an adult female authority figure. They recall that their first submissive desires were toward their teacher, babysitter or even their mother and they remember how pleasurable and exciting it was to have these desires. Usually as they happen upon Adult magazines or videos, the stories and scenes where an older woman dominates a young male is what causes them the most intense sexual arousal.

It is a very natural thing for a man to desire to be punished and disciplined by a woman. His mind reverts back to his childhood when the women that he loved the most (namely his mother, aunt, or an older sister) would punish and discipline him. He knew that these women loved him because they punished and disciplined him. An adult male still longs for the feeling of his childhood where his mother or female guardian punished him but then afterwards the male child would be hugged and nurtured by the same woman who punished him. Punishment and love go hand and hand. That is what loving female authority is all about.

As men become adults in this society that expects men to be the dominant gender, most men try to suppress their desire to submit to women. Some are successful at this but many are not. Therefore, the profession of being a Dominant Female was born and it thrives in our current society. The Dominatrix has never been more in demand. One just needs to search the Internet to see the thousands of women who offer professional Female Domination. Supply is becoming plentiful because the Demand was always there.

Where did the Dominatrix come from? Females have always been smart businesswomen. In the old days, there were not too many professions that society would allow women to be employed in. Prostitution is said to be the world's oldest profession and some women chose this guaranteed profit maker due to a lack of career choices. What many ladies of the evening discovered was that when they asked a potential male client what it was he desired sexually, many would say that they wanted to be dominated. Men would ask to be spanked or tied up and whipped. It didn't take the smart business-minded woman long to figure out that she could make more money and have less wear and tear on her body if she would offer men domination instead of sex. Before long, the professional Dominatrix was born.

Today, the majority of professional Dominant Women have never been employed as prostitutes. Dominant women have come to realize that the male urge to submit to a dominant woman is so strong that some men are willing to pay handsomely to be dominated by a woman. Some men are afraid to admit their submissive desires to their wives or girlfriends because they fear they will be rejected or called a pervert. So they seek out submissive fulfillment with a professional Dominatrix. The fascinating thing is that only a true dominant woman can satisfy a man's submissive nature. Today, a prostitute with a whip, who has not discovered her dominant nature, will not satisfy a submissive man. He is looking for a true dominant woman who has the attitude that she is indeed superior to him. Twenty years ago, that was hard to find. Today, however, there are thousands of professional dominant women who are educated and who truly believe that women are the superior gender. Men have never had so many choices when it comes to the professional dominant woman. Supply is starting to satisfy the demand.

A societal evolution is happening when it comes to the roles of the sexes. This bodes well for men because more women are starting to embrace their dominant natures. Women are beginning to desire to dominate men. Many males are finding out that they need not visit a professional Dominatrix to be dominated by a woman. I find it interesting that the number of men who desire to be dominated by women seems to be increasing at a time when women are becoming more liberated. Even though we still live in a so-called male dominated society, there seems to be a societal evolution that is taking place.

Of course we must not kid ourselves. Wives have dominated husbands behind closed doors since the beginning of human history. Single males have teased married men for centuries about being hen-pecked and pussy whipped by their wives. Men have always known deep inside that once they become married, the wife will run the show. But today's modern women are taking that domination a step further. What is different today is that women are not content with being the strong, hidden force behind their men. Women are starting to become dominant outside the home as they are flexing their superiority in college campuses all across our society. In the spring of 2002, fifty-seven percent of all college degrees were earned by women and this fourteen point gap (57-43 percent) is expected to grow more lopsided with each passing year. This dominance in the classroom is starting to translate to dominance in the workforce, in business and in politics.

As women start to excel and become dominant in the workplace and in the business world, this is causing women to exert even more dominance within their personal relationships with men. Whereas wives have always dominated their husbands behind closed doors in a subtle manner, now they are dominating their husbands more openly. They are taking charge of the bedroom, as they are becoming the initiators of sex. They are taking charge of the finances and they are taking charge of the decision-making within the marriage. As women are exerting dominance in these areas, men's submissive natures are stirring and men are desiring to be dominated in all areas of their lives by the female gender.

Some women are still restrained by traditions and societal expectations. Women naturally dominate men within the marriage relationship but not many women like to acknowledge that fact for fear of being a societal outcast. Some women still allow their husbands to appear as the in charge and dominant partner in order to conform to the model of what they witnessed from their parents. The female dominant nature still lies dormant in many women and it takes a male's submissive nature to draw it out. But as women become more successful and more aggressive in the classroom and in the business world, women will more readily embrace their dominant persona and will gladly accept and even demand their male partner's submission. In my opinion, the couples that practice Female Domination today are in front of the societal curve. Female Domination and male submission will be the foremost sexuality of the future. I believe that a majority of women will embrace it in the not too distant future. What some women still consider kinky and unusual today, these same women will embrace it in the future. Furthermore, their daughters will be stretching the limits and boundaries of female domination in areas that we cannot imagine today.

I am impressed with how confident and aggressive the younger women are today compared to when I was in college. The ladies are more intelligent and are out performing the males in the classroom. From talking to teachers and professors, this is happening in almost every area. I see a real occurrence happening in our society. One hundred years ago women could not even vote and very few were being educated. I suspect that in the future, women will be running our society. The societal evolution that is taking place cannot be stopped. Men are sensing this change and this is causing them to become more submissive toward women.

Of course the desire for Female Domination is nothing new. The book "Venus in Furs" by Leopold von Sacher-Masoch was written over 130 years ago. It is about a man with strong masochistic and submissive fantasies. He worships the Goddess Venus and he pursues his fantasies when he meets a wealthy woman named Wanda, with whom he starts a romance. He tells her of his masochism and his desire to be her slave. She agrees to indulge his fantasy out of her love for him but ends up loving being a dominant and sadistic woman and exceeds his wildest expectations. It is a very common story that has been played out in real life by couples over and over again. The man introduces the wife or girlfriend to his submissive fantasies and desires. The wife indulges the husband or boyfriend purely out of her love for him, but the woman grows to love her newly discovered power and dominant nature. Thus, she ends up taking her man deeper into submission to her than he ever dared fantasized about.

In this book, Wanda whips the male character Severin while wearing furs (at his request). This book was written in 1869 and to the author, fur was that day's leather. It was a common European male's fetish for the same reason leather is today. It was the power clothing of its day. Fur represented man's natural conquest through the hunting and dominating of the animal kingdom. When a woman wore fur and disciplined a man, it represented the female conquering and dominating the male. That is what leather represents today. It is the hide of an animal made into a smooth and sexy material. When a woman is adorned in leather, it sends off psychological and subliminal messages to the submissive male. Fur was the leather of the nineteenth-century, Venus is a Goddess, thus the title "Venus in Furs". If the book were written today it would probably be called, "Goddess in Leather".

Not only did Leopold von Sacher-Masoch write books about his desires to be dominated by a woman, he actually pursued these desires in his real life. His first wife actually changed her name to Wanda (after the female character in "Venus in Furs") and she whipped Leopold while wearing furs. Leopold even signed a contract surrendering his life over to his wife, much like the contract the character Wanda drew up in "Venus in Furs". The German neurologist Richard von Krafft-Ebing coined the word "Masochist" from the sexual desires of Leopold von Sacher-Masoch. Today, this book enjoys a cult like following from those who embrace the Female Domination lifestyle. Some have credited "Venus in Furs" with birthing Female Domination into the mainstream of society.

Leather? Whips? Masochism? So is Female Domination really S&M? Hardly! Female Domination is a broad umbrella with many forms and expressions. The desires of Sacher-Masoch are rather common within some men but they are only but one expression of the overall desire to be dominated by a woman. What many classify as being S&M is really nothing more than D&S. The abbreviations D&S (Domination and submission) and B&D (Bondage and Domination) have replaced S&M (Sado-Masochism) in the circles that practice alternative lifestyles.

Many submissive men have explored the world of S&M because that is where they were hoping to meet a lifestyle dominant woman. Most of these men are not masochists but merely submissive. Likewise, most of the women who join these groups are not sadistic but merely outgoing and dominant. Therefore, these groups are now considered D&S groups that cater to a wide range of alternative lifestyles. Some call them D&S groups, some call them BDSM groups (putting the emphasis on the Domination) and some call them Fetish groups.

Thanks to the occasional mentally disturbed criminal and Hollywood sensationalism, the term S&M triggers negative images in the masses. Therefore, the terminology D&S has replaced S&M in defining such groups or organizations that cater to alternative lifestyles that deal with one partner sexually dominating the other. Such BDSM groups like the Eulenspiegel Society in New York city or the Black Rose in Washington DC, attract submissive men as they search for dominant women. Once again, in my opinion, what many of these men are searching for is not merely an alternative form of sexuality but rather loving female authority.

One must understand the submissive male to understand how the female domination lifestyle is fulfilling to him. Not every female domination relationship is the same. Some are more advanced than others based on the desires of the individuals involved. Some couples keep it confined to the bedroom and female domination is a way to spice up their sex lives. Others take it outside the bedroom and into their everyday life. To these couples, female domination is more of a lifestyle and a belief system. Regardless of the degree of the female domination activities, I have found that a majority of the couples who practice female domination claim to have better marriages and relationships than they did prior to practicing female domination. They claim to enjoy deeper intimacy and more fulfilling sex lives.

This makes perfect sense because a female domination relationship requires trust and honesty. When a man trusts his wife enough to open up to her about his deepest, most hidden desires, this sets the stage for intimacy on a more meaningful level. How sad that so many men must keep hidden their innermost being from the woman they have chosen to share their life with. But for those couples who dare to be uninhibited about their desires, they open themselves up to a special kind of intimacy. The man who trusts his wife enough to submit his entire being to her will, bonds with his wife on a level that few husbands have experienced. Likewise, when the wife is trustworthy enough to rule her husband in love, this causes them to bond together in a way that most traditional marriages cannot offer. To these couples, Female Domination is more than sexual. It is also social, emotional and spiritual.

I believe that society is evolving into a female dominant society. Women are starting to take charge. Hollywood and Madison Avenue are capitalizing on the ever-growing male submissive nature as movies, television, and advertising are celebrating the powerful woman. Although the real strength of woman is in her intellectual, social and sexual power, it is easier to show female power via the physical realm. Thus, shows such as "Xena: Warrior Princess", "Dark Angel" and "Alias" are emerging. Men are yielding to the intellectual, social and sexual power in women and this is causing them to desire to be defeated in the physical by the female as well. That is where a lot of the female wresting fantasies within men are originating. That is also why Hollywood and television are celebrating the strong female.

It is hard for men to express and explain the inner power of women so they express it by showing them with physical power. When a woman kicks a man around on television or in the movies, chances are the male viewers are sexually turned on. This is because this act represents the power of the female and men want to submit to it. Just look at the movies that played this past summer at your local theater. "Charlie's Angels", Terminator 3", "The Matrix Reloaded", "Daredevil" and "Lara Croft, Tomb Raider". All of these films have strong, leather wearing female characters with scenes where they physically beat up men. Men know that the real power of women is sexual and intellectual but movies and television simplify it into the physical.

The one movie that truly displayed the sexual power of a woman was "Basic Instinct". The Sharon Stone character, Catherine Tramell, dominated the so-called intelligent men in the movie by using her sexual power combined with her sharp intellect. The director, Paul Verhoeven, was successful in showing the sexual power of women over men through the Sharon Stone character. Remove the psychotic and Hitchcock-like thriller aspects and "Basic Instinct" is a movie about a dominant woman who has her way with the weaker male gender.

Unfortunately, Hollywood rarely takes the time to develop this aspect of a woman's nature and will instead revert to only the physical when they want to show a powerful woman. In the movie "Batman Returns", a number of men went to see the leather wearing, whip wielding Michelle Pfifer as Catwoman. Too bad this film reverted to physical fighting instead of developing Catwoman's sexual power and obvious D&S interests.

Much like the book "Venus in Furs" in the late 1860's, the Catwoman character in the 1960's "Batman" television program played an important role in taking Female Domination and Fetishism into the mainstream. Catwoman was a major influence in igniting the submissive nature within boys as well as within grown men. When I counsel or interview men, it never ceases to amaze me how many of them will point to two female television characters from the 1960's when describing their earliest recollection of having submissive desires. They point to Julie Newmar as Catwoman and Diana Rigg as the leather wearing Emma Peel of "The Avengers". Both of these women were dominant, they wore leather or fetish clothing, and they radiated with a D&S sexuality.

Catwoman left a lasting impression on the sexuality of many men, as they would watch Batman or better yet, boyish Robin, being tied up and teased by the fetish clad and sexy female. The psychological and sociological symbolism of such a scene was very profound as it portrayed how a powerful woman renders men weak and helpless. It was fantasy but the males could identify with it because such scenes stirred their submissive nature.

The male desire for Female Domination is evident throughout Pop Culture and the smart female knows how to capitalize. Madonna has been able to combine music, sexuality and female power into a Pop Culture empire. Her popularity and fan following rivals that of the Beatles and Elvis. Madonna's music and music videos portray an aggressive, sexual and strong woman. Much like Pop Culture itself, Madonna has evolved from being suggestive about Female Dominance (Blonde Ambition) to openly portraying D&S in her music and videos (Erotica).

Shania Twain is another Pop Culture Diva who has successfully combined her music with a public image that depicts female dominance and power. Although her music is of the traditionally more conservative Country variety, Shania is not unaccustomed to posing in fetish clothing in her videos or while on stage (including in front of a worldwide audience during the Super Bowl) and many of her songs celebrate the strong woman. The music of Shania appeals to a totally different audience than that of Madonna, but both of these women have ascended to the top of their extremely competitive industry by appealing to man's desire for female dominance. While both women are very talented from an artistic standpoint, what has brought them success beyond imagination is the dominant and sexual aura they portray. The sexual, powerful female captivates men and Pop Culture in the new Millennium is not shy about promoting the dominant female or capitalizing on the submissive nature of man.

Here in the new Millennium, the battle of the sexes is over but women never viewed it as a battle. Women are no longer deceived into being submissive. Women are assuming their true natures and men cannot overcome dominant women. The submissive nature within men yields to the power of the female. In fact, men desire to submit to the female. It is within every man. The battle of the sexes is reduced to an internal battle within each male, as he tries to come to terms with his submissive desires in a society that expects him to be dominant. Some men take out that inner turmoil on women but it is a losing battle. The Genie is out of her bottle and women are liberated, educated and assuming their true, dominant natures.

Nevertheless, it still often takes a submissive man to draw out the dominance in a woman. Women react to genuine submission. I have had men tell me that after they had a session with a Professional Dominatrix, they returned home to their wife and she began to act more aggressive with them for the next couple of days, not knowing anything about the Dominatrix. It was if the wife could sense the submissive energy that was coming from her husband and was reacting to it. The Dominatrix had taken the husband to subspace and the wife could sense this, which caused her own dormant dominant nature to stir. I have heard a number of similar experiences from men.

Subspace or as I like to call it, the submissive zone, is a tranquil and somewhat hypnotic state that comes from the absolute surrender of the human will. Subspace is obtained within males when they surrender their will and their power over to a female. When a woman dominates a man (be it physical domination or mental domination) there is an energy and a power that she releases. This energy demands and desires submission. When a man surrenders to this power coming from the female, he enters into the submissive zone (or subspace). As he lets go and yields himself to the woman, he disarms his conscience guard and he allows his submissive nature to be released. This causes him to enter into that tranquil and near hypnotic state. That is what is known as subspace.

Subspace is a place of absolute surrender and a place where the female rules supreme. It is a magical place within the psyche of a man where he worships a woman with his spirit. It is powerful and it is beautiful. For only a man who surrenders his will to a woman and enters the submissive zone, can fully see a woman in all her beauty and glory.

One woman told me "After I've disciplined my husband, or humiliated him, or physically dominated him, he kind of lays there, he tilts his head to the side, he gets a grin on his face, and his eyes kind of get glazed over." Her man had entered subspace. That look she was referring to is the look of tranquility, contentment, submission, and genuine love. That look is what the female domination lifestyle is all about. By dominating and disciplining her husband, she struck a chord within him. The submissive male desires to be dominated and disciplined by a woman. Most men long for this inside and spend a good portion of their lives searching for this void to be filled within them. Once they experience the strong yet loving hand of a dominant female whom they trust and love, it fulfills them and it brings to them tranquility and contentment. Her husband had achieved deep subspace.

If all women could see that look on their husband's face or feel that kind of intimacy, they would flock to this lifestyle. Unfortunately, many women just see the leather outfits, the whips, and the techniques that dominant women use to get their men into that magical state of deep submission, and they think that this lifestyle is "strange" or "bizarre". If they would only look past the tools that dominant women use and the techniques that they utilize, and if they would instead focus on the results that they bring, then I believe that most women would openly embrace the Female Domination lifestyle. Women are searching for that kind of intimacy and that kind of relationship. If they would only understand that most men need to be dominated, disciplined, and controlled by a woman in order to be at peace within himself, then I am convinced the majority of women would assume their proper place, which is to be the dominant wife and the dominant woman.

Female Domination is still a minority lifestyle between couples. The professional Dominatrix thrives in our society because the majority of submissive men still must seek out Female Domination outside his home. Many men are eager to surrender themselves over to their wives but they hesitate because they fear their wives might reject them. The biggest obstacle to a female domination relationship is still the reluctance of the female. This just goes to show how successful our male dominated society has been in making women feel inferior to men. As women, we have been programmed since childhood that the man should be the dominant partner in a relationship or marriage. It is never easy to overcome our upbringing and our traditions. Women still struggle with thoughts that Female Domination is "abnormal". This is especially true if they were raised in a strict religious upbringing. Women struggle with the guilt that they may be going against what God has designed.

The first time I was exposed to this lifestyle, I thought it to be strange and perverted. I went in viewing these people as being sexually dysfunctional. However, I soon learned that most of these people were healthy and normal. There were people from all walks of life, religious backgrounds, and professions that were members of the D&S group I attended. Now I will confess that there are extremes that people go to with D&S that is not healthy but that is the same with all things. Eating is not a negative habit but taken to extremes, it can be unhealthy. The same goes for a person's sexuality. From my years of studying and living this lifestyle, I can tell you that the desire of a man to submit to a woman is not perverted. As a matter of fact, it is very common among men. I believe it is the number one sexual desire among men living in our society. Perversion is defined as that which is outside the sexual normal. Domination and submission is very much within the normal of people's sexual desires.

What women must keep in mind about Female Domination is the fact that men need it. It is almost always the man who will introduce the female domination lifestyle to the woman. A courageous man with submissive desires introduces female domination to his female partner. Why do men do this? It's because men desire and need to be in submission to women. No matter how hard society or religion tries to tell men differently, something deep inside of them yearns to surrender to a powerful woman. These desires grow stronger with age and men will spend countless hours dreaming and fantasizing about Female Domination. Men will pursue these desires and struggle with these desires trying to come to terms with them but sadly a man will not come to terms with these desires until he truly has a relationship with a woman that can explore these desires with him in a loving manner.

The other side of this dynamic is that women who embrace the dominant role and who allow their dominant nature to come out, end up absolutely loving this lifestyle. It never ceases to amaze me how many women who once were real hesitant about being dominant, end up loving it so much that they later say that they would never go back to being in submission to a man or only having vanilla sex (intercourse) with a man. This lifestyle is liberating to women and it is also liberating for men as they can now fulfill that yearning within them.

The number of couples who practice the Female Domination lifestyle has exploded over the past twenty years. Most of these couples keep it private but I can testify from the number of letters I receive that Female Domination is on the rise in our society. It may not enjoy a plurality yet but one only needs to look at the trends and the societal evolution that is taking place to see what is transpiring. As women continue to become dominant in college, in business and in politics, more women will naturally take the dominant role in their marriages and relationships. This is great news for the submissive male.

As far as the D&S stuff goes, that depends on each woman and on each relationship. A female domination relationship can take on many forms. Lots of dominant women do embrace the whole leather and B&D scene for these activities do provide great tools in the training and the disciplining of her man, as well as adding fun and excitement to their sex lives. Other women enjoy a softer D&S relationship, as they prefer a Victorian type of discipline and training of their men. Still other women love to be the dominant partner and love to rule the marriage but they do not like to incorporate D&S. Some women are Female Supremacists, while other women see themselves as Feminists and others see themselves as equals with men but with the belief that the wife needs to lead the husband.

The most important thing is that each couple must keep the lines of communication open, as honesty and openness are crucial in a female domination relationship. A woman needs to be open minded to explore new things as her submissive shares with her his deepest desires. It is all about negotiation and fulfillment. I ask women, what touches his submissive nature? Does he have a leather fetish? If so, then wear some leather. Does he have a foot or a boot fetish? Does he crave whippings or spankings? Does he enjoy the helpless feeling of being in bondage? I tell women to find out what stirs her man's submission and then do these things to him. A smart woman will take a man's submission and channel it into his service of her. A wise woman will use her dominance to draw out more of her man's submission and then use that submission to get her needs met and fulfilled.

I like to equate D&S as a dance. The man seduces the female's dominant nature with his submissive nature. She then begins to draw out more of his submissive nature with her dominant nature, which draws out even more of her dominance, which draws out more of his submission, and so on and so on. D&S works much like a magnetic force, with two opposites attracting. The Female's dominance feeds off of the man's submission and his submission feeds off of her dominance. The one needs the other to thrive and to grow. It is similar to how the plant world and the animal world function with the plants giving us the oxygen we need and we in return give the plants the carbon dioxide they need. As we breathe in their gift we give them our gift as we exhale. So goes it with Dominance and submission. The female gives the male what he needs by dominating him and the male gives her his gift by submitting to her and treating her like his Queen.

Most women would love to have a husband that loves, honors, worships, and obeys her. Young girls dream about a Prince who comes along and treats her like a Queen. What woman wouldn't want a man that would focus his energy and his attention on her all of the time? A man that would pamper her, give her foot and body massages, and who would get more pleasure out of pleasuring her than receiving pleasure himself. How about a man that would do whatever she told him to do, without arguing or complaining? A man that would not only do all of his chores like cutting the grass and washing the cars, but would also do housework, the laundry, the grocery shopping, and even the cooking. How about a man that would wine and dine her and shower her with gifts? What woman would not want a man that would love her with all of his heart and who would view her as his earthly Goddess? The dominant female lives this dream because she has learned how to motivate her man to serve her needs by meeting his need to be dominated. That is the beauty of the Female Domination lifestyle.

The Female Domination lifestyle is a large umbrella that encompasses a wide variety of lifestyles and D&S activities. The common denominator is that the woman is the dominant partner but as you will see, Female Domination can be expressed in many forms. Female Domination is important because while it is a desire that primarily expresses itself in a man's sexuality, it reflects the core desire within the male gender. It is that male desire for loving female authority that ultimately empowers women, one relationship at a time.

Chapter One

The Submissive Nature of Man

No temptation has seized you, except what is common to man.
(I Corinthians 10:13 NIV)

Henry Adams came to see me in the summer of 1998. Henry was a successful forty something businessman who had been married for fifteen years to his wife, Doris. He was a typical client of mine, a married man with a secret that he never shared with the woman who was the love of his life. Like a lot of men, Henry harbored a deep desire to be sexually dominated by a woman.

As Henry nervously fumbled through his confession to me, I could almost predict what he was going to say next. I had heard it all before from dozens of other men. Henry recalled having submissive fantasies since he was a teenager. He didn't know where they originated from but he recalled that whenever he saw a scene in a movie or television program where a woman was aggressive or dominant with a man, he became extremely sexually aroused. Whenever he saw a woman wearing leather or portraying any kind of dominant image in a magazine or a book, he would become weak as if he were being tied down without any actual ropes. Even just a certain look on a woman's face in an advertisement in a magazine would cause Henry to be overcome with submissive feelings toward the female gender.

Henry explained that as he discovered pornography, he noticed it was the images or stories of women being the sexual aggressor that excited him. Stories about older women who seduced and sexually dominated younger men especially aroused him. He also was drawn to pictures of leather wearing and whip wielding women, who collared men and placed them in bondage. Before he knew it, only pornography that dealt with women dominating men excited Henry. He would buy a Penthouse magazine and skim the letters in the front, looking for ones that were about a wife dominating her husband or an older woman dominating a younger man. Then he would fantasize and masturbate with the thought of him being the dominated husband or the dominated younger man. Eventually he discovered magazines that openly catered to the male fantasy of women dominating men.

Henry did not like viewing pornographic material. He was raised in a conservative, middle class family, he was active in his church, he had loving parents, and he was never sexually or emotionally abused. Henry had a very healthy relationship with his mother and was taught to treat women with respect. Henry was also taught that pornography was morally wrong and should be avoided. However, no matter how hard he tried to suppress his submissive fantasies, they kept coming back on him. He could not overcome his desire to be sexually dominated by a woman. Pornography was an outlet where Henry could turn to engage his submissive desires.

These submissive desires would come upon Henry out of left field, when he least expected them. All it would take was a scene of a dominant woman in a movie or a television program and his submissive desires would come over him and dominate his thoughts. Henry struggled with these desires his entire adult life. He dated and eventually met the love of his life, Doris. He never told a soul about his secret desires or his pornography habit. He tried his best to suppress these desires and live the kind of life that society expected out of him. Outwardly, he was the so-called head of his marriage (although his wife made most of the decisions because Henry usually yielded to her wishes). Henry loved Doris and he wished he could be in submission to her but he dared not tell her of his secret desires because he was afraid of being rejected by her and becoming a societal outcast.

Henry would suppress his submissive feelings the best he could but once he married Doris, those desires once again came upon him when he least expected them. Henry recalled the time he was watching television and the 1977 Robert Aldrich film "The Choirboys" aired. One of the characters in "The Choirboys" was a woman who was employed as a Dominatrix. There is a scene where this woman places one of her clients in bondage and whips him. Henry was not expecting this but that is all it took to send Henry deep into submission and back to wandering through Adult bookstores in the dark of night, searching for some magazines with images and stories about Female Domination. Henry felt powerless to resist whenever this desire to be in submission to a woman would come upon him.

In the early 1990's, Henry came across a magazine called DDI, "Dominant Directory International". It was a magazine dedicated to the professional Dominatrix. It was page after page of women advertising their services of professional Domination. Henry lived eighty miles from a major city where a half dozen or so professional Doms advertised in DDI. Henry decided that he needed for his fantasy to become a reality. Henry contacted some of these women from DDI and after backing out a number of times due to being nervous, Henry finally visited his first Pro Dom in 1994. He battled guilt, as he did not want to be unfaithful to his wife. However, the Pro Dom he chose reassured him that no sex would occur as she was only offering domination. Henry could not resist any longer. He had to experience what it would be like to be dominated by a woman.

Henry visited an attractive and reputable Dominatrix whom he met through her ad in DDI. She had him fill out an in-depth questionnaire to specify exactly what his fetish and submissive desires were. Henry did not know precisely what he wanted but he did know that images of leather-clad women with whips excited him and he wanted to be helpless in the presence of a woman. Henry also had a leather fetish and a boot fetish. Therefore, he marked on his questionnaire that he wanted to experience being whipped by a leather-clad woman, to lick a woman's boots, to be bound by a woman and to be teased to the edge of an orgasm but denied any sexual release. Henry figured that he would feel less guilty if he did not have an orgasm in the presence of another woman.

Henry got to experience all of this in his first session with a professional Dominatrix. Henry described his first session as being exciting but not completely fulfilling. Henry's struggle with guilt prevented him from really surrendering himself over to this woman during his session and his resistance prevented the session from being as fulfilling as he had hoped.

The session with the Pro Dom was exciting enough that Henry desired another one a few months later. With each session, Henry became more comfortable being dominated by a woman and before he knew it, he was seeing a Dominatrix about six times a year. At $250 per session, Henry was spending between $2000 and $3000 per year on these live sessions as well as some phone domination sessions and the purchase of some Female Domination magazines and videos. Needless to say, Henry's guilt increased about his little secret that he kept from his wife. Henry eventually discovered my ad, which offered more than just traditional domination. I also offered counseling.

Henry's story was a common tale. I had counseled scores of men who had similar stories. Ryan is such a man. Ryan is now a professional musician but when he was a teenager, he had an intense submissive experience while he was watching the 1978 film "Revenge of the Pink Panther". In this film, there is a scene where the Peter Sellers character investigates a crime that takes him to an oriental brothel. He is mistaken for a cross-dresser so the owner of the establishment thinks she knows what the good detective desires sexually. She summons for the house Dominatrix and the next scene is a humorous scene where the Dominatrix is trying to whip the naive French Detective. The scene lasts for less than a minute but it triggered something within Ryan.

Ryan never heard of a Dominatrix before but seeing this quick image of a leather-clad woman wielding a whip caused him to become excited and overcome with a submissive feeling. Like Henry, this feeling came over Ryan out of left field and consumed his thoughts and forever changed his sexuality.

Scott describes a similar experience. He was watching the 1983 movie "My Tutor", a comedy about a young man coming of age. In this film there is a scene where the high school boys pretend to be adults and solicit favors at a local brothel. In what is meant to be a humorous scene, the one unsuspecting lad (still a virgin) ends up with a beautiful blonde woman who wants to make his first time unforgettable. She binds him in an upright position against a device known as a Cathcrinc's Wheel. Once he is secure, she changes into something more comfortable but instead of lingerie, she appears in a leather outfit, at which the young man proclaims, "Oh my God!" After teasing her helpless young victim to the edge of arousal, she spins the wheel, sending him in circles and in a panic as he watches her open a closet door full of whips. The next scene shows the young male running for his life as the Dominatrix chases after him, cracking her bullwhip.

Once again, just a harmless scene in a silly movie meant to be comical but to a young man like Scott, it was a life changing experience. Scott experienced a sexual arousal he had never felt before and from that day forward, all of his sexual fantasies involved Dominant women. Scott would visit a dozen Professional Dominatrixes over the next couple of years.

Steve was overwhelmed with submission desires when he was a teenager while watching the 1987 John Ritter and Jim Belushi movie, "Real Men". As with Ryan and Scott, Steve was merely watching a mainstream comedy, not expecting to become aroused, when out of left field a scene involving a leather clad, whip wielding, dominant woman came upon the screen and caused Steve to experience an intense sexual arousal, unlike anything he had ever felt in his life. Steve could not shake what he felt and would spend the rest of his teenage years reading and fantasizing about Female Domination, which lead to a life of visiting Professional Dominant women and calling up Phone Domination services.

A number of men that I counseled mentioned the movie "Real Men" as containing the scene that they most identified with when it came to expressing what it was they were seeking sexually. In this scene, the James Belushi character meets an attractive, girl next-door type in a bar. She seems very sweet. He escorts her home and she invites him into her house. She knocks him out and he wakes up in bondage. This sweet woman is dressed in leather and she begins to verbally dominate him, she whips him and she shocks him with electricity. He resists in his male macho ways but she breaks him down and the movie cuts to a scene where he is confessing to her his inner most secrets while she is lovingly stroking his face. The next scene shows them in bed after having sex.

Why did this scene have such a profound effect on some men? After all, it was intended to be a comedy and the scene was meant to be funny. This scene was powerful because the woman represented loving female authority to these men. She was sweet and kind in public, but a real Bitch at home. She broke her male down through D&S but then was nurturing toward him once he was broken. Again, a short scene in a movie but to the submissive male like Steve, it triggered his desires and touched him at his core nature.

The reason FemDom stories, pictures and scenes in movies shake men at their core is because they touch men at their core. Their submissive nature becomes unleashed. It was there all the time but they never knew it was there until they discovered the world of Female Domination. Female Domination did not invade their brains through pop culture, literature or the media. No, their submissive desires were there all the time but those desires needed to be freed. The analogy I like to use is as follows.

A man could have a million dollars in his bank account, but if he did not know the money was there, he would never spend it. He would live his life thinking he was poor when in fact he was rich the entire time. Then if one day out of the blue, someone contacted him and said, "Hey, you have a million dollars in your back account", a light would come on and he would get excited and he would go and use that money. Did that money come out of left field and invade his bank account? No, it was there all the time but he needed a revelation that it was there.

That is what happens concerning Female Domination. A man's submissive nature is there all the time, birthed into him and cultivated by childhood and adolescent experiences but it is lying dormant. Then out of the blue, he comes across literature about Female Domination or a scene in a movie that portrays Female Domination, and that submissive nature comes alive. Now it will dominate his thoughts but not from without but from within. It is perfectly natural for a man to desire to submit to the female gender. Once he has that revelation, that revelation frees his submissive nature and brings it to the forefront of his thoughts and desires. It happens to men over and over again. Most of the time it happens when a male comes into puberty or is a teenager or when he becomes a young adult. But it also happens later in life in some males because they have not yet experienced that trigger until later in life.

Alan is a successful lawyer who counseled with me about his submissive desires toward women. Alan had submissive desires as far back as he could recall. When he was in his early twenties and had his first apartment, he would be overcome with the desire to be dominated by a woman (usually triggered by film, television or literature). Alan did not understand this desire but once it came upon him, he would seek out FemDom magazines or even mainstream magazines with dominant looking women. Alan would place himself in bondage and fantasize that a woman was whipping him or sexually dominating him. He would stand his mattress against the wall of his bedroom, tie himself up against the mattress (leaving one hand free), and he would gaze upon the pictures of the magazines that he had cut out and taped to his bedroom wall. Alan would then slap his erect penis over and over with his free hand, pretending that it was the woman from the picture who was slapping him.

Kevin is a financial advisor. He is successful, handsome and happily married. He confessed to me that when he was an adolescent, a picture of a sexy woman in a magazine would make him feel submissive. Kevin did not desire to have sex with her but rather he wanted her to dominate him. He remembers taking his brother's Sports Illustrated swimsuit issue or one of his mother's beauty magazines and he would flog himself with his belt (in the privacy of his bedroom with the door locked and the stereo turned up high) while he fantasized that it was the beautiful woman in the magazine that was flogging him. Why? Where did this desire originate from? He had loving parents who never abused him. It was as if he was born with this desire.

Phillip is a teacher and he recalls similar experiences in his childhood. He would sneak his father's Playboy magazines into his room and pretend that the naked models were dominating him. He even recalls the time he took a carrot out of his parent's refrigerator and took some Vaseline and penetrated his own rectum with the lubricated carrot as if it were a dildo. He fucked himself pretending that it was the beautiful Playboy model that was dominating him. Phillip was only ten years old at the time.

James had a reoccurring dream when he was only six or seven years old. In this dream, Peter Pan was a redheaded female and she would come to his room, take him by the hand, fly him up into the clouds and lay him in this pink cloud made of a sticky Jello-like substance. In his dream, James would struggle to get free but he could not move. The female Peter Pan would stare at him and enjoy watching her male captive struggle until he eventually surrendered to her. James was only a child but even as a child, he desired to be dominated by a woman. He did not seek this out. He had never viewed pornography or read any FemDom literature. He was an innocent boy, yet the desire to submit to the female gender was birthed within him and found its expressions through this dream.

Peter Pan was played many times by women on both television and the stage. Sandy Duncan played Peter Pan for years. Red hair represents dominance, as many redheaded women are aggressive and feisty. The cloud represents a state of subspace. The color of the cloud, pink, represents the feminine. The Jello substance represents bondage and fetishism. James knew of none of these things as a child yet he had this reoccurring dream.

James recalled another dream he had as a child. In this dream, he was a patient in a hospital bed and this redheaded nurse came to him and removed all of her clothes. She then climbed on top of him and sat her bare bottom on his face. He could not move and he struggled to get free but to no avail. He finally surrendered to her and he felt at peace.

James is a spiritual man who grew up in a Christian home. Later in life he married a Christian woman who had an out-going personality. He confessed to her about his submissive desires and after struggling with the concept of Female Domination, she finally embraced the lifestyle and took control over James and her marriage. Her name is Kathy and she is a redhead. She also once played Peter Pan in a school play and she now works as a nurse. A coincidence? Perhaps but Kathy and James like to think that Female Domination was their destiny.

Sometimes the desire to be dominated by a woman can become extreme and occupy a man's thoughts to the point where he becomes unproductive in life. Jeremy experienced this when his submissive nature was triggered from reading an article in an Adult magazine. Jeremy explains.

"Back in 1982, I was a freshman in college and I read an article in Club magazine titled the "Kalmann Diaries". It was a story about a

masochistic man that was tortured and dominated by a wealthy sadistic woman. This story contained some very intense and vivid details about how this woman whipped and abused this man. She had a sound proof room where most of this took place. When I read this story, something went off on the inside of me and from that moment, I became obsessed with female domination and sadistic women.

The thing that I found the most bizarre yet exciting in the Kalmann Diaries was how this woman trained this man to be her human toilet. She called it Immense Body Service (IBS) or something like that. The description was so disturbing and yet so sensual and exciting. This woman would always relieve herself in this man's mouth each night before she went to bed and then she would beat his balls. Like I said, she was very sadistic and this excited me to no end.

My life took a most unusual turn from that day. I was studying to be a computer programmer in college but I never finished getting my degree. I became so obsessed with female domination and the subject of sadistic women that my schoolwork and my social life suffered. I purchased every magazine and book on the subject that I could find. I was use to buying an occasional Penthouse or Club magazine for around 3 dollars a piece but now I was buying 8 and 9 dollar fetish and female domination magazines by the score. I bought videos and 8mm movies and I roamed from adult bookstores to old paperback exchange bookstores looking for any kind of books about sadistic women dominating men. The more I read, the more my appetite grew for female domination. I spent days upon days and weeks upon weeks fantasizing about being a masochistic male to a sadistic woman.

I went through my entire savings that my father had given me for my education. Once I was broke, I wrote some computer software and sold them for income. I worked as little as possible to live and to finance my obsessive habit of indulging in female domination. Most of my time was spent searching for literature about female domination and seeking out the sadistic woman of my dreams.

I joined Fetish and S&M groups, I attended fetish parties in California and New York, and I placed hundreds of personal ads in kinky contact publications. I met some interesting people and had a few wild encounters but I still had not found my dream woman.

36

Then I answered an ad that I found in the contact section of one of the fetish newspapers. It was from a woman and all it said was something like, "Sadistic girl seeks sincere male to torture". I had answered similar ads before but they usually were just a professional Dominatrix trying to add to her clientele. This time, however, was different. After some letter writing and one very long phone call, I met this woman at a public bar. Her voice sounded so sweet and innocent on the phone so I didn't think this woman was as at all as she had advertised. When she came over and sat down at my table in that bar that night, I thought I would faint right there. She was beautiful and very dominant. She was the very fulfillment of my fantasies."

Jeremy went on to experience his own "Kalmann Diaries" with this woman only to find that reality was nowhere as enjoyable as the fantasy. In fact, the reality was the opposite and left Jeremy feeling empty and totally unfulfilled.

"After I spent a week with this woman, I drove home and collapsed on my bed, a totally broken mess of a man. I wept and I shook and I just about had a total breakdown. I had no idea what day it was. I had stripes, welts, and deep bruises on my body from her whippings. I was ill to my stomach (from the IBS) and it would take me weeks to get my digestive system and bowels back to normal. Emotionally, I was a disaster. I never considered suicide or anything like that but I felt like I had totally wasted my life. I had thrown away my educational opportunity and wasted my money to pursue this obsession and now that I had experienced it, I was left unfulfilled and totally broken."

Fortunately, Jeremy got his life back on track, enrolled in a community college and got that degree in Information Technology. However, Jeremy is still seeking for submissive fulfillment. He no longer wants a woman to abuse him but he does desire to find a woman who will dominate him with loving female authority. His negative experience with the sadistic girl did not alter his desire to be in submission to a woman. Jeremy is wiser but still captivated by Female Domination.

Each of these men experienced the powerful desire to submit to a female. Something happened at different times in their lives that triggered this desire and that trigger opened them up to the world of Female Domination. For some men, that trigger happened in their childhood. For others, it happened in their adolescent years or teenage years. For some men, they did not experience such a psychological trigger until they were young adults. But somewhere and at some time, an event occurred that touched them at their core and unleashed a sexual desire to submit to women. Are these men rare? Hardly!

One need to only look at the growing profession of the Dominatrix to see how many males are searching for the experience of being dominated by a woman. Today there are literally thousands of websites where women are offering to dominate men in person or over the telephone. And more are coming on-line all the time. The supply is growing because the demand is growing. There is a real societal evolution that is occurring as the male desire to be dominated by the female is increasing at a rapid rate. Men will travel great distances and spend large amounts of money to find submissive fulfillment at the hands of a dominant woman.

Chapter Two

The Superior Sex

Woman was created as much superior to man as the name she has received is superior to his. For Adam means earth, but Eve is translated as life. And as far as life is to be ranked above earth, so far is woman to be ranked above man. (Henricus Cornelius Agrippa, "Declamation on the Nobility and Preeminence of the Female Sex", 1529)

Why do physically stronger males who live in a patriarchal world have this desire to submit to the so-called weaker sex? Is it sexual? Are men so captivated by the beauty of the female that they feel inferior? Sexuality does play a role. Men have feared the beauty and sexuality of women from the beginning of human history. That is why most religions have tried to cover up women and install man-made ordinances to keep women clothed conservatively. Man knows that he cannot resist the beauty of the female so the only way he can stay in control is to keep the female covered in conservative and unflattering clothing.

Be it Christian denominations that require women to wear a covering for their heads and forbids them to wear make-up or Muslim religions that require women to wear veils and dress in clothing that covers their entire bodies, religion fears the sexuality of women and places burdens on women because men cannot control their sexual thoughts and urges. Women are mysterious to men and men marvel at the beauty of the female. Women give off a sexual energy that men cannot resist.

Men also fear women beyond the sexual. Men have beaten down women and passed laws to keep women as second-class citizens for centuries. Why? If women were truly the weaker sex, there would be no need to mandate their dress or forbid them the same rights as men (such as the right to vote). Oppressive laws and customs to keep women in a subservient position suggest that it is not natural for women to be the submissive sex. If it were natural for men to be the dominant sex, there would be no reason for men to have oppressive laws and customs to keep women as second-class citizens. History is filled with examples of men suppressing women in order to maintain a patriarchal society. Yet, deep down men are fascinated by the female, they admire the female and they desire to submit to the female. What is clear is that men can only become the dominant sex by enforcing oppressive laws and customs against women. It is not natural for man to be the dominant sex if he has to put so much effort into keeping women oppressed. As these artificial laws and customs of a patriarchal society are removed, women will naturally rule. Deep down, men realize this.

Society has mistaken the softness and the gentleness of women for weakness and submission. Likewise, society has mistaken the toughness and the macho ways of men for strength. Men are only stronger physically. Women possess the real strength, which is Intellectually, Emotionally, Spiritually, and Sexually. Unfortunately, most women do not realize this due to centuries of being told they were the weaker sex.

Are women the weaker sex? The following data is from an article (The Weaker Sex) by Maggie Jones that appeared in the March 16th 2003 edition of the New York Times.

"Men start out ahead: 115 males are conceived for every 100 females. But it's downhill from there. The male fetus is at greater risk of miscarriage and stillbirth. Overall, more newborn males die than females (5 to 4). Sudden infant death syndrome is one and a half times as common in boys as in girls. Mental retardation afflicts one and a half times as many boys as girls. As teenagers, boys die at twice the rate of girls. Men are 16 times as likely as women to be colorblind. Men suffer hearing loss at twice the rate of women.

The male hormone testosterone is linked to elevations of LDL, the bad cholesterol, as well as declines in HDL, the good cholesterol. Men have fewer infection-fighting T-cells and are thought to have weaker immune systems than women. Men have a higher death rate from pneumonia and influenza than women. By the age of 36, women outnumber men. Men ages 55-74 are twice as likely as women to die of heart disease. In the United States, men are twice as likely to die from parasite-related diseases (in part, some speculate, because their greater average size may offer parasites a bigger target). Stroke, cancer, diabetes, heart disease and accidents -- all among the top causes of death -- kill men at a higher rate than women. American men typically die almost six years before women do. By the age of 100, women outnumber men eight to one."

Here are some biological facts that are undeniable when one looks at the research. Women have better senses (smell, touch, taste, and sight). Women tolerate pain the best. Pound for pound, women are in fact stronger thus men are physically stronger only because of their overall size advantage. Women have greater flexibility and endurance. Women, as a rule, eat healthier. Women are biological superior (and complex), less susceptible to certain diseases and they live longer.

So much for the weaker sex. But that is biological, what about intellectual? Are women more intelligent? Studies show that the human male brain is, on average, approximately ten percent larger than the female brain. However, certain brain areas in women contain more nerve cells. Women have a larger corpus collusum, the group of nerve fibers that connects left and right hemispheres in the brain. The part of the brain that allows us to think is known as "gray matter". Researchers wanted to know if women have as much gray matter as men. It was proven that women have 55.4 percent gray matter, vs. 50.8 in men. Men listen with only one side of their brains, while women use both, according to information on brain imaging presented in November 2002, at the 86th Scientific Assembly and Annual Meeting of the Radiological Society of North America (RSNA).

Here are some facts about a woman's intellect. Studies show women do better in memory tests. Women have better language and communication skills. As we will see, women have more success in small businesses and women are making better managers, directors and CEO's. Women use more areas of their brain. Girls mature faster than boys, from potty training to emotional development. As we will also discover, women have taken over higher education as many more women are graduating and getting degrees than men.

Perhaps the most influential person to come to the conclusion that women are the superior gender was Dr. Ashley Montagu, who died on November 26, 1999 at the age of ninety-four. One of the key forces behind the United Nations UNESCO statement on race, Dr. Montagu was the author of more than sixty books. Montagu wrote books on anthropology, human anatomy, intelligence, and marriage. His last book published was "The Natural Superiority of Women", originally published in 1952 and updated four times. The fifth edition was published in 1999 and has been expanded and modernized to fortify Dr. Montagu's theme that women are superior to men.

The book argues that the female of the species is biologically, sexually, emotionally, and even intellectually superior to the male. Dr. Montagu writes that women possess humane intelligence that will enable women to steer society toward a more humanized condition. Dr. Montagu used his knowledge of physical anthropology to dispel the myth of conventional wisdom that women are the "weaker sex" by showing how women's biological, genetic, and physical makeup makes her not only man's equal, but his superior. Dr. Montagu explains that his thesis is supported by scientific evidence. Dr. Montagu challenges his readers to distinguish between facts and opinions and he reminds us that facts are either true of false, and he welcomes all evidence that questions any of his facts and the conclusions deduced from these.

From "The Natural Superiority of Women":

"...the evidence indicates that woman is, on the whole, biologically superior to man."

"The evidence is clear: from the constitutional standpoint, woman is the stronger sex. The explanation of the greater constitutional strength of the female lies largely, if not entirely, in her possession of two complete X-chromosomes and the male's possession of only one."

"From infancy to adulthood the female superiority in verbal or linguistic functions is consistent and marked."

"Girls excel in most tests of memory. They do significantly better on tests of picture memories and such tests as copying a bead chain from memory."

"As far as intelligence scores and other indicators of what we call intelligence go, the conclusion is clear: Girls do better than boys. ...In short, the age-old myth that women are of inferior intelligence to men has, as far as the scientific evidence goes, not a leg to stand upon."

"...women continue to grow in intelligence; and in the kind of intelligence that is of the greatest importance for the survival of the human race. I think it can be shown that women far outdistance men."

"Studies carried out at both Duke University and at the University of London, uniformly agree that woman are far better judges of character of men, yet another evidence of woman's higher problem solver abilities."

"With respect to psychological and social qualities, the facts again, it seems to me, prove that women are superior to men."

"Women are the bearers, the nurturers of life; men have more often tended to be the curtailers, the destroyers of life."

The research does seem to suggest that perhaps the male gender is not the superior gender after all. As women continue to grow in power and become more assertive in our society, men will desire to submit to them. Women have become liberated in western civilization and now for the first time in history, women are seeing themselves in an equal and even superior light when compared to the male gender. A lot of women have come to believe that society would be better served if society were governed by women instead of men and that women should be in positions of authority. Women have gained equality but they are finding that equality is not enough.

How did women gain equality? Sure there were those great Female pioneers in the Feminist movement like Mary Wollstonecraft, Susan B. Anthony, and Alice Paul. But equality for women would not have been possible unless some men also desired for women to gain power. It was ultimately men of power and control who surrendered some of that power over to women in order to empower women. What is most surprising about the Feminist movement is the lack of male opposition. There was first a power exchange that occurred within the bedrooms and the homes that set the stage for women to gain equality in western civilization. It took men submitting to the female desire to be educated, employed and given an equal voice in politics that brought equality to fruition. The old saying, "behind every successful man is a strong woman" is true and well documented but eventually the strong woman behind the powerful man used her influence in the home to affect change in society.

It was the male desire for female empowerment that seduced the dormant desire within women and caused that desire for power to be unleashed. Societal evolution has always been driven by the empowerment of women, one male/female relationship at a time. Nature set this up as men are birthed into this world by women, nurtured by women and raised by women. The seeds for Female Domination have been implanted into the male psyche by nature. Societal evolution is often a slow, steady process but one just need look at the trends to see what has been transpiring.

Until 1920, women were not permitted the right to vote in America but now in less than one century, women are dominating men from elementary learning to higher education to the board rooms of International business. With each passing election, more women are being elected to political office from state houses all the way to the Unites States Senate. More and more companies are hiring female CEO's and the success of these women will only ensure more female hires for the top positions in the business world. Women now hold sixteen percent of corporate officer positions at large U.S. public companies (double the amount from only seven years ago). As women operate from these powerful positions, they will be hiring more women for lower level management positions, which will ensure even more future female executives and CEO's.

Even Dr. Montagu did not foresee such a rapid societal change. When he originally wrote "The Natural Superiority of Women" in 1952, Dr. Montagu commented on how men were fighting to maintain control of their role as the "breadwinner" and how that macho attitude was a reflection of man's insecurity and a way for man to compensate for his inner feeling of inferiority when compared to the nature of the female.

"I am not the first to suggest, and I am sure I shall not be the last, that the male's drive in work and achievement may actually be the consequence of his recognition of his biological inferiority with respect to the female's creative capacity to conceive and create human beings. One of the ways in which the male may compensate for this biological inferiority is by work and by achievement. By keeping the means of making a livelihood almost exclusively a masculine prerogative, men have unconsciously, as well as consciously, been able to satisfy themselves that they are by nature the "breadwinners", the pillars of society and the guarantors of the race. Hence, the great opposition to women when they begin to enter into "competition" with men in earning a living."

By the 1970's, that competition was a reality and after only three decades, the insecure male's worst nightmare has been realized. The trend toward women becoming the dominant financial partner within the marriage is growing at a rapid rate. In an article published in the January 2002 issue of Business Week, Michelle Conlin writes;

"After only three decades as members of the mainstream workforce, one in three wives now outearns her husband, up from one in five in 1980. Women with MBAs are doing even better: Nearly 60% have direct deposits bigger than their husbands. Look for the ranks of the female breadwinner to rise even more, with 20% more women than men graduating from college and more women swelling the managerial ranks every year."

Later in the same article Ms Conlin reveals a surprising discovery,

"...the more economic power the wife has, the more men help out at home. Minetor found that 51% of men with breadwinner wives are the major housekeepers. Finally, more career women are getting the one thing they say they need most: a wife."

The female breadwinner is becoming a rather common occurrence in our society. What a change from when Dr. Montagu first published his landmark book. Women are beginning to dominate the workforce. World War II saw women enter the workforce out of necessity but once the men returned from the war, they discovered that not all women were willing to return to the traditional role of stay at home spouse. This lead to much stress in the home as husbands and wives argued over the societal role of the female.

The fifties brought prosperity and ushered in the age of materialism. In order to afford the luxuries of the twentieth century, some men began to submit to their wives demands to work outside the home, as two incomes could buy more than just one. The sixties brought more social change and ushered in the age of Feminism. Women began to demand equal pay and equal opportunities in education and career choices.

The seventies saw women pouring into the labor force and the ascent up the corporate ladder began. Society continues to evolve and now women are beginning to earn more than their husbands. Women are ascending to positions of leadership and women are outperforming their male counterparts. Studies show that women are making better bosses and better managers.

Rochelle Sharpe writes for Business Week On-line;

"Twenty-five years after women first started pouring into the labor force--and trying to be more like men in every way, from wearing power suits to picking up golf clubs--new research is showing that men ought to be the ones doing more of the imitating. In fact, after years of analyzing what makes leaders most effective and figuring out who's got the Right Stuff, management gurus now know how to boost the odds of getting a great executive: Hire a Female.

That's the essential finding of a growing number of comprehensive management studies conducted by consultants across the country for companies ranging from high-tech to manufacturing to consumer services. By and large, the studies show that women executives, when rated by their peers, underlings, and bosses, score higher than their male counterparts on a wide variety of measures--from producing high-quality work to goal-setting to mentoring employees. Using elaborate performance evaluations of execs, researchers found that women got higher ratings than men on almost every skill measured. Ironically, the researchers weren't looking to ferret out gender differences. They accidentally stumbled on the findings when they were compiling hundreds of routine performance evaluations and then analyzing the results."

Joanna L. Krotz of Marketing Intelligence believes that it is genetics that makes women better managers. In her article "Why women make better managers?" Ms Krotz writes;

"As women gained traction in the workforce, gender differences among senior and junior staffers turned up in every workplace, from offices to factory floors to fighter planes. Now that women are pulling up chairs at boardroom tables and launching their own companies, the number of women-owned firms has increased by 103% in the past 10 years, those differences are increasingly playing out in executive suites, too. Studies show that both male and female styles of leadership can be effective. But when compared side by side, "female" has the edge.

Gender differences stem from nurture and nature alike. It's not only socialization that shapes men and women. It's also biology. Researchers are discovering physiological variations in the brains of men and women. For example, male brains are about 10% larger than female brains. But women have more nerve cells in certain areas. Women also tend to have a larger corpus collusum, the group of nerve fibers that connects left and right hemispheres. That makes women faster at transferring data between the computational, verbal left half and the intuitive, visual right half. Men are usually left-brain oriented. As girls and boys grow up, of course, they're also molded by differing sets of social rules and expectations. Gender obviously colors behavior, perception and just about everything else."

This societal trend is not limited to the United States. From an article in the January 9th edition of Scotland's The Herald newspaper by Helen Puttick,

"It is the news that the males of office life have secretly been dreading - women make better managers than men. A ground-breaking survey of 2000 UK workers found female managers were more highly regarded than their male counterparts in a wide range of areas - including taking risks and decision-making. Out of 14 new criteria for measuring managerial success, women were rated better than men in 11 and equal to men in the remaining three.

Male middle managers felt the opposite sex was significantly more effective at taking charge than their own.

High-flying men and women around Scotland yesterday admitted the survey confirmed their own instincts - although men in particular were reluctant to say so in public."

Women are beginning to dominate the corporate world. While men still hold the majority of CEO and management positions, they are losing their power with each graduating class from the major colleges and universities. Women are dominating the classrooms in higher education and thus more women are being hired for top entry-level positions with large companies. It is only a matter of time when women will ascend to top management positions at an accelerated rate. As it becomes apparent that women make better managers than their male counterparts, more women will be hired into these positions of authority. As women continue to ascend to these top positions, they will be more inclined to hire other women for middle management positions. Thus, the trend toward female rule in the business world will continue at an accelerated rate.

As impressive as women are doing in the corporate world, what is occurring in classrooms around this world is absolutely astounding. The societal evolution that is transpiring is quite evident. "Equality" is not the word that comes to mind when one looks at the data, but rather "Dominance". In the May 26 cover story of Business Week, Michelle Conlin wrote an article titled "The New Gender Gap (From kindergarten to grad school, boys are becoming the second sex)". In that article she states the following,

"When the leaders of the Class of 2003 assemble in the Long Island high school's fluorescent-lit meeting rooms, most of these boys are nowhere to be seen. The senior class president? A girl. The vice-president? Girl. Head of student government? Girl. Captain of the math team, chief of the yearbook, and editor of the newspaper? Girls.

The female lock on power at Lawrence is emblematic of a stunning gender reversal in American education. From kindergarten to graduate school, boys are fast becoming the second sex. ....Just a century ago, the president of Harvard University, Charles W. Eliot, refused to admit women because he feared they would waste the precious resources of his school. Today, across the country, it seems as if girls have built a kind of scholastic Roman Empire alongside boys' languishing Greece. Although

Lawrence High has its share of boy superstars -- like this year's valedictorian -- the gender takeover at some schools is nearly complete."

In the June 8, 2003 addition of the Grand Rapids Press, Melissa Slager writes the following in her article titled "Girls are better than boys";

"Girls have been walking up to graduation podiums in droves this spring, besting boys in the game of grades...Girls in recent years have dominated local valedictorian ranks -- this year, nearly two times the number of boys -- while guys continue to disproportionately fill classrooms for the academically and emotionally challenged."

Once again this trend is not limited to the United States. Lysiane Gaganon writes about Higher Education in Canada;

"The next generation of Quebec women might face a difficult love life. According to the September figures on student enrolment unearthed by La Presse reporter Andre Noel, in a few years the province will be filled with high-paid, ambitious, professional women. Across the dance floor will be a large group of losers -- uneducated men stuck in small, low-paying jobs. More and more women -- and fewer and fewer men -- enroll in universities. In 1991, 57 per cent of the students at Universite Laval in Quebec City were female. By 1996, the proportion was up to 60 percent; now it is 63 percent. The good news is that women are becoming more educated. The bad news is that the proportion of men with university degrees is decreasing every year...And women are much more successful. Three out of four female students receive their college diploma, while almost 40 per cent of the male students drop out or fail the exams."

In the May 31st edition of Canada's Globe and Mail, Margaret Wente wrote an article entitled "Girls Rule!" in which she ponders where this societal evolution is leading.

"Everyone knows that girls are doing well in school these days. What's stunning is how well. The girls have moved so far ahead, the boys can barely see their dust. This is something new in history -- an entire generation of alpha females, many of whom are destined to outearn the men as well as outperform them."

"Income is closely associated with educational status," says Paul Cappon, director-general of the Council of Ministers of Education Canada. "We've known about this tendency for a long time, but it's much more dramatic now."

"...on our doorstep is a social revolution. The graduating girls of '03 are confident, goal-oriented and self-sufficient. They're used to paying their own way, and don't expect to depend on men for much of anything. Who will they marry? How will they bring up their kids?"

"What does it mean when women are the main breadwinners and the main nurturers?" wonders Dr. Cappon. "We've never had a situation like this before."

Once can sense the concern in Dr. Cappon's comments as he asks this very profound question. What does it mean? Could it mean that society is headed toward female rule? The data is undeniable if one chooses to examine it. Society is headed toward female dominance. It is not there yet but the train has left the station and it is picking up momentum with each passing year. Women are beginning to dominate almost every profession and this is happening all around the free world.

In July of 2002, the BBC news published an article titled "Women Dominating Medical Schools".

"Too few men are training to become doctors, the British Medical Association's annual meeting was told on Wednesday. For the first time ever, more women than men graduated from medical schools. Six out of ten present students are women, according to figures, and some are worried that medicine may become overly-dominated by women in the future....Women were proving far more attractive candidates - both physically and because their "A" level grades were better. Stephen Sanders, another committee member, told the conference that at his school in Nottingham there were two women to every man."

Margaret Wente concurs in her article "Girls Rule";

"Speaking of doctors, women are now dominant in medical school. Only five years ago, they made up 49 per cent of first-year students. Today they make up 59 per cent. At Hamilton's McMaster University, 69 per

cent are women, and women make up more than two-thirds of incoming students in Quebec."

The data is overwhelming. Females are dominating males from grade school through post-secondary education. Kathleen Parker wrote the following for the Jewish World Review, "Battle of the Sexes Is Over and Clearly Girls Have Won."

"Four boys are diagnosed as emotionally disturbed to every one girl; two boys are learning-disabled for every one girl; six boys are diagnosed with attention deficit disorder to every one girl; two teen boys die for every one girl. Fifty-five percent of college students are female...girls outperform boys by 13 points in reading and 24 points in writing. Girls outnumber boys in all extracurricular activities...more boys than girls drop out of school."

In a June 2003 South African Sunday Times article titled "Girls knock boys off their perch", Gill Moodie writes;

"Male learners fall behind and drop out of school as a new breed of female teenager begins to dominate in class. Girls are trouncing boys in the blackboard jungle. Research shows that more girls are finishing school than boys. A paper to be published in EduSource Data News by the Education Foundation, a non-governmental organization, shows that more boys are dropping out of school. The paper, by independent education researcher Helen Perry, shows that last year 60% of pupils who got A averages were girls, and 57% of Bs and Cs were achieved by girls."

There is a societal evolution occurring and women are beginning to move from desiring equality to being the superior gender. What is transpiring in society is finding its initial expression within the male/female relationship. A lot of women have come to realize that there is no such thing as a 50/50 relationship. Anything with two heads is a monster. A 50/50 relationship means that every decision must be discussed and debated. That creates a lot of arguments and much strife and stress in a marriage. No wonder the divorce rate is so high. There has to be a leader in any unit. There has to be a CEO of a company, there has to be a General in an Army, there has to be a President of a Country, and there has to be a Dominant partner in a marriage. The buck must stop with someone. Women have allowed men to run the family, the work place, and the world for long enough. Now women are coming to realize that they are better equipped to lead.

As more women gain in power and come to the realization that they are indeed superior to men, they will dominate the men in their lives and our society will continue to evolve into a female controlled society. Women are beginning to come into this knowledge and society is beginning to evolve to a place where women are the dominant gender.

Once women were liberated and allowed to compete with men on an even playing field, it was only a matter of time before women began to excel. The most interesting aspect of what is taking place is the male reaction to the success of the female gender. At first, men fought it. They tried to convince society that women in the workplace was morally wrong and that it signaled a decline in western civilization. Men said that women could not function outside the home and that society and business would greatly suffer. Now that enough time has passed, men see that not only can women function in the higher institutes of learning and the workplace, they are in fact out performing men.

This has caused a different reaction within the male gender. Men are finding that they desire to be in submission to women. Deep inside, a lot of men would fantasize about being in submission to women in the bedroom but now those desires are evolving so men want to be dominated in every area of their lives by women. Men are desiring not only sexual domination but also social domination.

Women are becoming more confident and assured of themselves in not only the classroom but also in social settings. Women are becoming the decision-makers within relationships and men are more easily falling into the submissive role. Not all men, as there are still the macho males who hold to their father's traditions when it comes to the roles of the sexes. But more men with each generation are becoming more comfortable and at peace with being the submissive partner in a relationship with a woman.

As women continue to excel in colleges and universities, it is just a matter of time that they will gain the power in the business world and the political world. As this happens, the societal change will rapidly increase because of the natural submissive desire within men. When they see women as leaders and their bosses in the workplace, the desire to submit will become stronger. This will make it easier for the wife to run the marriage, as the man will be accustomed to submitting to a woman in all areas of his life.

The ramifications of this will only re-enforce and increase the rise of women to power. Young girls will grow up seeing Mommy as the main breadwinner and the dominant partner. This will tear down past stereotypes and instill in girls an expectation to succeed and excel in school. That will cause the cycle to continue and to grow with each passing generation.

The Genie is out of her bottle and there will be no going back to a patriarchal society. The male gender had absolute power in our society but man wanted to empower the female because man desires to be in submission to the female. There is a natural born desire within men that causes them to desire to be dominated by a woman.

It was men who encouraged women to rise up and to strive for equality. It was a stealth campaign, one never openly discussed among men because men fear being scorned and rejected by their male peers. However, deep in the recesses of his mind, the male gender could not escape his sexual and social desire to submit to the female gender. Men were hen-pecked and pussy whipped within their personal relationships with women behind the closed doors of their marriage but what surprised many males was their desire to see women become dominant and powerful outside of the home.

No matter how society tries to spin it, the fact is that men are aroused at the concept of women in power. An increasing number of men want the female to be the dominant gender. Society is changing but there is still a major roadblock in the transformation of power and the roles of the sexes. While scientific evidence does support the thesis that females are superior to males both intellectually and biologically, the primary reason men have been able to make women subservient to them for ages is not through Science but rather through the institution of Religion.

Chapter Three

The Latent Power of Eve:
The Spirituality of Female Domination

Woman is a more worshipful creature than man because she understands much more than man how much there is in the world to be worshipped. ...such wonderment are generative of the religious spirit. In this also, women show their superiority. (Dr. Ashley Montagu, "The Natural Superiority of Women", 1952)

If ever the world sees a time when women shall come together purely and simply for the benefit and good of mankind, it will be a power such as the world has never known. (Matthew Arnold, British poet, 1858)

Women have been programmed since they were little girls that the natural order of God ordained institutions (Government, Religion and Family) is for men to be dominant and women to be submissive. Most religions teach that the male is the superior gender (made in the image of God) and thus the husband should rule the marriage. Are men spiritually superior to women? Is it by God's design that men should be the dominant gender in society? Or have men perverted religion in order to keep women as second-class citizens?

We believe so much based on tradition. All religions are guilty of man made traditions passed off as God ordained truth. Christianity is the dominant religion of western civilization. The Christmas story about the three Wisemen is a perfect example of religious tradition. We all see the nativity scenes where the three Wisemen are in the stable presenting the baby Jesus with gifts. Those of the Christian faith were taught this story since childhood and most Christian adults believe it is factual. Yet, the very Bible that is the foundation for the Christian Faith does not substantiate this tradition. When one reads the Bible, one discovers that it never mentions how many Wisemen (or Magi) there actually were and in fact, by the time these Wisemen reached the child, he was two years old and living in a house with his parents. Some would argue that this is a minor detail in the big picture of Religion. Perhaps, but this is but one of many examples of how people believe stories from their childhood and accepts them by faith throughout their adult lives.

Another example is the widely quoted scripture that "God works in mysterious ways." The truth is, that so-called scripture does not appear in the Bible. It is a man made observation that has been passed down as scripture but in fact, it has never been in the Bible. Or how about "Money is the root of all evil". How many sermons have been preached on that subject when in fact the scripture actually reads, "The love of money is the root of all evil". That is a big difference because a person does not necessarily have to possess money to love money. Thus, poverty has been instilled as a virtue in many Christian denominations and some have taken a vow of poverty to show their righteousness.

Another example is the word "Rapture". The rapture of the Church is a widely held doctrine by most Protestant denominations, yet the word "rapture" is man made and in fact never appears in the English Bible or the original Hebrew or Greek texts or any translation of these texts. Neither the word "rapture" nor the teaching of the rapture of the Church is mentioned in any Christian literature prior to 1830. Apparently this doctrine was introduced into Christianity by a Scottish Minister after a fifteen year old girl by the name of Margaret MacDonald had a "revelation from God" during one of his Church services. The fame of this girl's "vision" spread through Christianity and now this doctrine is taught as Biblical fact.

Another Christian tradition is Good Friday. Any serious Biblical scholar will tell you that Christ was crucified on Wednesday and was buried for three full days and three full nights before his resurrection. Yet, because of tradition, the Christian church celebrates this on Friday and people believe it by blind faith, when even a child knows that Friday evening to dusk on Sunday is not three full days. Traditions, traditions, and more traditions. Jesus himself commented on how traditions of men render the word of God powerless. Over time, traditions are accepted as fact and the longer people repeat traditions that are false, eventually the majority of society will accept them as truth.

It is human nature to believe that which our elders have taught us as children. Most of the time, we rarely question what we are taught in church or synagogue. Back before the reformation, only the priests and the clergy studied the scriptures thus the masses had to trust the religious scholars and the church leadership's interpretation of scriptures. In the Catholic Church, the scriptures were translated into Latin under Roman influence but Latin was a language very few in the west could read or understand. After Martin Luther had his revelation that mankind is redeemed by faith and not works, the Protestant church was born and proclaimed a freedom from the traditions of the Catholic Church. However, in no time at all, the Protestant churches made up their own traditions and built their own denominations, which rarely agree on the meaning of the scriptures. Followers of Martin Luther became Lutherans, followers of Calvin became Calvinists, followers of Wesley became Methodists and so on until today there are hundreds of denominations just in the Protestant faith alone. Why so much disagreement?

The King James English Bible was written so any layperson could read the scriptures for themselves. However, the men who translated the King James Bible from the original Hebrew had to make many judgments as a word in Hebrew could have multiple meanings and thus could be translated numerous ways into English. While the scriptures may have been Divinely inspired, the human brains of the males doing the translating were not infallible. This has lead to endless debates and arguments and thus theological splits within the church. It is obvious to me that the translators of the English Bible (while their intentions were no doubt admirable) didn't always make the correct choices in their translations. This is especially true when it comes to the origin and the nature of the sexes. The translators of the King James English Bible no doubt believed in a Patriarchal society and this biased perspective influenced how they translated words from the Hebrew and Greek into English. Fortunately today, there are a number of other translations of the English Bible and anyone can research the original Hebrew and Greek meanings of scriptures through a Bible Concordance.

The three large patriarchal religions (Judaism, Christianity, and Islam) all trace their origins back to the Garden of Eden with the belief that Adam and Eve were the original male and female. Genesis is the recorded account of creation that most mainline religions and denominations use as the foundation of their faith. So what does Genesis say about the original nature of man and woman?

When one reads the Bible and the story of Adam and Eve in the original Hebrew, it is apparent that Adam was originally created both male and female (Genesis 1:27). Adam was the first man but man did not mean male. Man was the species just like a Lion is a species; an Elephant is a species and so forth. God created Man (the species) and God made Man both male and female, just like God made the Lion both male and female and the Elephant both male and female. So when the scriptures refer to Man, it is not necessarily referring to male. That is why one must look at the original Hebrew to see if a name is masculine or feminine.

God created Woman (the Man with the womb or the female Man) from Adam by pulling the female nature out of Adam. This is represented in scripture by God taking the rib out of Adam's side and forming the female but the spiritual truth of this is that God took the nature of the female out of Adam and made a unique creation, then joined them back together through marriage. Adam was made in the image of God so God must also be both male and female. The scriptures do not describe God as a male but refer to God as a Spirit with both male and female traits. To authenticate this, the Jewish names for God in the Old Testament are both male and female. Jehovah/Yahweh is YHWH, Y/El, father; H/Asherah, mother.

In addition, the word that describes Eve as being Adam's helpmate is the Hebrew word "ezer" which means that she was to assist Adam from a position of authority. It is the same word the Bible uses to describe God when it refers to how God will assist us when we need help. God assists us from a position of power and authority and Eve was created to assist Adam from a position of authority. Eve's subjection to Adam in the Bible was the result of the fall of mankind due to sin and not God's original plan for Adam and Eve. Woman's subjection to man was called a curse in the Old Testament (Genesis 3:16-17). The New Testament says that Christ has paid mankind's debt in full and has restored mankind back to God and has delivered mankind from the curse. However, most Christian denominations are still based on a patriarchal view of God and they refuse to see what the scriptures truly say about the true nature of Woman.

I personally believe that Eve was God's last and greatest creation, thus women are the superior gender. I am not alone is this interpretation of the scriptures. The following is fom "Declamation on the Nobility and Preeminence of the Female Sex" by Henricus Cornelius Agrippa, written in 1529;

"We know that, among all that was created by the best and greatest God, the essential difference consists in the fact that certain things live forever, while others are subject to corruption and change, and that, in the course of this creation, God advanced following an order that consisted in beginning with the more noble of the first group and ending with the most noble of the second. Thus, he created first the incorruptible angels, then the souls (for Augustine affirms that the soul of our first parents was created at the same time as the angles, before the body was fashioned). Then he created the incorruptible bodies, such as the heavens and the stars, and elements that, although incorruptible, are nonetheless subject to various changes. And from them he formed all other things that are subject to corruption, proceeding again by ascent, from the more insignificant through all degrees of humor to the perfection of the universe. Thus were created first minerals, then vegetables, plants and trees, followed by animated beings, and finally brute beasts, in order: reptiles, fish, birds, quadrupeds.

Again after all this he created two human beings in his image, man first, then woman, in whom the heavens and the earth, and every embellishment of both, are brought to perfection. For when the Creator came to the creation of woman, he rested himself in this creation, thinking that he had nothing more honorable to create; in her were completed and consummated all the wisdom and power of the Creator; after her no creation could be found or imagined. Since, therefore, woman is the ultimate end of creation, the most perfect accomplishment of all the works of God and the perfection of the universe itself, who will deny that she possesses honor surpassing every other creature? Without her the world itself, already perfect to a fault and complete at every level, would have been imperfect; it could only be perfected in the creature of all others by far the most perfect."

A number of Biblical scholars over the centuries have come to the conclusion that the female is closer to Divinity than the male. The voices of those with such an opinion have been called heretics and have been severely persecuted. Women have been indoctrinated by religion that they are the weaker sex and thus, wives must submit to their husbands.

In the New Testament, there are scriptures that men have used to keep women in the subservient role. Men have argued that women cannot be in any leadership positions in the church because of the charge by the Apostle Paul that women should remain quiet in the church. That is another misinterpretation of scripture. Neither women nor men are perfect by themselves. They both have strengths and weaknesses, which is why they need each other. One personality trait of most women is that their minds are very active and they tend to talk more than most men. Women are more social creatures. The early church obviously had a problem with the women socializing a bit too much, so the Apostle Paul felt that he had to address this. Therefore, he told them to be quiet while church was taking place. That's all there is to this doctrine, yet male dominated religion has taken this scripture, as well as others that have been misinterpreted, to push down and rule women.

Ephesians 5:24 is another passage in scripture that men have used to get women to be in subjection to them. *"But as the church is subject to Christ, so also the wives ought to be to their husbands in everything."*

The phrase *"in everything"* was added by the English translators of the Bible in an obvious attempt to drive home their patriarchal viewpoint. Men could thus point to that phrase *"in everything"* and rule over women in every area of life. This is another misinterpretation of scripture. This passage is talking about the man being the Spiritual covering of the woman. It has nothing to do with a wife obeying a husband in earthly things but is talking about the woman submitting to the Christ nature in her husband. It was the husband's responsibility to pray for his wife and family and to cover them with prayer.

Often when this doctrine is preached, the scripture right before this passage (Ephesians 5:21) is omitted, which states that the husband and the wife should submit one to another. In other words, the wife should submit to the spiritual covering of the husband but the husband may submit to the wife in other areas, if they so choose. Nowhere in scripture is the act of a man submitting to a woman in the bedroom or in the natural things in life, forbidden by God. As a matter of fact, when one views how woman was created to help man from a position of authority, it is obvious that the woman is better equipped to rule the marriage. The scripture just after this passage (Ephesians 5:25-28) tells men that they need to love their wives like Christ loved the church and gave himself for it. In other words, husbands should be willing to sacrifice for their wives. Sacrifice is the ultimate form of submission. Religious men are quick to quote Ephesians 5:22-24 but they eagerly omit Ephesians 5:21 and 5:25-28.

Some have said that the Apostle Paul did not like women since many of his writings seemed to be talking down to women, treating them as second-class citizens. When reading scriptures, it is important that people realize the culture that they were written in. Women were not educated during the Apostle Paul's time and thus men had to be in charge of most institutions. Paul was writing to a male dominated society where women were viewed almost like children. But God's plan is ever unfolding and now women have been liberated and educated. They are now equipped to be Pastors and leaders in the church, as well as in the home, in government and in business. Paul also told slaves to obey their masters but we know that God is against the institution of forced slavery. As God's plan unfolded, God freed the slaves and God liberated women. Society evolves and women are coming into their rightful positions. Back during Biblical times, women were ill-equipped to rule due to a lack of education and being held down by a male dominated society. Today is a new day and women are liberated. So one must keep this in mind when reading the scriptures.

It is also important to read the scriptures in the manner that the scriptures invite. The scriptures are described by the scriptures as manna from heaven, food for the spirit. However, carnal man tries to intellectualize a spiritual book and this leads to endless debates and arguments and thus theological splits within the church. The Bible proclaims that the letter kills but the Spirit brings life. In other words, read the Bible more with your spirit as it applies to your life today and less with your logical reasoning. If one reads the Bible as a dead, historical book, it becomes just that, a record of Biblical times that is a spiritually dead book with outdated doctrines and traditions. However, if one views the Bible as a spiritual book which is to be read with one's spirit and with an open heart, then it becomes a living book that is relevant today. Blessedly, educated women are not so easily indoctrinated or controlled by a patriarchal society. Thus, the patriarchal society is diminishing and society has evolved toward equality and is now evolving toward female dominance.

In addition to the three major religions, today we are witnessing a return to many forms of Goddess Worship and Goddess religions. It has been estimated that in the United States alone, hundreds of thousands of people are now active in churches that believe in a female deity. Most of these churches can trace their origin back to ancient civilizations that actively worshipped a Goddess.

The Egyptians worshipped Isis, great Mother, Goddess of fertility, Giver of Life and Queen of Heaven. The Greeks worshipped Artemis, protectress of children and the great Huntress; and the Romans worshipped Diana, Goddess of the moon and sister of Venus. Venus was originally Goddess of gardens and fields, later identified with Aphrodite, love and beauty. Worshipped as Venus Genetrix, mother of founder of Rome; Venus Felix, bringer of good fortune; Venus Victix, bringer of victory, and Venus Verticordia, protector of feminine chastity.

Then there is the Goddess Cybele. The name Cybele or Cybebe predominates in Greek and Roman literature from about the 5th century BC onward. Cybele was the Titan mother of the Olympian gods, who held domain over fertility and the earth. The Goddess Cybele held significance as a Goddess of the moon and of fertility, but was also worshipped in her earthly aspects as a fertility deity. The moon throughout history has been seen as a symbol of the feminine; its regular cycles correspond to the lifecycles of women.

A cult like religion was formed based on the mythical stories of Cybele. This whole belief was further developed and refined by the Greeks around 6,000 years ago. They created a temple and an order of priesthood. These priests would have to be castrated following a ritual act of sex with the Goddesses representative. They would then serve her for life. To show their devotion they would have to dress in female clothes.

Three thousand years ago the state religion of Phrygia (in what is now Turkey) was centered around the worship of the Mother Goddess, there called Cybele. In many parts of the eastern Mediterranean, the Mother Goddess (under a variety of names), was served by a priesthood that often consisted of feminized males.

The Romans followed a Sibylline prophecy that the enemy could be expelled and conquered if the Goddess were brought to Rome, together with her sacred symbol, a small stone reputed to have fallen from the heavens. By the end of the Roman Republic, the Cybele religion had attained prominence and under the empire it became one of the most important cults in the Roman world.

Cybele's priests, the Galli, castrated themselves on entering her service. The castration was justified by the myth that the Goddess Cybele had a lover, the fertility god Attis. The fable goes that he had emasculated himself under a pine tree, where he bled to death. Violets were created and sprung to life from the blood of Attis. In this fable, the Goddess Cybele later raised Attis from the dead as a woman.

Galli priests, often temple attendants or servants of Cybele and her female representatives, were eunuchs attired in female garb, with long hair fragrant with ointment (representing the masculine taking on the feminine, based on the story of Attis). Together with priestesses, they celebrated the Great Mother's rites with wild music and dancing until their frenzied excitement found its culmination in self-scourging, self-laceration, or exhaustion. Self-emasculation by candidates for the priesthood sometimes accompanied this delirium of worship. They would accept flagellation by women for the sins of the patriarchy (male dominance).

Other Goddesses that people worshipped throughout history were Aphrodite from Cyprus, Astarte from Phoenicia, Demeter from Mycenae, Ishtar from Assyria, Kali from India and Ostara, a Norse Goddess of fertility.

Today, many in western civilization look at such religions of old as being based on fables and mythology. Yet, many are joining New Age religions that center around the same beliefs of the Goddess religions of old, such as the worshipping of nature. Wicca is one of many earth-based religions. Traditional Wicca was founded by Gerald Gardner, a British civil servant, who wrote a series of books on the religion in the 1940's. It contains references to Celtic deities, symbols, and seasonal days of celebration. As a religion, Wicca is a reconstruction of the pre-Christian religions of Europe, especially Northern Europe (Celtic or Norse traditions), sometimes elsewhere incorporating Greco-Roman and Egyptian traditions.

Many of our western Christian Holidays were in fact founded as Goddess holidays. The Christmas holiday is an adaptation of the pagan winter solstice rites. Called Yule, it was one of the traditional Celtic fire festivals and marked the return of the light after the longest night of the year. Pagans (peasants, rustic people) in northwestern Europe conducted a yearly celebration, which is remarkably similar to the Christmas we know today. The Christmas Tree is left over from the pagan winter solstice rites. As Europe was evangelized by Christians, the pagan holiday was replaced with a Christian holiday celebrating the birth of Christ. Most Biblical scholars believe that Christ was in fact born in September but since there was already a celebration in December, Christmas was substituted for Yule.

Easter is another Christian holiday that was originally based on Goddess worship. Easter was named after Eostre (a.k.a. Eastre). She was the Great Mother Goddess of the Saxon people in Northern Europe. Easter falls in the Spring, right around the Vernal Equinox. Spring has been, and is, the season for much merrymaking and fun, much of the time with an emphasis on sexual fertility. Easter falls on the first Sunday subsequent to the first full moon after the vernal equinox (March 21). Thus, it can occur as early as March 22nd and as late as April 25th.

Christians celebrate Easter as the Resurrection of Christ. Obviously, since this was an actual date in history, it should be the same date each year. Originally, Easter was celebrated on the same day as the Jewish Passover. Since the Jewish calendar is lunar, Passover can fall on any day of the week, and some Church fathers were distressed that the Lenten fast should end on any day other than a Sunday. They argued about it until the 8th century, when the church officially adopted the pagan date of Easter for the celebration of the resurrection of Christ.

It has been argued by those who are active in Goddess worship that as women become more liberated, patriarchal religions will lose their appeal and there will be a heavy return to Goddess religions of old. It has been my experience that the majority of couples who practice Female Domination come from all religious affiliations, Christian, Jewish, Muslim, Buddhist, Goddess Worship, New Age, Agnostic and Atheist. A person's faith is a private matter and most people are unwilling to change their Faith. I have known some dominant women who left the Christian Church and who have since embraced Goddess religions, as they are more comfortable worshipping God as a Female. But I also know many women that are active in the Female Domination lifestyle, who are at ease with their Female Supremacy beliefs and their Christian faith.

Dominant women who are active in Christianity will point out that their religion is not a patriarchal religion. Men have perverted it into a patriarchal religion but Christianity is really about a personal relationship between a person and their Creator through Christ. One need not change their religion when they have a revelation of the true natures of women and men. I chose to study my faith in more detail to see if what I was being taught was indeed so. I discovered that Christianity was very compatible with my Female Supremacy beliefs and the Female Domination lifestyle.

Why is all of this important? Because one of the major stumbling blocks for women when it comes to embracing the Female Domination lifestyle is religion. Deep down, most women believe that they are equal or superior to males but they still are uncomfortable with being in charge because of a feeling of guilt that religion has shackled them with since they were little girls. It is one thing to oppose a male dominant society based on Science or Ethics but it is hard to oppose God or Nature. Religion uses fear and guilt to keep people enslaved to theologies that would otherwise have no chance of surviving under the light of truth. Once the light of truth is shown and women begin to see that they are not going against their Maker or Nature by expressing or embracing being dominant, the shackles of religion can come off and the inner power of the female can be exercised with a guilt-free mind and a heart of confidence.

There is a spiritual dimension to Female Domination. Females have a power over males and that power is not physical. That power is expressed through the sexual but it resides in the mind and originates in the spirit. This power is within and women need to release it. I call this power the latent power of Eve. I believe that women were created to be in authority over men, not to lord it over them but to complete them with loving female authority. We are spiritual beings so no matter how the mind has been programmed by society or religion, the spirit strives for truth. This may explain why man yearns for Female Domination even as he lives in a so-called patriarchal world. Be it the male followers of Cybele during the Roman Empire, the men who frequented the Brothels of Flagellation in 18th Century Europe or the American businessman of today who frequents a House of Domination. Something within man longs to be in subjection to a woman.

The latent power of Eve can do wonders in the life of the female, not only in her personal relationships, but also in her social life, in her career, and in every other area of her life. Right now in our society, men hold most positions of power and authority. However, they hold these positions by deceiving women into allowing them to be the dominant gender. The truth is that women are the superior gender and once a woman unleashes her dominant power, few men are able to resist her. Men become submissive and like little puppy dogs when they are confronted with a powerful woman. Attitude is the key. The woman who believes she is superior will permeate that attitude and thus she develops an aura of dominance and power. *"As (she) thinketh in (her) heart, so is (she)." (Proverbs 23:7).*

Deep down, men know that women are not their equals, no matter how politically correct our society tries to be. Women are different and mysterious to men. Women are sexual in a way that men do not understand. Women have a power that men do not understand and cannot resist. This female power is active during the courtship between a man and a woman. Men are under the spell of the female during the dating and courtship process. Most males are in the submissive role and most women are in the dominant roles during the courtship. They may not recognize those roles, but that is what in fact happens. The female uses her sexuality (knowingly or unknowingly) and the man is helpless under her power. Men will try to prove to the female how he is worthy of her time and attention and how happy he will make her if she will accept him as her mate.

During the courtship, men shower the female with flowers and gifts. A man will romance the woman and write her poetry and sing her songs. Even macho and overly masculine men will show their softer side around a woman whom they are interested in forming a lasting relationship. Men become selfless and will agree to do whatever the woman wants to do, just to be near her. But once they become married, this all stops. The male usually reverts back to his old ways and becomes selfish and begins to take the woman for granted. He hangs around his old friends again and he watches lots of television, ignoring the love of his life. He becomes cheap and the flowers and the gifts stop. He begins to refuse to do things with his wife and refuses to visit her family and friends. Everything becomes a fight and an argument. Then there is the sex. Sex use to last all night and be so exciting but now it has become boring and fast. Once the man gets his sexual release, it's time to go to sleep. Forget about the female. After all, bringing her to orgasm is too much work. What happened to the passion? What happened to the man of the courtship?

What happened is that the female didn't realize how she had him under her spell. Her female beauty and her sexuality had captured the male and he fell for her. He would do anything for her during the courtship. She didn't realize it at the time, but she was the dominant one and he was the submissive one during the courtship. She didn't have to know about D&S or Female Domination as her sexual energy and female ways naturally caused the man to become submissive towards her. For a short time, his macho ways and male pride was overcome by her female power.

However, once the two of them were married or entered into a serious relationship, his male pride and societies ways caused him to become the dominant one and she surrendered that power and the spell was broken. Now he expects her to be the good little wife and he expects her to obey him. He starts to call the shots and the euphoria is over, for the both of them.

That power is still within the married woman. As a matter of fact, she only used a little of her sexuality and power during the courtship. There is much more power within her that if released, will not only bring back the man that she fell in love with, but will drive him into total submission to her. Not just her husband either, but all men will sense her female power and they will either desire to serve her or they will be afraid of her. Some women recognize their sexual and female power but other women need to have that dominant nature seduced and brought to the forefront by a man's submissive nature. There are many more men who realize that they are submissive than women who realize that they should be in charge.

Female Domination has always been a male desire tucked away in the depths of his mind and expressed in his sexual thoughts and urges. The dominant nature of woman usually lies dormant due to the programming a girl receives from a patriarchal society. But the submissive desire of man is easily ignited and brought to the forefront of his mind through his sexuality. It is only a matter of time when the male will try to introduce his fantasy to be sexually dominated to a member of the female gender. Some men will have the courage to confess this desire to their wife or girlfriend but most men will elect to confide in a stranger, like a professional dominant woman or a phone domination service. That way he can pay for domination and still remain anonymous thus not risking rejection by family or society.

With the liberation of the female and the societal empowerment of the female, men are beginning to feel more at ease confessing to their female partners a desire to submit to her in the bedroom. Some men choose a wise approach and take small steps to slowly seduce and awaken the dominant nature of the female. Others get impatient and spill their deepest secrets on a woman who is not prepared to hear such confessions. This leads to conflict and strife as the woman misunderstands and sees her man as a pervert. The male who wisely seduces his wife's dominant nature, has much more success, as he shows her the advantages of being the dominant partner within a male/female relationship.

Chapter Four

The Seduction of the Female Dominant Nature

You have put yourself in Fortune's power; now you must be content with the ways of your Mistress. If you try to stop the force of her turning wheel, you are the most foolish man alive. (Boethius, "The Consolation of Philosophy", c520)

What does the submissive male do who is in a relationship with a woman who has yet to come into her dominance or who is blinded to the societal evolution due to her traditions and upbringing? Society is changing but the submissive male is living his life in the now. The submissive male desires to submit to his wife or girlfriend of today. So what advice do I give these men when they open up about their submissive desires? Let me finish the story of Henry Adams who came to visit me in 1998.

The advice I gave to Henry Adams is the same advice I give to every submissive man who confesses to me his desire to submit to his wife or girlfriend. First of all, I was able to get Henry to see that his desires were very common within males and I was able to get Henry to be at peace with his submissive desires by convincing him that he was not a pervert. I pointed out to Henry that the many ads in DDI and the thousands of Dominatrix ads on the Internet demonstrated how many men are just like him and how there is a hunger within the male gender for Female Domination. The professional Dominatrix is simply filling the need that exists within a male gender that is too afraid to come clean with their wives about their submissive desires.

Once I sat Henry's mind at ease, I then proceeded to give him some practical advice about how he could introduce the Female Domination lifestyle to his wife. I explained to Henry that what he really desired was to submit to the woman he loved. I was able to get Henry to understand what true submission is really about. True submission is not looking inward at getting your own fantasies and desires fulfilled but true submission is to serve a woman in a selfless manner. For only the man who serves a woman in a manner that the woman desires will experience the submissive fulfillment that he has been seeking.

The professional Dominatrix is only a temporary submissive fix and not permanently fulfilling because the exchange of money causes the Dominatrix to focus on her clients needs instead of the male client focusing on the woman's needs. What Henry needed to do was to seduce his wife's dominant nature and thus liberate the dominant Genie from her bottle, not by buying her a leather outfit and a whip, but by genuinely serving her needs. I explained that the fetish outfits and the D&S may indeed manifest later but that was not to be his focus if he wanted to experience true Female Domination.

Henry took my advice and began to focus on his wife's needs. Henry channeled his submissive desires into serving his wife Doris. The first thing that Henry did was he stopped seeing professional Mistresses, he stopped calling phone services that offered phone domination and he quit buying FemDom magazines and videos behind his wife's back. Henry began to view his money as his wife's money. He changed his attitude and renewed his mind to the fact that he worked for his wife and that his paycheck really belonged to her.

Doris and Henry had been married for fifteen years. It was a good marriage but over the past five or six years, the romance had pretty much gone out of their relationship. Doris is a beautiful woman, outgoing and full of life. Henry adored her but like most husbands, he had taken her for granted. This began to change with Henry's new attitude.

Henry took my advice and started out slowly. Henry began by treating his wife like a Queen. He opened doors for her, pulled out her chair at dinner, and acted like a real gentleman around her. Henry brought her flowers and gifts of appreciation on a regular basis. Doris became most appreciative of this new attention and her warm reaction to his warm actions re-kindled the romance in their marriage.

Like so many other husbands, Henry had developed the bad habit of ignoring his wife and would go straight to the television or the Internet when he got home from the office, but not anymore. He now focused on ways to serve his wife. Doris worked as a saleslady in a department store and was on her feet most of the day. When she came home from a hard day's work, Henry got in the mode of serving his Queen. He would kneel at her feet, remove her shoes and give her a tender-loving foot massage. It didn't take Doris long at all to learn to relax and receive this loving submission from her husband.

On some nights, Henry would draw his wife a bubble bath and would bathe and pamper her. Henry loved fondling his wife's beautiful naked body as he bathed her with his soapy hands. After the bath, he would towel her off, blow dry and brush her hair while she sat in the vanity chair in their bedroom. After tending to her personal needs, he would offer to give her a back rub or a full body massage. Doris began to wallow in pleasure and she could not believe this sudden change in her husband. All of this attention reminded her of their courtship when Henry would do anything for her or go anywhere with her, just to be near her. Many of these nights of pampering ended in sex with one noticeable difference in their newly ignited sex life. Henry focused on Doris' pleasure. Henry got in the habit of orally servicing his wife and focusing on her orgasms, and not his. Henry got in the habit of asking for permission to have intercourse with his wife and when she allowed it, Henry would ask Doris for permission to climax. Doris always obliged when Henry asked for such permission, but she began to enjoy the fact that the sex was centering on her pleasure and her desires.

Henry also began to do the chores around the house that he knew his wife wanted him to do. Doris would have to beg Henry and nag Henry to mow the lawn, wash the cars and to put out the trash on garbage night. Henry was not a man who enjoyed doing household chores but he renewed his mind to the fact that by doing these chores, he was serving his Queen. Of course, I was the one who made these suggestions to Henry in the first place but he quickly grasped the concept and before he knew it, he was enjoying his status of being his wife's servant. Henry even jumped in and helped Doris with some of the so-called woman's chores like washing dishes, vacuuming and dusting.

Henry's service of Doris led to many discussions where Doris would ask Henry about this sudden change in his behavior. Henry took my advice and used such opportunities to tell his wife that he needed to serve her and he needed to submit to her. Henry took these opportunities to lightly bring up the subject of Female Domination without going into the fetish or D&S aspects. Henry just simply told Doris that he had an urge to submit to her their entire marriage but he suppressed that urge due to his thinking that the man needed to be macho and the leader. However, after fifteen years of marriage, he now realized that life was passing them by and that he got no greater joy in life than serving his wife.

Naturally, Doris responded favorably to this. She felt a bond to her husband unlike anything she had experienced since their courtship. Henry's servitude and outward submission began to stir her desire to dominate him. Doris knew nothing about Female Domination, as Henry was wise in not mentioning such things at this point. Henry simply focused on serving his wife and while he missed the leather and the D&S he got from the Pro Doms, he discovered that what I told him was true. Serving his wife in an unselfish manner was the most submissive fulfilling experience of his life. In addition to that, their marriage had become stronger than it had ever been.

Henry's servitude of Doris seduced her dominant nature. Doris was an out going woman with dominant urges but she suppressed them her entire life because of how she was raised. Doris believed that to be happy, a woman needed to marry a strong man and then allow the man to wear the pants in the family. Henry appeared to be such a man when she met him but it didn't take long after their marriage for Doris to realize that her husband was not a natural leader. Doris pretty much ran the marriage but it was more from being a strong, silent force behind her husband then being openly in charge. Doris considered herself to be a feminist but her strong religious upbringing programmed her that men were better equipped to run society, as well as the family.

Like most women, it did not take Doris long to realize that women could do as good of a job, if not better, when it came to making decisions and running the show. She realized this on her job and she realized this in her marriage. Henry did not know that Doris entertained such thoughts but as Henry was now seducing her dominant nature with his openly submissive attitude, Doris began to verbalize to Henry how she believed that perhaps the woman should run the marriage and other societal institutions. One thing was certain, she was enjoying being pampered and served by Henry. She had never been happier.

As Henry and Doris bonded over the next year from his submission and service of her, Henry began to feel more comfortable opening up to Doris about his submissive nature and desires. Had Henry discussed such things from the outset, Doris would have rejected such talk, as she would have responded to him from her preconceived ideas of what D&S and Female Domination were all about. Had Henry showed Doris a FemDom book or website right from the outset, her defense mechanism would have slammed her mind closed. However, after experiencing first hand the benefits of Henry's submission, Doris was now more comfortable and open to discuss Female Domination with the man she loved.

Henry continued to take things slow with Doris, but he became bolder in telling her about his adolescent years and his teenage years and how FemDom stories and images always excited him. Doris was now open to accept this part of her husband and his openness to her allowed them to bond on a more meaningful level. Henry eventually showed his wife some non-pornographic websites and books about Female Domination and while Doris was not overly enthusiastic in the beginning, she maintained an open mind and was willing to explore this with her husband. Henry had seduced her dominant nature and that taste of dominance over her husband was pleasant enough to Doris that she began to desire more.

Once Henry finally confessed to Doris about what he desired as a submissive man and about how he wanted to submit to her in deeper ways, Doris began to do her own research on the Internet and she began to desire to experiment with FemDom in the bedroom. It started out very mild, with Doris ordering some leather lingerie and a leather paddle. Doris also ordered a couple of WHAP magazines (Women Who Administer Punishments), a FemDom publication with a retro 1940's look with stories and articles about real women who were dominating their husbands, with a heavy emphasis on discipline. The more Doris learned about Female Domination, the more she became interested. Doris began to administer light spankings to Henry during sex with her paddle. This felt more natural than she had imagined. Henry responded very favorably to this discipline. Doris got the idea from the WHAP magazines to assign Henry regular chores and to have a weekly discipline session with him where she evaluated his performance in his service of her. Before long, the weekly discipline session became a regular part of their relationship.

Doris and Henry kept the lines of communication open and freely discussed what they each enjoyed about their D&S play and what they disliked. Henry could not believe what had happened. By the year 2000, he was in a full-blown Female Domination marriage with his wife Doris, complete with regular discipline sessions. Henry began to do most of the household chores as Doris expected that out of him. Doris agreed to dominate Henry in the bedroom, complete with fetish outfits and D&S activities, as long as Henry would obey her outside of the bedroom.

Doris enrolled Henry into a cooking class at a local community college and Henry began to do all the cooking as well as the majority of the household chores. Doris loved this new arrangement and it was like a dream come true. Henry served her needs, did the chores and treated her like a Queen. In return, Doris disciplined Henry to motivate him and to train him to become an even better servant to her. Henry's submissive nature was fulfilled and Doris blossomed into a confident and take-charge wife. The Genie was out of her bottle and by Doris' own admission, she would never go back to a non-FemDom marriage. Theirs was now a win/win relationship and neither of them had ever been happier.

Henry's approach to introducing his wife to the Female Domination lifestyle is the most effective method. While not all wives so easily embrace the D&S aspects like Doris did, most women will at least come to enjoy being served by their husbands in such a selfless manner. The key is that a man must first serve his wife and show her the benefits of the FemDom lifestyle before he can open up to her about his fetish and D&S desires. Even if his wife will never totally embrace Female Domination, I believe that the submissive male will still enjoy more submissive fulfillment from placing his wife's needs ahead of his own than he will by merely fantasizing about Female Domination. After all, true male submission is about denying self and focusing on the needs of the woman.

Once a woman's dominant nature has been seduced and she begins to feel those dominant urges, a man still must be patient and allow her the room to grow. Depending on a woman's upbringing, she may have a number of issues to work out within herself before she can openly embrace her dominant nature. Societal programming and religious upbringing can be major stumbling blocks for a woman as she begins to express a side of her nature that goes against what she was taught to be the norm for a member of her gender. Nevertheless, once the dormant dominant nature begins to come alive, most women will be able to overcome their inhibitions and blossom into that beautiful and confident dominant woman.

Kathy is an experienced dominant woman. She and her husband James have been active in Female Domination for over seven years. Kathy does phone counseling with submissive men under the name Ms Kathleen and she heads up a Female Domination support group in the Maryland/Virginia suburbs of Washington DC. Kathy absolutely loves Female Domination and is a firm believer in Female Supremacy. One gets the impression that Kathy was the one who brought James into this lifestyle for they seem so natural in their current roles. But that was not the case. James had to seduce Kathy's dominant nature and allow her the space to overcome her doubts and questions.

Once James had confessed to his wife his lifelong desire for Female Domination, Kathy agreed to play some D&S games with him in the bedroom. She struggled with this kind of sexuality and although she had fun, she had problems reconciling this lifestyle with her conscience. Kathy loved being dominant in the bedroom but she would go back and forth. She even threw out the riding crop and PVC outfit James had given her as a gift. But something about this lifestyle appealed to her at the same time. Kathy describes her metamorphosis into a dominant woman.

"My love for my husband has never waned. I was a blissful bride on my wedding day. I can't imagine a bride being more ready to get married to a man. The wedding day was great, the honeymoon was fun but I did not particularly care for the early years of our marriage. It was great being

74

married to a man that I considered my best friend. What I loved the most about being married was that there was always someone there to talk with and to do things with. We had a lot of fun together.

The problem I struggled with the most was trying to be the submissive wife that our society, our religion and our families expected. I was a twenty-eight year old single and independent woman when I entered into marriage. Now I was expected to submit to my husband. We both worked but somehow I was expected to cook the meals and clean the house. My husband expected this out of me, after all that is what he witnessed from his parents. I witnessed the same thing from my parents as my father worked and my mother stayed home and cared for us kids and the house.

Therefore, I thought that I needed to be the submissive wife and the homemaker. I agreed to this family model in theory but once I began to live it, I found myself hating it. I felt trapped and I guess I started to resent my lot in life. After six years of marriage, my husband and I began drifting apart. I never envisioned divorce but I could see us heading down the road that so many marriages do. I could see us being friends forever but not having that intimate loving I so desired.

I agreed to submit myself to my husband. After all, it is a man's world. I work for men, men run our country, and I was told that God is a man. So it made sense to me that a woman should submit to her husband. But why was I not happy being the good, obedient wife? It's not as if my husband was a tyrant. Far from it, he was a sweet, meek and easy-going man. If anything, he was too easy going. I would get frustrated at his inability to make a decision.

I am a go-getter. I have always been outgoing and aggressive. I am physical; my husband is passive. I am fiery and spirited; my husband is laid back. I am a doer; my husband is a thinker. I like to meet life head on; my husband likes to let life come to him. So who is better equipped to be in charge? If a company was interviewing someone to be a manager or a supervisor and my husband and I were the only two candidates, whom should they hire? Wouldn't it be the one with leadership abilities? That would be me. So why does society require that a man be the head of a marriage? Is it just because he has a set of balls? That makes no sense and if society has the marriage relationship wrong, I believe they have all the other institutions wrong as well."

Once Kathy had settled most of her doubts within, she finally agreed to pursue this lifestyle but she felt she needed to learn about Female Domination from an experienced dominant woman. Since she did not know of any, she decided that they needed to visit a professional Dominatrix. James had visited a couple of Pro Doms prior to marrying Kathy and he recommended a reputable Dominatrix with whom he once had a session. She lived in the DC area but Kathy didn't want to be influenced by James. She wanted to choose the Dominatrix based on her own research. Kathy chose Mistress Morgan in Pittsburgh. Mistress Morgan's website portrayed the kind of sophistication that was appealing to Kathy.

"Morgan advertised welcoming couples which was a major selling point for me. I sent her a polite e-mail introducing myself and informing her of what it was I was looking for out of someone in her line of work. She promptly replied to my letter and graciously gave me her telephone number along with the best times to call her. When we talked on the telephone, I knew she was the one. She quickly put my mind at ease, assuring me we would do nothing James or I felt uncomfortable with. What sold me on her was when she informed me that she was a Lawyer who did Professional Domination on the side."

Kathy and James drove to Pittsburgh for their joint session with Mistress Morgan. It would be a day that would forever change their lives, as Kathy was able to come to terms with her dominance and the FemDom lifestyle.

"We arrived at the restored Victorian residence which was located minutes from downtown Pittsburgh in a safe, upscale neighborhood. We made our way up the long staircase, rang the bell and Morgan's friendly face appeared around a half open door. She was stunningly beautiful with long black hair and big brown eyes. The inside of her place was clean, bright and spotless. Morgan wore a gorgeous one-piece black leather corset with buckles down the center. She also wore thigh-high black leather boots. This was the perfect outfit for my husband as he has an enormous leather fetish.

Morgan had told me to bring along an outfit. Since I had thrown out what little fetish attire I owned, I brought a short, sexy, black dress that exposed major cleavage. James had told me that I looked very dominant in this dress. Morgan showed me to her bathroom to change while she entertained James in her living room. Morgan had my husband strip totally naked and she placed some wrist and ankle cuffs on him. She made him sit on the floor of her living room awaiting my entrance. When I emerged in my tight dress, Morgan complimented me on how beautiful I looked. She invited me to sit on her couch and she asked me if I wanted James to sit next to me or did I prefer that he remain on the floor. This totally shocked me but I must say that the sight of my husband naked at the feet of two women did turn me on.

I made the decision that James had to remain on the floor. Morgan sat across from us and she took her time as she interviewed us about our past experiences and our future goals in the female domination lifestyle. After answering a series of her questions, I took another look at my husband. I loved seeing him in such a vulnerable state.

What I found fascinating about Morgan was how she was so open and honest about everything. We could have been two women discussing interior decorating or gardening. She discussed D&S and the Female Domination lifestyle with a complete confidence and assurance. She was a kind and considerate woman. She joked with us and she loved to tease my husband. Whenever my husband said anything that she found to be cute or funny, she would smile and lightly tap his cheeks as if he was a little boy and say something like "Awww, isn't he cute?"

After we talked for close to a half an hour, Morgan gave us a tour of her place. Besides the living room, kitchen and bathroom, she had two plays rooms in the back. Neither of which were very big. They were obviously two bedrooms she had converted into her play space. Morgan then began to show me what all the equipment was and how she used them. She experimented on my husband, taking the time to teach me how to dominate him and engage in D&S activities in a safe manner. We took things slowly and Morgan showed me how to do all the things I was interested in trying.

She calmly explained every item she used and answered all my questions. I was impressed with how she could teach me but also hold James attention at the same time. Morgan attached some mild nipple clamps on my husband. He was Ok at first but then he complained that they were hurting him. Morgan was merciful and removed them from him but not until she showed him the nipple clamps she used on her fiancé. The ones she put on James were rubber-tipped. The ones she used on her man were made of metal with sharp teeth. They were nasty looking. I wondered to myself if this sweet woman and intelligent lawyer didn't have a serious sadistic side.

Next, we moved to the larger of the two rooms. Morgan tied James, bent over this padded horse. His behind was vulnerable, exposed and sticking up in the air. Morgan began to teach me how to whip a man. We both disciplined him. I really enjoyed this as having someone else join in with you validates your own actions and desires in some way. We used various types of whips and paddles and she ended his discipline with her showing me her favorite activity, caning a man. My husband's ass was all red from having two women go at it. My husband can be a wimp at times, like how he whined when she put the nipple clamps on him. But I must say that my husband can take a good paddling and whipping across his buttocks. When Morgan used the cane, however, he jerked and let out a scream. It was priceless. He would squirm to try to avoid each strike of her cane but to no avail.

Finally, it was my turn. Morgan showed me how to place the cane against his butt and then bring it back slowly before striking it with a flick of my wrist. I loved the sound of the cane swishing through the air and the stinging sound of it making contact with my husband's flesh. I have never entertained any sort of sadistic desires in my entire life. I am a kind woman who loves to hug and kiss people and animals. However, something was definitely unleashed within me as I whipped and caned my husband that day. I found myself getting aroused as I caned my husband. My husband was relieved when we finally released him from his bonds. His cute little butt was a nice shade of pink and red with a few stripes of dark red from the cane.

I had one more surprise for him before we left. Morgan asked me if there was anything else I wanted to try before our session ended. I knew that James had this fantasy of being humiliated by me in front of another woman. So I asked Morgan if I could dominate my husband in front of her.

I didn't know that I had it in me but I ordered James to his knees in my most bitchy and demanding voice. I began to verbally humiliate him in front of Morgan as I told him what a worm he was and how our marriage relationship was going to change. I told him that I was taking over and I would call the shots from here on out because he wasn't man enough to make decisions. As I was berating him, I grabbed one of Morgan's whips and I struck his sore ass sharply. I then ordered James to lick and kiss my shoes and to grovel before Morgan and I. James snapped right to it and for the first time during our session with Morgan, he had a total erection. I was touching something within him and I knew I was on to something here. I made James confess his place in our marriage by confessing to Morgan how I was superior to him and how he was going to be my servant. I could tell that Morgan was impressed with my performance.

Afterwards, Morgan really encouraged me by telling me what a good job I did. She also presented me with a parting gift. She gave me my very own cane. I promised to put it to good use. James and I got dressed in our street clothes, as there was a knock at the door. Morgan went down to talk to a gentleman and he hurried on his way. I asked Morgan if that was one of her clients and she said that he was in fact a client of hers and he had stopped by to get his list of assignments and tasks that she wanted him to do for her. Now I was the one who was impressed. Men stopped by just to do chores for her and probably paid her for that privilege. I could get use to that.

Morgan gave us both a big hug and told me to write or call her again if I had any questions or needed help with anything. I was certain that I would take her up on her offer. After the session I was extremely motivated to get serious about this lifestyle. In fact, Morgan gave us the address to a fetish store in her area and we stopped on our way home to purchase some toys and some new fetish outfits for me. I spent over a thousand dollars on my new wardrobe and toy collection. My husband was not about to complain. I think he was grateful just to be standing around the store. His sore bottom needed a break before the long car drive home."

Although Kathy still had to work through some of her issues as far as society and religion were concerned, from that day forward, Kathy never looked back. She totally embraced the Female Domination lifestyle and James and her developed an even deeper love for each other.

The stories of Doris and Henry and Kathy and James are not unique. I have interviewed dozens of other couples with similar experiences and I have received hundreds of letters and e-mails from couples who have a similar story to tell. Female Domination is a growing and thriving lifestyle within our society.

Chapter Five

The Greatest Sex Organ:
The Psychology of Female Domination

Love looks not with the eyes, but with the mind, and therefore is winged Cupid painted blind. (William Shakespeare, "A Midsummer Night's Dream", Act I, Scene I)

Most of the time, it is the husband that introduces his wife to the female domination lifestyle. She usually embraces it out of love for her husband and then she ends up loving this lifestyle as well. She experiences first hand the intimacy and the improved sex life and she loves the benefits outside of the bedroom like the extra attention and the help around the house. With women in the workforce, the need to have the male perform domestic chores around the house is a great motivator for women to explore the sexual aspects of the male's desire to be in the submissive role. Women are discovering that to dominate a man in the bedroom can lead to a man's submission outside of the bedroom and the rewards to the female are plentiful. Furthermore, women are discovering that the male sexual desire to be dominated in the bedroom leads to a fresh and exciting form of sexuality and provides for intense sexual fulfillment for the female. Women usually indulge the male fantasy to be dominated out of love for their partner but end up discovering a new area of their own sexuality, namely a desire to dominate men.

The male that seduces the female dominant nature unleashes that Tigress within and many females fall in love with her new power, both inside and outside of the bedroom. Women I have interviewed claim an increase in their self-image once they embraced their dominant nature. They claim a higher sex drive and more intense orgasms. They claim more confidence outside the home, in their career. A real power exchange occurs within the home when a man seduces his wife's dominant nature with his submissive nature. Thus society continues to evolve, one female/male relationship at a time.

Not every female domination relationship is the same. Some are more advanced than others based on the desires of the individuals involved. Some couples keep it confined to the bedroom and this satisfies them. Others take it outside the bedroom into their everyday life and this satisfies them. What is obvious from talking to couples that practice this lifestyle is that they have better marriages today than they did prior to embracing Female Domination.

Powerful women both excite and frighten men. When you have talked to as many submissive men as I have, it becomes apparent how strong the desire to submit to women is within the male gender. When I got involved in this lifestyle, I had no idea how deep these desires ran in men. It is not just D&S games to balance out ones life, as many believe.

A lot of very successful men find out that their lives are still not fulfilling, even after they have succeeded in business or their chosen profession. The more prosperous and powerful a man becomes, the more his weakness is magnified. A lot of men walk around thinking that if they only had more money or success, all would be well. The men that have the money and the success realize that these cannot satisfy them emotionally, socially, and spiritually. Successful men have the resources to explore their submissive desires at a greater length than does the average middle class male. But regardless of a male's financial and social status, the desire is still there to submit to the female gender. This just goes to show further that the desire to submit is present within all men and economical and social factors do not play a major role in the development of these desires. A man's childhood and his interactions with female authority figures when he is a child and an adolescent, play the biggest role in the development of that submissive seed that I believe is present within all men.

Another widely held viewpoint is that a person's temperament will determine if they will be dominant or submissive within relationships. In my opinion based on my years of study and participation in the Female Domination lifestyle, dominance or submission cannot be measured by a person's temperament.

The human temperament has been broken down into sixteen categories under four distinctive types, Sanguine, Choleric, Melancholy and Phlegmatic. The Sanguine is an extrovert, a talker and an optimist. They are emotional, demonstrative, enthusiastic, expressive and loud. Likewise, a Choleric is decisive, strong-willed, and bossy. It has been thought that a person who is a Sanguine or a Choleric would gravitate toward the dominant role within personal relationships. It has also been assumed that a Melancholy and a Phlegmatic would gravitate toward the submissive role. A Melancholy is a person who is an introvert, a thinker and a pessimist. A Melancholy is analytical, creative, sensitive, self-sacrificing, and usually has a low self-image. A Phlegmatic is also an introvert and is easy-going, relaxed, quiet, indecisive and tends to be shy.

From my years of counseling and interviewing submissive men, it has been rather obvious that the male desire to be in submission to the female gender has very little to do with temperament. There are submissive men who are introverted, shy and passive and there are submissive men who are aggressive, outgoing and extroverts. The male desire to submit to the female cannot be over analyzed. Some have tried to explain the popularity of the professional Dominant woman (a.k.a. the Dominatrix) as being a way for the aggressive businessman to obtain balance in his life. It has been said by some who have examined the phenomenon of the D&S lifestyle that D&S attracts men of power and of a "Type A" personality because FemDom gives these alpha male types a chance to be on the receiving end of aggression and power instead of being on the giving end. In other words, Female Domination gives the macho male an avenue to find balance.

Then there are those who have claimed that FemDom attracts men who have a low self-image because they harbor a secret desire to be abused. Some in the field of Psychology believe that the Melancholy is most likely to develop masochistic desires. These two theories contradict each other. If FemDom primarily attracts shy and insecure males, then why do so many aggressive and extrovert males also desire to be dominated by a woman?

Just as a man's temperament cannot be used to determine the source of his submissive desires, a woman's temperament cannot be used to measure her potential to be dominant. Women who are Melancholy or Phlegmatic are just as capable of being Dominant as women who are out-going. Dominance is primarily an attitude. It is an inner nature and it is authoritative. Out-going and aggressive women are more easily turned on to Female Domination but they do not necessarily make the best Dominants. Some of the most dominant and authoritative women that I know are very laid back and quiet. They dominate more with their aura and their self-confidence than they do with strong outward personality traits. One woman I know rarely raises her voice when she dominates a man but she has the most intense stare and controlling aura about her that men crumble in her presence. She believes that she is superior to men and she walks with that confidence and that authority.

I have found that the more laid back and soft-spoken Professional Doms are the most popular. While some men fantasize about a strong and aggressive woman overpowering them and having her way with them, far more men fantasize about a mysterious and confident woman seducing them with her sexuality and than enslaving them with her mysterious female power. Men are attracted to a confident and sophisticated woman, whether she is out going or laid back. Domination is all about attitude. If a woman believes she is superior to men and walks in that authority, men cannot resist her no matter what her temperament.

The primary reason outgoing women make the most likely candidates to embrace the Female Domination lifestyle is because they are already accustomed to being aggressive with men but still struggle with the roles that society has shackled them with. Once that barrier is removed through willing male submission, an out going woman usually runs with this lifestyle much like a caged animal who has been freed. A woman who is a Choleric may be more open for physical domination play such as corporal punishment whereas a Phlegmatic woman may enjoy softer and sensual D&S activities better. Nevertheless, one should not mistake the softness of a woman for weakness or submission. Some of the most dominant and slightly sadistic women I have known were Phlegmatic.

They may not like to forcefully take a man but they enjoy the psychological domination play like the teasing and denial of the male, forced feminization of the male and even enforced chastity of the male.

These are generalizations of course, and it would be a mistake to assume that a woman would prefer a certain D&S activity over another simply based on her temperament. Many aggressive and out going women also enjoy softer and sensual D&S activities and likewise a laid back woman may indeed love administering corporal punishment on her man. One of the beautiful things about D&S is that it allows an arena where people can experiment with different sides of their personalities and natures. One never knows what hidden desire is within until that desire is touched, unlocked and freed through experimentation and exploration. A person may not be able to change their temperament but a person may indeed free a part of their personality that was previously locked up due to inhibition and fear.

Our true natures come from the inside out but unless one opens their mind, our natures can be held captive and thus remain dormant. When this happens, our natures try to break forth via the sub-conscience. That is why a man will be going along in life and all of a sudden a scene in a movie or a story in a magazine about female domination will trigger something within his sub-conscience (bypassing his conscience) and he will experience desires he previously had no idea were there. Dreams will also express thoughts of the sub-conscience mind, as was the case with James with his dreams from his childhood.

Domination and submission is about a sexuality of the mind. Physical sex is about bodily pleasure obtained through the sensual sensations of touch and physical contact. D&S is a sexuality about mental stimulation that triggers sexual arousal. Within the submissive male are psychological triggers that when stimulated within his mind, will trigger an intense sexual arousal. These triggers are childhood experiences and every thought, sight, sound, smell, taste and physical experience that a person encounters in life.

The human brain can be viewed as a computer. It stores every experience a human encounters. The eyes, the nose, the ears, the mouth and the senses are all input devices that transport data into the human brain. A person's sexuality is influenced by the collection of the data within the brain. The brain becomes the greatest sex organ and physical contact is not necessary to rouse the sexual senses if an intense image, sound, taste or smell can access the data within the brain and thus trigger a sexual reaction. D&S is a sexuality that stimulates these triggers within a person's psyche.

I have discussed a man's core nature and how certain sexual desires and fantasies are the expression of a man's core nature. I have also discussed how I believe the seeds of submission are implanted in men at birth and are cultivated through his interactions with female authority figures. This can also be described using the computer analogy. Think of a person's core nature as being the pre-loaded software or operating system, whereas a person's life experiences are the data that is created and accumulated over time.

Each person has a human will to make decisions in life but some decisions are made for us by nature. For example, we blink our eyes every couple of seconds, our bodies maintain a core temperature of 98.6, we have a built in air conditioner unit when we overheat known as sweat glands, our heart pumps continually, our lungs breath in and out, and etc. The brain controls all of these bodily functions but we do not have to will them to happen, they are automatic within healthy human beings. Our core nature is also preloaded through genetics. Our temperament and personality is pre-loaded as is our skin color, eye color, hair color, and body type. Nature also preloads sexual programming in our minds thus sensual touch causes sexual arousal. The caressing of the skin feels pleasurable, as does a warm bath, as does touching one's genitalia. God has created us to have certain given responses to certain forms of stimulation. This programming exists in our brains and it is preprogrammed.

On top of this preprogramming goes all the data that our senses collect throughout our lifetime. Males are pre-wired to be visually oriented and Females to be sensually oriented. Thus, men react more to sight and women to touch within the arena of sexuality. This gives women an incredible advantage sexually because the female form is a masterpiece of nature and mortal man has great difficulty controlling his sexual urges when he sees a woman naked or scantily clothed. The data enters into his eyes, goes to his brain, is processed, and his programming sends a signal to his genitals causing the penis to become stimulated, without any actual physical contact.

A man is born with the seeds of submission (a preloaded program) and that core nature is further built upon through childhood experiences with female authority figures. A boy might be bathed by a woman, spanked by a woman, scolded by a female authority figure, nurtured and loved by female authority figures and all of these interactions goes into the male psyche. As the male enters puberty, the beauty of the female captivates him and his sexuality begins to develop according to his core nature and his childhood experiences.

In addition, the female has a natural sexual power that permeates from her and this power (be it the latent power of Eve or nature's way of procreating) captivates men. The sexual desire of human beings has been called animalistic but unlike animals, the sexuality of humans is not instinctive. The sexuality of humans is about more than just physical sex. It is also spiritual and mental. Desire begins in the mind but desire is based on what is in the heart. Human sexuality is about romance, love, commitment, partnership and yes, dominance and submission. The need for love, romance and sex is stronger than the need for food, air, water and sleep. While a person needs the later things for survival and can exist with out the former things from a physical perspective, from an emotional perspective the desire for love, romance and sex is more important to the condition of the human soul.

Unlike animals, humans possess the ability to imagine, dream and create with thought. Thought is faster than the speed of light because a person can travel to a place in their mind simply by thinking. While their body does not leave its current location, the imagination can go anywhere. Humans can dream big dreams and create buildings, cities, and civilizations. The physical follows the mental thus each creation begins in the mind in the form of thought before the physical reality is realized. While the great feats of mankind is seen in big buildings and large cities, the greatest creations are those that cannot be touched with human hands but are rather touched by the human spirit. Music, poetry, literature are all creative thoughts transferred to the hand via the spirit by way of the brain.

The spiritual comes first and then the natural. Just as God created the Heavens and the Earth first through thought, then the spoken word and finally through the works of His/Her hands, so does humankind create first through thought, then word and finally through the works of the hands. The species of Man is not an animal for an animal cannot design a building or build a city or compose music. Likewise, sex between a human female and a human male is not purely physical. Sex exists in the spiritual realm first, then the mental and finally the physical. Those who only practice a physical form of sex are only scratching the surface of the possibilities, for the soul of woman and the soul of man is creative.

The brain contains both the core nature of a person and the totality of the person based on that person's life. Just as the scriptures describe sex between Adam and Eve as Adam "knowing" Eve, so should sex be between a husband and a wife today. To "know" someone is not purely physical contact. To "know" someone is to tap into the vast resources of the psyche, to touch them at their core nature and to find those triggers that make each person unique and who they are. D&S provides the vehicle for such a sexuality because D&S is all about the sex of the minds. It takes truly knowing someone to have a D&S session with them. A woman cannot effectively dominate a man she does not know or understands. That is why the Pro Dom must have a client fill out a questionnaire. She needs to learn about her male client, so she can know a little about him to ensure the D&S session is going to be fulfilling to him.

Within the psyche of the male is the desire to be dominated thus D&S play becomes sex of the psyches between a dominant woman and a submissive male. D&S is about a power exchange and the surrender of the masculine and macho ways of a male over to the feminine ways of the female. Women permeate a sexual power and the beauty that is the feminine touches man at his core nature.

When a man surrenders to this power coming from the female, he enters into the submissive zone (or subspace). As he lets go and yields himself to the woman, he disarms his conscience guard and he allows his submissive nature to be released. This causes him to enter into that tranquil and near hypnotic state. That is what is known as subspace. Women love what subspace does to men. It makes them meek, obedient, loving, and worshipful. This feeds a woman's dominant nature and she feeds off of the submissive energy coming from the man.

Subspace or as I like to call it, the submissive zone, is a tranquil and somewhat hypnotic state that comes from the absolute surrender of the human will. Subspace is obtained within males when they surrender their will and their power over to a female. I analyze subspace from a psychological perspective, not from a biological perspective. Men who are masochists claim that they enter subspace via endorphins that are released in the brain to block the pain and this causes the man to obtain a sort of a high from the endorphins. Endorphins are hormones that bind to opiate receptors and they reduce the sensation of pain and can affect the emotions. I do not doubt the validity of the high that endorphins provide to a masochist. Runners who push themselves beyond their threshold claim to have a runner's high from endorphins. However, I feel that this is different from subspace. While a masochist may indeed enter subspace, I believe this is due to the mental stimulation that he encounters as he surrenders his will over to the female.

The reason I do not believe in the correlation between pain and subspace is because different D&S activities will transport a man to the submissive zone and most of these activities do not involve physical pain. A man need not be a masochist to enter subspace. Humiliation play will transport a man to subspace. Being cuckolded (a husband who willfully accepts his wife's infidelity) transports men to subspace. Strap-on play, light discipline, worshipping the female body, even the sight of a woman in fetish attire will transport some men to subspace. So what do these activities have in common? The mental stimulation of a man surrendering his will over to the woman.

The D&S activity is what triggers the mental stimulation and it is the mental stimulation that transports the man to subspace. Subspace can last a few hours or it can last for weeks at a time. It depends on the trigger and the depth of that trigger. The male psyche is like an onion and it needs to be peeled back layer by layer. The deeper you go, the more potent the trigger. Once you discover these triggers, they can be touched and stimulated with the expected results. In my opinion, all men are capable of achieving subspace if they will let go and if they will surrender to a dominant woman.

Subspace is a place of absolute surrender and a place where the female rules supreme. It is a magical place within the psyche of a man where he worships a woman with his spirit. It is powerful and it is beautiful. For only a man who surrenders his will to a woman and enters the submissive zone, can fully see a woman in all her beauty and glory.

Subspace is different for each male. Every man is unique with a unique nature, a unique personality and with unique life experiences. Depending on his nature and his experiences, a man's sexuality is developed and is stored within his mind. It often takes experimentation to explore and discover exactly what will trigger a man's submissive nature. It is initially explored through the sexual but once touched and released via sexual and mental stimulation, it will cause a man to lay down his guard (his human will) and if he lets go and surrenders himself to the female, he will enter into subspace. The D&S is a merely a tool that a woman uses to explore the hidden areas of the man's mind, looking for that trigger that will cause the man to surrender his will to her. Once he does, it opens them both up to embrace their true natures.

Since the male psyche is like an onion, the deeper the dominant woman explores, the more intense the scene and the more potent the trigger. Once a woman discovers her man's triggers, they can be touched and stimulated with the expected results. If is it a negative trigger (childhood hurts, abuse, etc), a woman can bring healing to it through nurturing and love. The trigger remains and the woman can use it to take her submissive to subspace, thus she can turn the negative into a positive. If it is a positive trigger or a trigger with an unknown origin or quality, she can use it to her advantage to further her control and power over her submissive.

In my opinion, all men are capable of achieving subspace if they will let go and if they will surrender to a dominant woman. It need only be a short and temporary surrender if it is a man having a scene with a Dominatrix or a Professional Mistress. A man can surrender, enter subspace, and worship a woman whom he does not have a relationship with. The subspace will last for the session and perhaps hours after the session, but then he returns to his normal life. However, if a man is married (or in a permanent relationship with a dominant woman) he can experience an even greater level of submission. His time in subspace will vary and although he will still live most of the time out of subspace, the dynamics of an ongoing relationship will enable the man to live a life of worshipful and meaningful service of his dominant woman. His time in subspace will be multiplied and weekly sessions will ensure the power exchange and the power dynamics of the female domination relationship.

What men are discovering is that freedom does not come from trying to maintain control. Freedom will come only when they surrender. That which restricts and confides a submissive man is his analytical and logical thinking. But the man that surrenders to a woman will experience true inner freedom. A train is restricted by its tracks but that which restricts it also allows it to freely move across the country. Take the train off the tracks, it is no longer restricted by the tracks but it also cannot move at all. That which restricts it is that which frees it. A woman's dominance and control will restrict her man and confide her man but if the man will yield to her power, he will find that he enjoys more inner freedom under her control than he ever did under his own control.

Female Domination can bring an incredible amount of harmony to a marriage. One couple shared with me how female domination can be used to end arguments and defuse fights. To quote from the husband Brett:

"When we are in the middle of a heated disagreement, my wife will sometimes pull out some fabric strips (that are normally used for romantic purposes) and tie me to a chair; we have an understanding that I will not resist this act no matter how angry I might be. After then gagging me with a scarf or bandana, she will leave me for an hour or two to think about it.

The strong emotions that I experience during this time are always the same: I go from fury (at being helpless and unable to continue the argument) to frustrated resignation to regret about having upset her to burning passion for her.

When she returns and loosens the gag (leaving me still tied), I am dying to apologize to her and "make it up to her" by serving her sexually. At this point she accepts my apology and calmly explains how I am expected to change my behavior in the future. Then when she is satisfied that I am contrite, we exchange "I love you's" and she goes away again leaving me bound to the chair for another half hour or so. By the time she finally releases me, I am ready to explode with both lust and loving emotion for her.

I know that some BDSM writers believe that female domination practices must only occur in romantic or sexual scenarios, but we believe that since she is the boss 24/7, that it is even more important that she be able to assert herself during disagreements. I can testify that emotionally, it is very effective for both of us."

What this wise woman has discovered is she's taking a negative experience and turning it into a pleasurable and positive one for her husband by incorporating female domination. She realizes that by placing him in bondage, eventually his submissive desires will come to the forefront and overpower his anger and frustration. She knows that he cannot resist her dominance and authority. His anger melts away and he chose submission over anger and frustration. She is one smart lady.

If only more women would use their sexual and dominance weapons to defuse arguments and fights in their marriage. Once a wife knows what causes her husband to become weak and submissive, she needs to use that knowledge whenever her husband steps out of line and displays negative behavior. I have defused many of potential serious arguments in my own marriage by ordering my husband, in my most bitchy and commanding voice, to drop to his knees and to kiss my feet or lick my shoes or kiss my tush. He fumes and he is reluctant but he can't refuse me when I get bitchy with him, so he reluctantly falls to his knees and begins to unenthusiastically kiss my feet. In a matter of seconds, his anger flees as his submission and passion explodes and he begins to kiss and lick very enthusiastically. Then if we have time, I take him to the bedroom for a little attitude adjustment or if we don't have the time, we just hug, make-up and go on our merry way. Female domination is very powerful and a smart woman will use that power to keep harmony in her home.

A temper is an outward expression of an underlying insecurity. A man with a temper has issues within him that when touched, will cause him to act childish. D&S is a wonderful lifestyle for a man with a temper because he needs the firm discipline of a loving woman to give him an alternative outlet to release that pent up anger. The whip used correctly can drive anger out of a man if he will surrender to his wife's female power during the discipline session.

Keep in mind that childish behavior often needs to be dealt with in a parental manner. A child needs lots of nurturing and reassurance as well as discipline. When a husband becomes angry and expresses his childish behavior, the worst thing a woman you can do is to express anger back at him. A wise woman who understands female domination will stay calm and under control, knowing that she will have her chance for retribution. If she becomes angry, then it is best that she remove herself from her husband's presence until she cools off. Two angry people should not be in the same room. That is always a condition for trouble. A wise woman will walk away and collect herself before returning to deal with her grown male child. Just as a woman should never discipline her children when she is angry, the dominant wife should never discipline her husband when she is angry.

A wise woman will walk away from him, collect herself and return with a strategy. That strategy depends on her husband's submissive nature. Through the female domination lifestyle, she has come to know him better than he even knows himself. What is it that stirs his submission? Does he have a leather fetish? Does he have a foot fetish? What is it that turns him submissive? The wise wife will get his submission to overpower his anger so she can reconcile with him first, then she can punish him for his temper tantrum.

I know my husband has a strong leather fetish. After I cool down, I might dress in a sexy, leather outfit, return to him and order him to his knees. I can see the struggle within him as his hurt and anger wants to continue the fight but his submission wants to bow before me. I love watching that internal struggle within him. I will order him again in my most bitchy voice to bow before me and to kiss my boots or feet. Notice, I do not mention what we were fighting about. I approach it as a regular D&S session. Usually, my husband will submit and once he is kissing my boots or feet, his anger begins to leave his body and passion and submission will overtake him.

If that does not work, I go to another weapon that I know he cannot resist. I will walk over to him, hug him and kiss him. I will not say a word but I will lead him by the hand to our bed. I will lay him face up on the bed and I will proceed to sit my tush on his face and I will order him to kiss and worship it. This will cause most men to melt into submission. The face sitting also prevents him from speaking, so that will defuse the argument at least momentarily until his submission overtakes his anger.

Regardless which approach I use, my goal is to get him into a submissive state. Then I bring reconciliation by telling him that I love him. After that, I might make him confess his place in our marriage. I will make him tell me how I rule over him and how I have authority over him. Once I see that he is in a submissive state, only then will I re-visit the argument by making him apologize to me. Again, I do not seek this apology outside of our D&S session or else it might re-kindle the argument.

After he apologizes, I will tie him face down on the bed and now it is time to punish him for his behavior. He is already in a submissive mood so I will give him a spanking and that is when I let him know how upset he made me and he will feel my displeasure through my loving but firm discipline. My husband says that he can feel the hurt and anger leaving his body as I discipline him. Afterwards, I will hug him and love on him as we confess our love for each other. It works like a charm.

Once a woman understands the correlation between love and discipline, D&S and specifically Female Domination will seem less unusual and will begin to make more sense. It is the female gender that possesses the ability to discipline and punish in a loving manner. Grown men never out grow the need or the desire for loving discipline at the hands of a woman. While most men desire some form of correction from the female gender, I believe that the less discipline a man had from a woman when he was a child, the stronger the desire for discipline will be when he is an adult.

As our society goes away from the spanking and physical disciplining of children, I am finding that men desire to be spanked even more as adults because that important part of nurturing is missing from their upbringing. I really believe that physical punishment (done in love) is an important part of the nurturing process that boys need and men still crave it as adults inside of their psyche.

Chapter Six

Love and Punishment:
Female Domination through Discipline

Do not consider painful what is good for you (Euripedes, "Medea", 431 BC)

She is frequently kind and she's suddenly cruel, She can do as she pleases, she's nobody's fool. (Billy Joel, "She's Always A Woman To Me")

Beverly and Vince have a wonderful relationship. They have been happily married for twenty years and rarely can one be seen without the other. Together they run a successful Bed and Breakfast in the New England state where they live. Both are well educated with Masters degrees. Beverly worked for fifteen years in Real Estate and Vince worked in the Investment field before they realized their dream and bought the B&B.

Beverly is a beautiful woman, feminine, fit and full of grace. She makes the perfect hostess at the old New England Inn that doubles as their residence and place of business. Vince is a dapper gentleman who does most of the manual labor and shares in some of the domestic chores with the hired help. Vince is extremely courteous and kind to the guests with noticeable manners toward women. Vince is a throwback to when males would treat women like ladies. Vince's manners are especially obvious in his relationship with Beverly. Vince treats Beverly like a Princess and his devotion and love for her is obvious to anyone who sees them together.

Their private quarters exist on the top floor of the large Inn, complete with a private entrance. While running the Inn affords them little free time from the late Spring through the early Autumn, they still manage to steal away plenty of time for romance. Beverly describes her relationship with Vince as a fairy tale come true. Their sex life is full of passion. Blissful, is how Beverly describes it. An outsider would consider Beverly and Vince as the perfect couple and that they are. Yet, Beverly and Vince have a little secret about their successful marriage, one that very few people know about. So what is the secret ingredient that causes them to have such a wonderful relationship?

"I run our marriage and I dominate Vincent both inside and outside the bedroom", Beverly shares. "At least once a week, I discipline Vincent much like a loving Mother would her mischievous son. We are into good old-fashioned over the knee spankings. I like to dress up in various outfits to set a certain mood and then I scold Vincent about the things he did during the week that bothered me. I order him to lie across my lap and I proceed to discipline him. We have been doing this for the past ten years and it has worked miracles in our relationship.

When I am done disciplining Vincent, he radiates with peace and contentment. Then I take him in my arms and we both become full of passion. It is rare if our discipline sessions do not lead to blissful sex. Our weekly discipline sessions bring harmony to our relationship as I deal with all strife and anxiety while I discipline him, thus we work through our differences in a fun manner. The result is that we are free to go about our business the rest of the week in perfect agreement and harmony. I always take Vincent's needs into consideration but I rule the roost and I make the decisions. We would have never realized our dreams if I hadn't taken Vincent to where we needed to go as a couple. He is a very cautious person, which is good as that brings balance to our marriage, but I am a go-getter and I am able to motivate Vincent through our discipline sessions."

So exactly how does Beverly discipline her husband and how does this build intimacy?

"What I do during a discipline session with Vincent is as follows. I will first dress up in an outfit that I know will excite Vincent, as well as prepare him for his spankings. I have come to realize that the best way to get a man to become submissive is through a man's sexuality. I know that Vince has a real leg fetish, so I wear sexy nylons, stockings or pantyhose along with a short skirt, high heel shoes and usually just a bra. Such a look drives Vincent into submission and mentally prepares him for his discipline. I change up the outfit by changing the material and look of my skirt as well as utilizing the array of stockings and pantyhose I have at my disposal. But regardless, my overall appearance highlights my shapely and sexy legs that Vince finds so attractive.

Next, I will order Vince to undress and kneel before me. At that time, I will being to critique his weekly performance of his chores around the Inn, as well as how he treats the people he comes in contact with, especially those of the female gender. I will scold Vince if he disobeyed me during the week or displays a negative attitude. Once I have told Vince of what he has done to displease me, I will sit down on the edge of our bed, order him across my lap and then I discipline him accordingly.

I may spank him with my bare hands or I may use a tool of discipline like a hairbrush or a paddle. I start out with slow and sensual blows to his bare bottom, carefully rubbing his butt cheeks with tender loving caresses. I talk to Vincent in soft whispers, challenging him to be a better husband and informing him of my demands of him for the week ahead. Vincent yields to my dominance and surrenders his will over to me. This brings peace to Vincent and love and harmony to our marriage."

As Beverly described, their discipline session usually leads to a night of passion and sex. Beverly gets turned on by the act of spanking Vince's behind and Vince is overwhelmed by Beverly's sexuality and dominance. So how on earth did they happen upon such a lifestyle?

"Vincent and I have always enjoyed the kind of relationship where we communicated about everything. We have always been open with each other and unafraid to discuss our dreams and desires. It didn't take us long into our marriage before we both realized that I was the dominant

partner. Vincent was your typical American male who tried to act macho but I never put up with that. I knew that Vincent was meek and sweet and I just naturally took the reigns of the marriage.

One time about ten years into our marriage, Vincent confessed to me about the excitement he felt when he read stories about dominant females. He showed me a couple of erotica books that he had purchased that had stories about female domination. I read them and rejected some of the stuff I viewed as being unrealistic but I incorporated that which I felt would mesh with my personality. Discipline was one of them. I was willing to experiment with Vincent in the bedroom in an effort to add some spice to our sex lives and one thing lead to another and it became a lifestyle to us. What can I say? It all seemed very natural to Vincent and I and the positive results it yielded to our lives was evident right from the outset."

Beverly and Vincent are not alone. It is hard to estimate how many couples practice Female Domination behind closed doors or how many wives incorporate discipline into their marriages. One thing is certain, Beverly and Vincent have lots of company in the lifestyle they have chosen. In my research, I have discovered all kinds of organizations and groups that share the common interest of wives disciplining their husbands. Whether it is the DWC (Disciplinary Wives Club), ClubFEM (Females Enslaving males), the AKS (Alice Kerr-Sutherland Society), one of the many Spanking clubs like Crimson Moon or Shadow Lane or one of the smaller and more secretive groups. The facts are obvious that more and more couples are incorporating discipline into their relationships and marriages, and having fun and fulfillment in the process.

Whipping and spanking a man is an art and a skill that is developed over time through practice. People who are repulsed at such a lifestyle between consenting adults have never taken the time to understand the psychology and the sexuality of such an act. The skilled woman does not discipline a man in a violent manner. She starts out light and makes it sensual, than she slowly builds it up to harder and more severe. She does not start out too hard or it will not be erotic. Disciplining the man you love can be an extremely sexual activity, not to mention it can be very productive in training the man you love to become the type of husband you desire.

The goal of the physical punishment is not what it does to a man's body but rather the effect it has on his mind. Spanking or whipping a man is not an act of violence but rather an act of love. The more a woman does it, the better at it she will become and the more her husband will desire it. Discipline and nurturing are the flip sides of the same coin of love. Men desire physical discipline and men need physical discipline. It is satisfying to their soul as it acts as a sort of a relief valve that releases pent up stress and frustration, as the submissive male surrenders his will over to the woman's will. Discipline is a very natural and healthy activity between two committed and loving adults.

When I discipline my husband, I touch his inner child and this transports him to a place of peace and tranquility. He doesn't always enjoy the actual spankings and whippings as they do sting but he enjoys the effects they have on his psyche. It causes him to lose control and it causes him to surrender. Men have told me that physical punishment drives rebellion and stress out of their bodies. I believe this to be true because I can sense and see the anger and frustration leaving the body when I physically discipline a man and I see that look of peace and contentment on the man's face afterwards. Not to mention as a woman, I feel powerful and liberated when I discipline a man. Based on the feedback I have received from other women, I am not alone.

Victoria is a Professional Dominatrix with over twenty years of experience in disciplining men. I asked her if she could supply some practical advice to the novice female when it comes to disciplining a man.

"*If a woman decides to incorporate physical discipline or corporal punishment into her relationship with a man, it is important that she start out slow and that she be willing to experiment. I would advise that she start out with an old fashioned over the knee spanking with her hands or a hairbrush. I recommend that women prepare for the discipline session by dressing sexy to stir a man's sexuality and submissive nature. Then she should order him naked across her lap. It is important to start out with soft blows, rotate between cheeks, always wait a few seconds between blows, and then build up to harder and faster blows. Nurturing is part of the discipline process so I would advise for the dominant female to caress her partner's ass cheeks during and after the spanking. A spanking should be erotic as well as punitive.*

I would also recommend that after a woman becomes comfortable in administering a mild spanking that she purchase a paddle or a whip and then experiment with them. She should always start out light and build up to harder and more severe. It is vital that physical discipline stay primarily confined to a man's buttocks and if the woman wants to discipline other regions of the male anatomy, she should try his thighs, the backside of his upper legs and the upper region of his back. The lower back (where the kidneys are located) must be avoided, as should most regions in the front side of the male anatomy.

Also, it is important to give the man a safe word that he can use if he becomes too uncomfortable or experiences serious pain. It will take time to build a man up to where he can receive a rather hard whipping or paddling but his endurance will increase the more he is disciplined.

Most important, I advise women to hug and love on their submissive man after the discipline session, as she should always be willing to balance discipline with nurturing. Women will be impressed at the level of intimacy and love that will form between a couple that incorporates regular discipline within their relationship. If you don't believe me, give it try."

A woman should always keep in mind that the effect on the man's body is not as important as the effect on his mind, so the severity of the discipline is not as important as the purpose of the discipline. Disciplining a man purges his conscience of guilt, his mind of negative thoughts and his soul of negative emotions. Sometimes people are too busy being grown up and acting like mature adults that they tend to close their minds to the fundamentals of the human nature. Men need structure and discipline in their lives in order to become productive in life. Men crave to be disciplined and when necessary, punished by the woman they love.

Is there is a difference between Discipline and Punishment within a Female Domination relationship? Yes and while the terminology is often interchangeable, both can be valuable tools to the Dominant Female. Discipline is a lifestyle of correction toward a positive goal. Punishment is a judgment for violating rules. A lawbreaker that is sentenced to prison is being punished for his crime. The athlete who is trying to obtain a positive goal lives a disciplined life and makes sacrifices in order to be trained so he can achieve those goals.

In the FemDom lifestyle, the woman disciplines the man so he becomes a better servant to her. The man is disciplined in order to be corrected so that he becomes that better husband and that better servant. A weekly discipline session is so the Mistress or Dominant Wife can grade the man's performance in his assigned goals and tasks. He is given correction via discipline so that his performance will improve and so that he is properly trained in how to better serve his Mistress or Dominant wife.

A punishment is a judgment or a sentence for the violation of the law that the Dominant woman has laid down. The man that knowingly has violated one of his Queen's commands is punished to pay her retribution for his unlawful behavior. An example would be, say the Dominant Wife forbids her husband to masturbate. If he violates her known rules, he then would be punished to learn his lesson and to pay her retribution for his infraction.

Contrary, the submissive husband is regularly disciplined, whether he has violated any rules or not. He is discipline because his Dominant Wife is training him. A D&S activity like a whipping or a spanking can be either a discipline or a punishment. But the purpose and the severity will vary depending if it is for training or for rebuke. A punishment would be more severe than a discipline.

Discipline is a good thing and the submissive man can be taken to subspace by the loving yet authoritative hand of correction from his Mistress. Discipline is necessary for the Dominant Female to properly train her husband. A man without regular discipline is usually a disobedient husband who becomes self-centered and lazy. By nature, men need to be disciplined by a woman. The more a man is disciplined, the less he will need to be punished because he will be more obedient.

Punishment is a negative and is not intended to be submissively fulfilling. It is intended to punish wrong doings in a manner so that the wrong doings do not happen again. A punishment is also an act of love but its purpose is to rebuke and reprimand. The terms discipline and punishment are easily intermingled and sometimes people refer to a punishment as discipline and vice versa. However, the terminology is not as important as the purpose of the correction. If it is to train, guide and alter a male's behavior and attitude, then it is Discipline. If it is to reprove, penalize and chastise a male for disobedience, then it is Punishment.

The need for discipline is a part of the human condition. As a society, we have allowed fear to rob us of this important tool of life and thus the desire for discipline is becoming stronger within the male gender. Unfortunately, some people abuse the weaker among us. Society has been horrified at the abuse of children at the hands of adults. Therefore, society has been placed in fear and thus has overreacted to that fear. Instead of making the obvious distinction between loving discipline to correct a child's behavior and the criminal act of physically abusing a child, most psychologists and sociologists have instead come out against all forms of physical discipline in order to protect those that cannot protect themselves. While that goal is admirable and understandable, the result is that society has thrown the baby out with the bath water. While children are better protected from the potential of abuse, they also grow up lacking the love and security that comes through normal and healthy discipline. Thus, we end up with a generation of rebellious and undisciplined adults who experience much restlessness within themselves. The world of D&S can be very appealing to those adults who want to experience some physical discipline in their lives.

The need for discipline in human beings is expressed across all forms of society. Some men join the military to get discipline and structure in their lives. The military is all about discipline and submission to authority and such a life is appealing to a certain portion of the male population. In most religions the command to be in submission to spiritual authority and to live a disciplined life are the cornerstones of these Faiths. Religion has recognized the importance of discipline and submission on the human condition. While some religions and denominations within certain religions have abused power and used their man made doctrines to control people and to rule over their lives, the majority of people still seek out faiths that require them to live a disciplined life.

Every Christian child learns in Sunday school about Jesus and his twelve Disciples. A Disciple is merely a learner under discipline. Most religions portray God as a God of order and a God of authority with a designed hierarchy. This is very comforting to people and the spiritual nature of humankind is of such that desires to submit to a higher power.

One of the most ironic things to me is that most Christian denominations are based on a Patriarch view of society and thus do not embrace any form of Female Domination. Nevertheless, no matter how hard society or religion indoctrinates men with the teachings that they need to be in charge of society, something within the male nature causes him to desire to submit to the female gender, at least within a personal relationship. Some men struggle with this for their entire lives, never able to fully come to terms with that internal struggle within. People are triune beings with a body, a mind and a spirit. One can easily be programmed to accept a certain reality but the inner nature of man cannot be changed from what God or nature intended. In my opinion, the male gender needs to be in submission to the female gender and the male gender needs to experience loving discipline at the hands of the female gender. Therefore, the act of a wife disciplining her husband seems very natural to me. I am no longer surprised to hear the many testimonials from FemDom couples about how regular discipline sessions have greatly improved their bond of intimacy.

Crystal and John have such a loving bond as they both enjoy their regular discipline sessions. Crystal uses her creativity to make her loving discipline sessions with her husband special. She disciplines John at least once a week but to her it is so much more than just tying her husband down and whipping him. Crystal likes to draw it out and make it erotic with the goal of transporting John to subspace. She uses these sessions to build intimacy and romance. Crystal explains.

"We have grown in this lifestyle and our discipline sessions reflect that growth. I was your typical novice, unsure of what I was doing and conflicted about why John needed this in his life. Today, I look forward to our discipline sessions as much if not more than John does. I like to be creative and make them erotic and romantic, as well as using them to train John to be obedient to me outside the bedroom.

For example, one time I had John read the novel "Venus in Furs" and he had to underline the passages in the book that spoke to his submissive nature. The author was able to convey to the reader through the character of Severin what goes through a submissive man's mind when

103

he is being dominated and whipped. I had John underline any passages that he felt related to how he felt when I disciplined him. Once he was finished with the book, I read it and underlined the passages that spoke to me as a dominant woman.

The next discipline session we had, I incorporated "Venus in Furs". I secured John to our bed, face down, with the wrist and ankle cuffs I keep tied to our bedposts. After my usual warm-up session with my soft, deerskin floggers (I like to use two on him at the same time, flogging him with a rhythmic pace), I began to read the passages that he had underlined in the book, while I continued to whip him. I changed to my riding crop and later to my cat-o-nine tail whip as I continued to read the erotic words from "Venus in Furs". It was an incredibly erotic experience for us both. John kept growing more excited with each passage and the more excited I got, the harder I would whip him. The more excited he became, the more he could take from me. We have a safe word but John went deep into subspace and did not use his word. I read from the passages I had underlined as I switched to my Spencer paddle (a paddle with holes) and eventually to my cane. This session lasted for well over an hour and it led to a night of deep intimacy and romance.

It is not uncommon for my discipline sessions with John to last well over an hour. We have gone two hours and even longer. I drag them out and most times we talk very little during these discipline sessions. There is a calm and a quiet and we both drift off into our roles. I discipline him with love and he receives his discipline with love. The only times I get verbally forceful with him is when I want to point out an area that he needs improvement or when I tell him about an upcoming event that I know he will not be enthusiastic about (like me going away to visit my family or one of them coming to visit us). These discipline sessions provide me with the perfect venue to get my loving husband to agree to whatever I want."

Crystal and John are perfect examples of how Female Domination and loving discipline can be a romantic experience. Crystal will be the first to admit that the years since she embraced FemDom are by the far the best years of her marriage, both socially and sexually.

Chapter Seven

Victorian Discipline and Domination

Providence is the Queen and Governess of the world (Thomas Watson,
"Body of Divinity", 1686)

Trudy and her husband Norman live on the eastern shore in Maryland.
To meet them, they would strike you as a conservative couple. Trudy is a
voluptuous woman who dresses immaculate in public. Norman is a quick
witted and fun-loving gentleman who has a million dollar smile and a
knack at making a stranger feel like a close friend. They are a refined
couple that enjoys the Arts and the finer things in life. When one spends
time with this couple, the word "sophistication" immediately comes to
mind.

Trudy and Norman are accustomed to hosting social events at their
home. Trudy is active in a number of civic organizations and she loves to
organize socials and entertain friends and associates in her home.
Besides her mainstream civic duties and social parties, once a month,
Trudy hosts a different kind of ladies social that would no doubt shock
and surprise the people of her community. Trudy is a member of the
Alice Kerr-Sutherland Society.

The Alice Kerr-Sutherland Society (AKS) is a society that was founded
in England based on the alleged writings of Alice Kerr-Sutherland, who
advocated the disciplining and training of young males by Adult women
for the purpose of ensuring that young males grew up to become

respectful and well mannered gentlemen. The AKS is big on using Victorian style discipline with the cane as the instrument of choice for the female members when it comes to disciplining males.

The Alice Kerr-Sutherland Society International was founded in 1992 as people in the United States discovered the controversial book "A Guide to the Correction of Young Gentlemen" in which Alice Kerr-Sutherland advocates physical discipline and corporal punishment of young males at the hands of females. According to the members of the AKS, "A Guide to the Correction of Young Gentlemen" was written in 1924 but before it could be published all known copies were seized by England's Vice Squad and, after a sensational trial, burned by order of the judge, except One! Supposedly, "A Guide to the Correction of Young Gentlemen" was reprinted in 1991 and the AKS was founded on Ms Sutherland's philosophy, but with the modification that Victorian discipline should be conducted on husbands, boyfriends and young Adult males.

Based on my research, the story of Alice Kerr-Sutherland and her book is a fable. The book was, in fact, written by the writer, Jacqueline Ophir, prior to her forming The Alice Kerr-Sutherland Society as a tribute to the non-existent author. Regardless of the author or the book's origin, "A Guide to the Correction of Young Gentlemen" details the philosophy, equipment and techniques for the successful administration of physical discipline to males by females. The book and the AKS developed a following in England and in the United States. The AKS became so popular that they began to publish a quarterly publication, "The Governess". When it was published, "The Governess" had the reputation as being an elegant and refined journal of disciplinary literature. The magazine itself is no longer published but copies are still available. Although the AKS has evolved into a society of Adult women who discipline Adult males, "The Governess" stayed true to the original philosophy of the book "A Guide to the Correction of Young Gentlemen". The original twelve issues of "The Governess" consisted of dozens of letters, essays, articles, poems, reviews, and intriguing archive material about the disciplining of young men at the hands of Female Guardians.

A more recent publication that caters to a sophisticated form of Female Domination through the discipline of the husband is WHAP magazine (Women Who Administer Punishments). WHAP is a FemDom publication with a retro 1940's look with stories and articles about real women who dominate their husbands through spankings and regular discipline sessions. Much like "The Governess", WHAP has a design and a format that appeals more to the female. It is non-pornographic with tasteful illustrations that accompany the articles and stories.

Today, the vast majority of the AKS members are well-educated and upper mobile individuals who believe in and practice Female Domination through discipline between consenting adults. Most of the members of the AKS are not into leather or BDSM but rather enjoy an eloquent and sophisticated type of Female Domination based on the Victorian era.

The Victorian Era is the eclectic period of time between the mid and the late 19th century, covering the sixty-four year reign of Queen Victoria from 1837 to 1901. Though Queen Victoria's reign over England ended in 1901 when she passed away, the era which bore her name continued on for several more years, creating styles, fashions, and symbols of a gilded age, rich with elegance and romance.

At the AKS socials held at Trudy's house, the women dress in Victorian era outfits and their husbands or male partners dress in tux pants and black bow ties (no shirts) or feminized maid outfits. The men prepare the food and refreshments and serve the women as the women socialize. These socials are not a monthly masquerade party but rather a celebration of their secret lifestyles. All the women present at these AKS functions have a Female Domination marriage or relationship with their male partners. These monthly socials are merely an opportunity for the women to show off their progress in the training and disciplining of their spouses and significant others. Trudy and her female AKS friends believe in Female Domination but enjoy a more traditional and historical form of FemDom. They love the Victorian era and would rather wear the clothing from that era rather than leather or fetish attire.

Like many of the women of the AKS, Trudy owns quite an extensive wardrobe that consists of not only Victorian era dresses but also Victorian era lingerie, corsets and petticoats. Most Victorian undergarments are very pretty and elaborately embellished with lace, ruffles, and embroidery. Petticoats especially, are trimmed extensively at the hem with ruffles where they might be seen. Dressing in such attire becomes somewhat of a ritual and a major production or as Trudy likes to call it, "a celebration of the feminine".

The clothing of the Victorian woman was so elaborate and cumbersome that getting dressed during the Victorian Era was indeed a complicated chore. Ladies literally had to develop a careful, well-thought-out routine for dressing. Because the corset was quite rigid, which made it so difficult for the woman to move or bend, several items went on prior to the corset. First would have been her stockings; cotton for everyday wear, silk for special occasions and wool for the winter. Stockings were held in place by garters, which attached directly to the corset. Boots of some type were the typical everyday wear for the Victorian women. Drawers would be pulled on next. Drawers were almost always open-crotched and they were usually made of cotton and ended just below the knee. Next, a chemise would have been slipped on. A chemise was a cotton garment, similar to what we know today as a "slip". It usually had extra trimming over the bust-line to add fullness. Bras were not worn, but there was the "comfort bosom supporter" for the endowed, and the "bust-enhancer" for the smaller woman.

Next came the corset. There were as many different types of corsets as there might be occasions to wear one. There were rust-proof corsets for swimming, short corsets for horseback riding and corsets with elastic inserts for everyday wear. Today, the corset has become popular in the world of Female Domination. A lot of submissive men (like Norman) have a fetish for seeing a woman in a corset. The Professional Dominatrix is accustomed to having a male client request that she wear a leather corset as part of her Dominant outfit.

I find this to be fascinating because during the Victorian era a corset was confining and really a social statement to the restrictive plight of women in a society that rarely educated women and a society that had few employment choices for women. Now women like Trudy have turned the tables and are taking what was once a symbol of subjection (the corset) and have turned it into a symbol of power and liberation, using man's fetish against him. The corset and the hourglass figure it enhanced in the female form, made the Victorian woman appear even more beautiful and sexual and thus society began to change during the Victorian era. While the uncomfortable, complicated, and time-consuming task of dressing up may have been a dreaded chore for Victorian Ladies, it seemed that the inconveniences were a small price to pay for the pleasure of looking beautiful.

The benefits to the Victorian woman became well worth it as she used her beauty to live a life of comfort and luxury if she were fortunate enough to be married to a man of means. During the reign of Queen Victoria, England grew very rapidly into a rich nation. Many of her citizens became wealthy or middle class and some were able to afford to pay others, Nannies, Governess' and Tutors, to take over the raising of their children. The Governess was to teach the female children skills that would be attractive in marriage. Victorian parents sought a woman who had the ability to teach their daughters the genteel accomplishments. This was the aim of female education. The ideal woman was one of leisure, who preformed no housework, and whose husband could support her leisurely lifestyle. To Trudy and the other ladies of the AKS, the Victorian era and feminine wardrobe is a celebration of the beauty of the feminine as the Victorian female used her feminine beauty to rule her husband in a subtle and secret manner.

Trudy and her female friends of the AKS enjoy dressing in Victorian era attire for their socials while their submissive husbands and significant others serve them tea and wait on them as their servants. For hostesses during the Victorian era, Tea Time was an opportunity for the ladies to compete with each other in the elegance of their settings, as well as in the refreshments that they might offer to their guests. Noblewoman, Anna, Duchess of Bedford, created the custom of drinking and serving tea to friends in the late afternoon. Because she grew impatient with the late hour for dining which was fashionable in the 18th Century, she began to invite her friends to visit her and share a snack of tea, bread, and butter. These "tea parties" quickly became a popular social event, where women could share conversation and the latest gossip. By the 19th century, afternoon tea was a regular event in upper-and middle-class homes in both Europe and in the United States. While Trudy's socials usually take place at night, the women get into the spirit of the Victorian age by their attire and by having their male partners serving them tea and refreshments.

The AKS women demand obedience and respect from their husbands and they enforce their loving female authority by administering regular over the knee spankings or for more serious offenses, they use the chosen implement of the AKS, the cane. In Trudy's marriage, Norman does the majority of the housework and she requires that he don a maid's outfit when he cleans her house and irons her clothing. Once a week, Norman's weekly performance is graded and if he has done a satisfactory job, Trudy will discipline him by administering an old-fashioned over the knee spanking. Trudy will usually dress in a Victorian corset or undergarments, as she spanks her hubby's bottom with her bare hand or her hairbrush. The purpose of this discipline is to motivate Norman to keep up his excellent performance as her submissive husband and household maid.

If Norman's weekly performance is ever graded by Ms Trudy to be "unsatisfactory", he will be dealt with in a more severe manner. For such occasions, Trudy will bind Norman in a standing position to the posts at the bottom of her bed. Trudy will dress in one of her Victorian outfits, then choose from her large array of wooden canes and she will administer a rather stern caning to Norman's buttocks. The cane is very painful but luckily for Norman, Ms Trudy has become quite skilled and although she leaves an assortment of stripes on Norman's butt cheeks, she never causes him any real harm or injury. Nevertheless, the sting of the cane is enough to teach and instruct Norman to improve upon his efforts for the coming week.

The Victorian concept of discipline is well known, and many boys became so sexually oriented to whipping and flagellation that it became known in Europe as the "English Vice". A Governess was a woman invested with authority to control and direct the children of the household. The status of the Governess was ambiguous because she was neither family nor servant. The Governess most likely suffered from "status incongruity," which means she was neither a servant nor thought of as full member of the employer's class.

The Governess was often responsible for disciplining the children and she usually was more punitive and firm with the male children. During the Victorian era, it was thought that it was better for a boy to be disciplined by a Lady than by a man because it humiliated a boy far more to be punished by a Governess or a School-Mistress than by a man. Humiliation was a common tool of discipline during the Victorian era. Often, punishments included being ordered to write lines over and over, or having to memorize long passages. In school, teachers shamed their students by making them wear a "dunce cap", or wear a humiliating sign around their neck. A boy might be made to put on a girl's bonnet and sit on the girl's side of the room, or students were forced to balance themselves on a small block of wood in the corner of the room. "The Peg" was a severe and dreaded punishment. The disobedient child's hair was fastened to a clip which was pegged into the wall at a height which kept the pupil standing on his or her tiptoes until the teacher felt that the student had learned his/her lesson. During the Victorian era, it was perfectly acceptable to slap a boy's face, or pull and twist his ears.

The Governess often handled the young males under her care with a very firm hand. Of course, the most common punishment for male children was a whipping with the dreaded cane (thus the reason for the cane as the chosen implement of discipline for the AKS). The Governess' strategy was to administer the punishment in such a way that the young male would think as much as possible about the caning he was soon to receive. The slow nature of ceremonial punishment induced the young male to think more than he wished about the punishment. It was believed that fear made the rebellious boy more attentive to detail. It was thought that fear enhanced perception, thus fear enhanced the effect of the cane. For this reason, the Governess could play her mind games as she prepared her young male for punishment. She often used such tactics as making the boy wait for a considerable amount of time after he was bent over, perhaps placing the cane in his line of vision, making him think about the cane while he waited for his punishment at the hands of the Governess. When the cane was finally picked up, she would take a few practice swishes or even tap the cane lightly on his seat. It was more than likely that while the cane was swishing through the air from the Governess' practice swings, she would give the young male a lecture on the value of corporal punishment and explain to him why he was being punished.

When the Governess stood behind the young male with cane in hand, his sense of helplessness and apprehension became strong. It was useful for the Governess to tease him by standing behind him in a position where her feet and other parts of her body would encroach on his peripheral vision. The awareness that she was standing behind him, watching him, and contemplating her delivery made the anticipation worse than the actual caning. The punished male was left with a sore posterior and a determination to do better. That was the desired result of the Governess' mind-game. Trudy uses similar psychology when she disciplines her husband, playing those same mind games. Her goal is for the impact of the punishment not to be limited to Norman's bottom, for she also desires to impact his mind and his soul.

Trudy loves this form of Female Domination and it is hard for one to argue with her methods when one meets her loving and well-mannered husband. When one looks closely at her marriage, it is easy to understand why Trudy enjoys Victorian discipline and the AKS. But what does Norman get out of this type of marriage? After all, he works full-time and he is required to do most of the domestic chores around their very large house. Does he ever desire a different kind of marriage?

"I wouldn't trade my marriage or this lifestyle for anything", proclaims Norman. "I have harbored submissive desires toward women since I was a teenage boy. Trudy didn't ask for this type of marriage, I introduced it to her. The AKS was a form of Female Domination that appealed to her. She had no interest in BDSM. She believes in Female Supremacy but she liked the way the women dominated boys and young men during the Victorian era. She grew up watching her Mother being firm with her brothers. Trudy loves the clothing, the corsets, and the whole mind-set of the AKS. I needed discipline in my life and I love to serve my wife by doing housework for her.

What do I get out of it? Being disciplined by my wife brings me contentment. I feel loved. Only a wife who loved a man would be willing to discipline him for his own good. I needed structure in my life and Trudy brings me that structure. Besides, you should see her in her corsets. Wow, I would gladly endure all of her canes just to behold her beauty and her hourglass figure that her corsets enhance. I realize that those corsets are not comfortable to wear and I am a lucky guy that she enjoys wearing them. She also loves the Victorian dresses and outfits. She gets to live a fantasy life and also be a vital part of our community. We keep the two separate but this life enhances that life. We have a fantastic marriage and I owe much of it to our life of Female Domination."

Female Domination and Discipline need not be confined to marriage. A Female Domination relationship that incorporates discipline can exist between two consenting adults in a non-intimate relationship. Not all FemDom relationships need be about sex. The story of Kristen and

George is a perfect example of how Female Domination in a non-intimate relationship can be beneficial and fulfilling to both parties. Kristen is a former member of Trudy's group and was willing to share her story.

"I am a librarian at a local college, divorced and in my early forties. My ex-husband had introduced me to D&S and Female Domination. I thought he was weird and perverted at first. Actually I still do but that is another story. Anyway, we met some people who are into the scene and I got to know a few women who were self-proclaimed Dominant women. They were members of a FemDom group that enjoyed a softer and more maternal form of D&S. They were into spanking and punishing their husbands in order to train them to be well-mannered gentlemen. They were not into leather, BDSM, or anything real kinky. They liked to dress up in Victorian era clothes, have old-fashioned tea parties, and have their husbands serve them. If their husbands ever displeased them or disobeyed them, they would be disciplined through over the knee spankings or if it were a serious offense, they would be caned.

I enjoyed my times with these ladies and I really got into the Victorian era. I loved the clothes and the way these women handled their husbands. Unfortunately, it wasn't enough to save my marriage so I eventually got divorced.

Once on my own, I went to work as a librarian at a local University. There was this nice young student, George, that kept coming around and he seemed to really like me. I didn't encourage this, as I was not interested in college age males. I was looking for a man more my age but this young man just kept coming around and he would flirt with me. He eventually got up enough nerve and he asked me out to dinner and a movie. To my surprise, I accepted. He is a good-looking kid and I did feel that I needed to get out.

I picked up immediately that he was submissive. I sensed it the first time I met him. I think this is what really attracted him to me and vice versa. We went out a few times and I found myself enjoying this young man's company. I had no real romantic feelings for him but nonetheless a special friendship was formed between us. I also saw that George needed a woman to help him out in life. He didn't have a clue about all kinds of things from how to treat a Lady to some personal hygiene issues. So I decided to take advantage of the situation and help this kid out, as well as have some fun in expressing my dominant nature.

One night (after we had been out on a few dates) I invited him over to my apartment and after a pleasant conversation, I excused myself and went into my bedroom and I dressed up in one of my old Victorian outfits. It was one of my sexier pieces that consisted more of lingerie than anything else. His mouth was watering when he saw me in my outfit and I could feel his submission growing. I had this strong urge to dominate him so I ordered him to undress down to his underwear and I ordered him across my lap. I took my hairbrush and I gave this young man a hard spanking. As I did this, I scolded him about how I needed for him to shape up. I really enjoyed disciplining this boy and his cute derriere was nice and red in no time. He was really squirming but I didn't let up until I got my point across. After the spanking, I made him leave. I knew that he wanted to have sex with me but I wasn't about to allow that.

For the past two years, I have had a non-sexual relationship with George. I make this young man do chores for me and run errands for me most days. He corrected those areas that needed correction as far as his hygiene goes and other areas of his life. We have regular discipline sessions and I even broke out my cane and I have caned him on a few occasions when he needed some extra discipline. I have trained him to be a very obedient and polite young gentleman. I was exactly what George needed in life.

Now my apartment is spotless, my car is waxed and always clean, and I don't have to go to the grocery store very often. My young college gentleman takes care of most my chores and errands. He benefits in that I have trained him on how to be a proper young man. He comments on how many girls have taken a liking to him since I got his act together. His grades are improving in school and he is becoming a well-balanced individual. We also enjoy going to dinner and taking in a show as friends. We get some stares, as I am quite a bit older. I have started to date another man for romance but George and I enjoy a very special relationship. For the time being, this relationship is fulfilling for the both of us."

It could be said that Kristen is a kind of a modern day Governess to George. Although Kristen draws the line at sex with George, according to George, his feelings toward Kristen are both submissive and sexual and he readily admits that he would have submitted to any sexual advances from Kristen had she desired to take their relationship from friendship to intimate. When I interviewed George about his relationship with Kristen, I was able to get a glimpse into the mindset that must have been prevalent in young men toward their Governess during the Victorian era.

"There was something about Ms Kristen that attracted me to her. First, I thought she was stunningly beautiful. She dressed conservatively but even so, her female form and her pretty face had me spellbound. I especially loved how she looked in her glasses. She had this intellectual but sexual appearance when she wore her frames. College aged girls could not compete with the mature, sophisticated and sexual look of Ms Kristen.

She also had this demeanor of a no-nonsense woman. She was firm and serious and I found that to be attractive. Some of my college friends saw me out in public with her and they teased that I had this Mother-figure thing going with Ms Kristen. I though about that but I really can't explain why I wanted to date her. I just found her to be exhilarating and so intelligent.

She definitely took charge of our relationship from the beginning. I made a suggestion on a movie but she immediately changed it to one she wanted to see. She told me where she wanted to eat and she basically controlled our relationship from the start. I definitely felt submissive toward her. I think I was the one who first brought up the subject of my attraction to dominant women during one of our dinners and when she told me about her former involvement in Female Domination, I couldn't believe my ears. It was like a fantasy come true. She said that my hands began to shake as she was telling me about her female domination past.

I was hoping that our relationship would become sexual but I respect her for not wanting to become emotionally attached to a much younger man. She is right, we have no long-term future. I am just grateful that she decided to discipline me and to train me to become a gentleman. I was in real need of that in my life.

When I saw her in her lingerie and she ordered me across her lap, I was so excited that I almost climaxed. Had the spanking not re-focused my attention, I think I would have had an accident. After that night, I would do anything for her. I love doing chores for her and running errands for her. She is more interested in my grades and my life than even my parents, and I find that I can't wait for my next discipline session with her. To her, our discipline sessions are a social engagement and an extension of our friendship. To me, our discipline sessions are sexual. There is energy between us when she disciplines me. I worship Ms Kristen and I admire her more than any woman I have ever known. I just hope I can meet a girl more my age who is just like her."

Since during the Victorian era all female teachers in the school house had to be single (once they married, they were no longer permitted to teach) and a Governess was also required to be single, it has been widely recorded that there was a sexual element to the act of a Governess (or Female school teacher) disciplining a male child. It has been documented how some boys during the Victorian era developed a deep affection for the one who punished him, namely his Governess.

There were actual instances in which the Governess became the corrupter of the young male that was entrusted into her care. Instead of guarding his mind in innocence and purity, she initiated him into temptation, as he would hold sexual thoughts toward his Governess throughout puberty and into young adulthood. Such instances may not have been accidents but rather well planned by the Governess who feared for her uncertain future. A middle-class male had a tendency to stay at home until he married at an age as late as thirty. Unprotected by her own family, the Governess was open to sexual approaches and there are numerous tales of Governesses in their thirties or even older having sexual relations with the twenty something male of the household, the very same male who was once under her care. The relationship between Kristen and George has many of the same elements of the Victorian relationships between a Governess and a young male.

Kristen, Beverly, Crystal, and Trudy have all successfully incorporated discipline into their relationships with men. Each has a slightly different style but they have all incorporated FemDom to fit their individual needs and lifestyles. One area the Trudy has stretched the limits of Norman is in his attire when he does his household chores. Norman had no desire to wear a maid's outfit or women's clothing but Trudy got the idea from some of her friends in the AKS. She observed some of the husbands wearing feminine attire at AKS socials and this excited Trudy enough that she wanted Norman to wear similar attire when he did his housework. Norman was reluctant but of course, Trudy wields the cane of discipline, so she was able to get Norman to agree to his new work clothes. As we will explore in the next chapter, what Trudy has successfully introduced into her marriage is the FemDom activity known as "Forced Feminization".

Chapter Eight

Forced Feminization, Sissification and Domestication

I know the boy will well usurp the grace, voice, gait and action of a gentlewoman ... A' will make the man mad, to make a woman of him.
(William Shakespeare, "The Taming of the Shrew")

Nadine is a thirty-two year old woman from Europe who has been married for seven years. As with many other girls, she suffered during her studies at her University from the macho attitudes of the male professors and male peers in a very male dominated career in her country, Architecture. The attitude of many of her male colleagues clearly showed that they thought that women were only fit to achieve the rank of second-class professionals. She has proved the contrary and now she is the owner of her own company and the boss of a nice group of University trained male professionals.

Seven years ago she married one of her close collaborators. Ned is a handsome man but what Nadine found most attractive was that Ned is a respected professional and very good at his job, while at the same time very collaborative, friendly, and gentle. Although she was the dominant member of the couple when they dated, their relationship was not an overt female dominated one. Ned's macho male ego was on display one day and this led to some unplanned changes in his relationship with Nadine.

Nadine happened to overhear Ned's colleagues teasing him about her assertiveness and they teased that she would wear the pants in their marriage. His response was a typical male response as he stated for the record that although Nadine was the boss at work, at home he would be the ruler and, of course, he would wear the pants. Later that day, Nadine confronted her fiancé about this. He explained that what she heard was simply men talking, joking, and making some silly comments. Nadine did not accept his excuses. Instead, she asked him what would he have thought if she had stated and boasted in front of all her female colleagues, that she planned to be the boss in the marriage and furthermore that she planned to be the one responsible for the decision-making. In other words, she would wear the pants.

Ned said nothing so Nadine laughed and added, *"I might also add to those comments that I will wear the pants and that you will wear ... the knickers ... pretty lace knickers ... that I will choose for you. Would you like if I boasted about something like this?"*

Ned blushed and quickly apologized to her, saying once again that he was only joking. Nadine explained to Ned that his comments had humiliated her and that she did not accept macho attitudes and she wanted to make this clear. As this conversation progressed, Nadine found that she was getting excited about dominating Ned. She could see his humiliation and fear as she teased him about her wearing the pants and him being feminized. She became so excited that she made a bold declaration.

Nadine gave Ned two choices. One choice was to forget their plans to marry since he was obviously not the kind of man she wanted to marry. The second choice was that Ned had to accept that Nadine would be the dominant partner. She told him that this would be something private between them, not to be shown openly, and that she would not embarrass him in front of anybody. However, he would have to change his boasting to other non-humiliating comments like, *"You know, Nadine is very strong willed and most times, she manages to get anything she wants from me."*

Ned insisted on how much he loved her and how much he wanted to marry her. He agreed that she was the one ruling most things in their relationship and that he did not object to that. Nadine was pleased but still not satisfied. She had Ned right where she wanted him so she decided to drop a bombshell on him.

"Apart from this, I think that I have to punish you somehow and at the same time make clear that you will obey me when I tell you something. I think that what I suggested earlier fits very well. You were boasting that you would wear the pants but will instead wear the knickers. Do you agree?" Ned looked at Nadine in stunned silence. He never would have imagined something like this. He asked Nadine to please explain what it was she was trying to say to him.

Nadine responded in total female confidence, *" I mean that you are going to wear panties and female lingerie that I will choose for you, all the time, and with no complaints. But don't worry, I am not going to tell other people about this. I am not going to shame you in front of others. But we both will know that you are wearing panties and feminine lingerie under your clothing. I am going to ask you one last time. Do you agree or do you prefer the first option of ending this relationship or will you submit to me? The choice is yours."*

Ned knew Nadine and he knew that she was serious about this. He hesitated, argued with her briefly, complained and hedged but finally he yielded completely. Nadine was so excited. She could not get over the power rush running through her body and she was now wet between her legs. She knew how much this was going to change her marriage with Ned. She knew how much it meant for him to agree to her wild demands.

"Do you still want to marry me and will you wear feminine clothing in the marriage?" She asked one final time. Ned agreed to her demands and Nadine set the date for the wedding and Ned immediately began to wear her panties under his clothing.

Nadine bought him a very nice set of bridal lingerie, set their wedding night and Ned did not dare to say a word. *"That meant a lot for me and for our marriage"*, Nadine stated with all the pride as if she was talking about her engagement ring. Nadine continues with the story as she describes their wedding night.

"On our wedding night, we went to the bridal suite and I undressed him from his tux and I kissed him tenderly and caressed my hands over his

lace lingerie. I led him to bed and pushed him back and kissed him and instructed him in how to sexually please me orally. I know that my words were tender, soft, sensual, but at the same time my instructions made clear his role in bed: pleasing me and submitting to me."

Nadine continues, *"In the following years I pushed further his submission and expanded my dominance. And his love for me increased over these years. My husband wears feminine lingerie under his clothes and he is in total submission to me. Last year on our anniversary, apart from other presents, I told him that for the first time, I would allow him to be as dominant with me in bed as he wanted and that I would submit to him. I wanted to see how he would react. Ned felt lost, he felt so absolutely inappropriate in his performance that I had to end the experiment and return to our normal roles. He felt relieved when I asked him to put on his lingerie again and he immediately accepted."*

Ned had no desire to be dominant with Nadine. His forced feminization had caused him to accept the submissive role and he was happy in the submissive role. At work, around family and out in public, Ned carried himself with his normal masculinity. However, behind closed doors, he was Nadine's feminized hubby who adored her and who submitted to her authority in the marriage. Neither of them knew about Female Domination or Forced Feminization when they began to date but their relationship evolved into this area and for them it worked.

Forced Feminization also works for Hillary and Raymond. Hillary is a female executive with a large corporation in Texas. She has climbed the corporate ladder and now is responsible for many employees under her charge. Raymond was once a cutthroat corporate type. He was an executive with a different company and he was very high up in management. Then one year in the late 90's, his company was bought out by another company and he lost his job when they eliminated his position. Fortunately for him, Raymond had accumulated lots of stock options over the years and due to this merger, his stock options made him enough money that he could afford to retire.

Hillary and Raymond are both aggressive individuals with strong personalities. However, at home Raymond has always encouraged Hillary to take charge of him in the bedroom and they played many D&S games. Hillary loves being in charge so she took to the Female

Domination lifestyle very quickly. Once her husband lost his job (but had made enough money through the stock options to never have to work again) she decided to fulfill a fantasy of hers. She made Raymond into her feminized sissy maid. Hillary totally feminized him and now he spends his days cleaning her house and doing chores for her. Raymond has been completely domesticated.

"It was a process and it took time and determination on my part to feminize Ray", Hillary explains. *"I developed a technique where I used my dominance and sexual power to force him into deep submission to me."*

Raymond was crazy about Hillary and he loved to be dominated by her, so she used his submissive desires to take him to where she wanted him to go in their relationship. Hillary began to dress Raymond up in woman's clothing each day and used his submissive excitement to motivate him to do household chores for her. She also started to have sex with him only when he was dressed in woman's lingerie. She began to get more dominant with him and she turned the tradition sexual tables by incorporating the use of a strap-on rubber phallus on Raymond when he was dressed feminine for her. Finally, Hillary discarded most of Raymond's male clothing and she made him dress in primarily woman's clothing.

"I can't tell you how excited and how powerful I felt doing this to him. He was so macho and he use to treat women that worked for him quite poorly, but now I have transformed this corporate man into my little sissy maid. I could tell that he enjoyed aspects of this as well. Sure he would fight me at times and cop his male attitudes, but I learned how to discipline and control him long ago, so I used my dominant female nature to put him into his place. Now he seems at peace in his new role as my full time house slave. I never would have believed it was possible.

As I ponder where we were and where we are now, I realize that I really didn't "force" Raymond into this but I rather took him where deep down, he wanted me to take him. He now knows what real Female Domination is about and I love having this power over him."

So how did Hillary feminize a man who showed no previous signs of desiring to be her sissy maid?

"You must use a man's sexuality against him until you have him trained. I played off of his submissive desires to explore how he would react to being feminized. I had my husband go to this room we designated as his slave room and I had him undress and bow facing the door. When I came into his presence, I always had on a sexy outfit. I dressed in lingerie or leather, or even just bra, panties, and high heel shoes to stir his sexuality.

Then I would have him worship my boots, shoes or feet when I came into the slave room. If wearing boots, I might sit down and allow him to lick them all over and suck the heels in order to capitalize on his boot fetish. Next, I would dress him up in his outfit, which would be woman's lingerie, or pantyhose, or a French-maid's outfit, or whatever feminine outfit I chose. It is important for the woman to dress the man in the beginning of his training. Don't just tell him to put on the clothes. As you dress him, be real sexy and caress his body with the material. Squeeze his balls and lightly stroke his penis. Make it a sexual experience. You are developing a fetish within him. Also, whisper softly as you dress him and tease him about how you are going to feminize him and how he is going to be your slave.

After he was dressed, I would assign him some chores. I started out slow, maybe only one or two the first few times. Later I built it up to many chores but I wanted him to enjoy being feminized so I made it fun in the beginning. As he went about his chores, I would occasionally check in on him and fondle his body. Again, I used sexuality to control him. Plus, it made things fun for me. The housework was getting done and we both were having a good time.

After he finished all his assigned chores, I would drive our new role-reversal home. I put on my strap-on harness, I strapped on my dildo, ordered him to assume the position and I took him from behind. Oh, it is crucial that he is still dressed in woman's clothing as you take him with the strap-on. This is important. He must equate the feeling of the lingerie with the sexual feeling of being taken by a woman. We had participated in strap-on play in the past so he was use to this activity but now that he was feminized, strap-on play took on a whole new meaning. I wanted him to equate the feminine clothing with being the receiver of penetrating sex. This made him docile and more eager to obey me outside of the bedroom. I was touching his submission and his sexuality and this eventually caused him to desire to be feminized.

I did this routine consistently with him and after I had him trained, I got rid of most of his male clothing and I made him my feminized houseboy. So, that is basically how I feminized my husband."

Hillary may come across to some as being a bit cruel in her treatment of her husband. Yet, when I talked to Raymond, it was obvious that he found her aggressive ways to be sexually stimulating and submissively fulfilling.

"I can't say that I wanted to be feminized to this degree. I mean the first time she paraded me in front of a mirror and I saw myself, I felt totally ridiculous. I felt degraded and humiliated. Notwithstanding, I must confess that I felt a sexual arousal that was out of this world. At that time in our marriage, I was having some challenges with my erections and this was prior to the popularity of Viagra. But who needs drugs when you are married to such a dominant woman? When she began to feminize me and forced me to be her maid, I would go around with an almost constant erection. That hadn't happened for I don't know how long. Our sex life might not be traditional but our sex life is intense and exciting. How many couples approaching fifty can say that?

I didn't want to be feminized but what turned me on was that she wanted me to be feminized. I have always enjoyed it when Hillary would make me do something that I didn't want to do. I have always loved watching her become aggressive with me. The feminization was a battle of our wills and although I didn't want to be feminized, I wanted her to win. I wanted to submit to her will, which I did and now I am very content in my role as her maid.

Nadine and Hillary are not alone in their desire to feminize their husbands when they are in the privacy of their own home. I am surprised at how popular the forced feminization of the male is with Dominant women. Of all the different D&S activities, there seems to be a real enthusiasm with the female when she engages in this practice with her husband. The more macho and reluctant the male, the more personal satisfaction and sexual excitement there is with the woman when she feminizes him.

I believe it is because deep inside, women love seeing the feminine conqueror the masculine. Feminizing a man is the ultimate symbol of the feminine defeating the masculine. That is a rare feat in our society. We are so use to seeing the masculine having his way with the feminine. That is why it can be such a rush for a woman to feminize a man. It causes a woman's dominant energy to flow out of her and she loves the social statement it makes at the same time.

Forced feminization allows a woman to be more aggressive. Forced Feminization causes a man to become weak and submissive. His ability to resist and object go by the way side and he is very vulnerable. Women love this because now they can do whatever they want with their helpless victim. Now the woman can be the aggressor and she can have her way with the man. The man is not threatening to her and she no longer fears his strength or masculinity. Women (such as Hillary) have told me that they have a very strong desire to take a man forcefully with a strap-on dildo when he is feminized. The desire to be the giver of penetrating sex becomes very real to the aggressive female and the actual act becomes quite satisfying to her. Again, it sends such a message to the man and society. It says that the woman is the aggressor and the giver and the man is the weaker sex and the receiver.

Forced Feminization may become attractive to a woman who has previously been abused by a man. Some women fear men due to being mistreated or abused and feminizing a man may cause him to be less intimidating to her. Now she can have her way with him because he is just a little sissy boy. A number of women have rejected the macho and masculine male and prefer a submissive and boyish male instead. Women who have had negative experiences with macho types may feel more at ease with a softer male. Carolyn describes how she enjoys feminizing her husband.

"I am a 34 year-old woman married to a submissive man. We're a middle class couple with straight friends. Basically, our sex life is pretty well based on my husband passive in panties. It all evolved slowly and pretty innocently...fun that got serious. He is not a fulltime sissy. I wouldn't want that. But in the bedroom he is less than a man and I like that because I met him after an abusive relationship with an impossibly "masculine" man.

My husband is not effeminate...but slender, almost hairless, a potentially feminine body. He likes to be spanked and soon that became a ritual. He began to wear unisex white briefs for these punishments and I noticed he always pulled them tight up the crack of his bottom. Then I began to do that for him before the spanking began. Anyway, it all slowly evolved into the wearing of panties for spanking. Now most of our sex life is built around his pantied bottom. He is only allowed to have an orgasm at my command while playing with his pantied "peepee".

He satisfies me orally...front and back. I use a cane and strap, administer golden showers over his body and face, tie him into positions,.....oh a lot of things. We have different styles of panties for different roles...punishment panties, sissy panties, slut panties, schoolgirl panties etc. Often his genitals are tucked down so you don't see anything male at all between his thighs. I don't seem to be able to help myself and he is always excited by whatever new thing I demand."

Like so many things about this lifestyle, it is hard to pinpoint for sure why women love to feminize a man. But this we do know; there is something inside the psyche of a woman that causes her to become excited by the thought and activity of making the masculine submit to the feminine through forced feminization.

Of course, not all men object to being feminized. Some men desire to be forced to dress in female attire. I have had many males confess that they wish that their wives would dress them up in feminine clothing during sex and be the aggressor with them. Other men would like to be dressed in female attire and then humiliated by the female. Still others just like the feeling of being adorned in soft, feminine clothing as it puts them in contact with the world of the female.

Mary Jane met such a man when she was taking a computer course at a college in Minnesota.

"The instructor was a small, slim man in his late 20s who wore his hair in a ponytail. He was a good teacher, kind and patient. He was also what I would call "almost pretty." I thought he had a feminine appearance, but I know some younger women in the class thought that he was really cute in a way they found attractive.

We had some casual conversations in which he learned I owned my own salon and I half-jokingly told him I could improve his look if he let me cut his hair. I didn't give these conversations much thought because they were like conversations he had with every student.

Eleven months after the class ended, our paths crossed again at a Barnes and Noble bookstore. His very first words to me, after calling my name, were "Are you still interested in cutting my hair?" We ended up visiting for about 30 minutes during which he asked if he might come to my town to take me out to dinner. My impression of him, from my time in his class, was of a kind, considerate person, sincerely interested in others. Our dinner date confirmed those impressions and we ended up talking for more than six hours that night. Among the many things I learned about him in our very comfortable conversation was his desire to dedicate himself to a dominant woman. Although he claimed that he is heterosexual, he also expressed a desire to know what it feels like to (in his words) "live like a woman." Although I did not communicate, straight out, my dominant nature, I shared my true acceptance of his desires and he was very grateful for that acceptance.

During this same time period, I was having trouble getting reasonably priced, high quality custodial service for my shop. I asked him if he would be willing to come in and clean my shop nightly if I would help him develop a more feminine appearance. He couldn't have said "yes" more enthusiastically if I had asked him to accept a Million dollars as a gift! For the next two weeks, every evening and each Saturday afternoon, he cleaned my shop like he was polishing silver. On several occasions he even swept up the parking lot!

Most remarkable of all, was something he did in response to a comment I made during our first dinner together. I briefly mentioned to him that I thought he could easily "pass" as a woman, and off-handedly said that it was too bad his lips were not fuller. Near the end of his second week as my custodian, he arrived with the fullest, most feminine lips imaginable. He had arranged to receive a medical treatment to enhance his lips, and although he tells me it is not permanent, until they recede, his appearance is remarkably feminized. I decided I needed to find ways to take fuller advantage of this man who is kind, considerate, sincere, and is so compliant that he does exactly what I say, even when my wish is expressed as a subtle hint.

As his reward (he was not being paid for his custodial efforts) for two weeks of excellent custodial work, I told him that he needed to anticipate staying late on Saturday while I changed his appearance. In response to my questions, he assured me that there was no limit to the feminizing procedures I might perform, and considering the lip enhancement he had undergone, I certainly believed him. I required him to arrive with his body waxed, and had referred him to a shop near his home where he could get that done ahead of time.

Several women rent work stations in my shop, and we rotate the responsibility of closing the shop. On the Saturday afternoon of Ronni's (a derivation of his true name) feminization, only my last two clients and I were in my shop when he arrived. If it can be said that cleaning can be done with passion, that is exactly how Ronni attacked his cleaning responsibilities that afternoon.

Although it took quite a while to pluck the relatively small number of course facial hairs Ronni had on his chin and side burns, once that was done, and his brows had been thinned and shaped, the rest of the procedure was like serving any other female client. Ronni really does have a head of hair "to die for" and the full, long, cut and color I gave him was no unisex hairstyle. Even without makeup, his hair, full lips, fine skin, thin face and shaped brows, gave him an appearance almost anyone would "see" as a woman's face.

As I applied his makeup, Ronni was actually trembling and whimpering with excitement. His excitement, and repeated thanks and claims that he would do anything for me fueled an overwhelming sexual rush in me. The chairs we use to wash clients' hair have a safety rod that prevents the seat back and headrest from reclining too far. I put Ronni in one of those chairs, removed the safety rod, and reclined the chair until the seatback and headrest were resting on an overturned wastebasket. With Ronni reclining in the chair, his face was now about 24 to 30 inches above the floor. I disrobed from the waist down, and wearing only a long black smock over my bra (my usual work attire), I straddled Ronni's chest and invited him to please me with those puffy, pouting lips to which, only moments before, I had applied blood red lipstick. He was already bucking in the chair when my vaginal lips met his beautiful mouth.

What has happened since is like an out-of-control fantasy, made possible by the fact that Ronni does not teach in the summer. He is living with me and serving me in every conceivable way. Except for the money he needs to maintain his residence, he gives all his money to me, and does virtually everything I ask of him. My house is spotless, I have him wash my car almost every day, and his sexual ministrations are totally centered on me. It is common for me to require him to slowly apply lotion to my entire body, ending with lotion being applied to my bottom then penetrating my anus with his tongue while I climax with a vibrator. His naturally androgynous appearance is more feminine than masculine (thanks largely to my attention to his very feminine hair) and almost everyone perceives him as a female. It is unbelievable to me that I have this sweet-smelling slave that will do anything for me and keeps me so turned on that I am having more orgasms now than I have ever had in my life."

The desire to be feminized is more common among men than one would surmise. Everything about women and the feminine excites males and causes them to be curious. Women are mysterious to a lot of men. Wearing female clothing, shoes, etc can be sexually exciting for a man. It is like embracing the feminine and exploring the feminine. This is a rather common fetish among submissive males. Many young boys have their first sexual urges and excitement from touching and even trying on their Mother's bra or panties or pantyhose, etc. Again, this is exploring the mysterious world that is the female. Many adult men never outgrow this fascination or excitement. By wearing these articles of female clothing, it is natural for this to cause submissive desires within the male and cause him to want to submit to the female.

The male that willingly accepts feminization has laid aside his macho male personality and ego and has embraced that which is feminine and forbidden by society. This causes his submission to stir within him. It says to him "If the mere clothing of a woman has this power over me, how much more power does the female herself have over me?"

Self-Feminization (or Cross-Dressing) and Forced Feminization are two distinct desires. Cross dressers are men that want to dress up as a woman. Most of these men are not gay, but there is something within them that desires to dress like a woman. It is kind of a fetish. These men usually enjoy being dominated as well as being dressed up as a woman so cross-dressing can be a form of Female Domination.

Forced feminization is totally different. The key word here is "forced". Forced feminization is where the dominant female forces her submissive male to dress up like a woman, against his will. This is a form of domination and humiliation. The idea of forced feminization is to make a man who has absolutely no desire to dress in woman's clothes, to do so for the woman's entertainment. Forced feminization is fun because the woman knows that the man "hates" to do this. She will force him into woman's clothes, add make-up and maybe even a wig, than she will parade him in front of a mirror and force him to look at himself. She will then proceed to humiliate him. Finally, she may even strap-on a dildo and penetrate her "sissy slut" to further control him and dominate him. Hillary and Raymond enjoy Forced Feminization while Mary Jane and Ronni enjoy assisted Feminization.

So the main difference between these two activities is that the one involves forcing the submissive to dress like a woman, whereas the other involves assisting a man who desires to dress like a woman. Over time, the man who is drawn into this activity by his wife usually will grow to enjoy it to the place where he begins to desire it on his own.

Forced feminization can be exciting to the male, even if he does not start out enjoying wearing female attire. Forced Feminization can be mentally satisfying to a man because he wants to be stripped of his masculinity and he wants the Feminine to overpower the masculine. There are many psychological and sociological reasons why more and more men are having these desires. As women gain in power and authority, men's submissive natures are becoming stronger. As women continue to invade areas that once were the worlds dominated by men (business, politics, sports) this causes the submissive nature within man to stir. Some men when confronted with a powerful woman become weak and thus the male no longer views himself as the woman's equal. He now wants her feminine power to overpower his masculinity and strip him completely of it. He wants the female to conqueror him. He wants to yield all control over to her. Being forced to wear female attire and do domestic chores around the house can bring submissive fulfillment to a man as he now gets to serve the gender he considers to be superior to him.

Some men enjoy serving women even if there is no sexual contact or chance for intimacy. Harold is the domesticated servant of Kay. Harold works for a large computer company where he makes six figures a year. He is forty-eight years old, single and successful by many societal standards. Kay is thirty-seven and happily married to her husband but has chosen to keep FemDom with her husband confined to the bedroom. Kay prefers for her husband to be her social and domestic equal.

Kay met Harold through a local D&S group she and her husband frequent on occasion to stay educated about D&S practices. She formed a relationship with Harold based on her need to dominate a man outside the bedroom and his need to be the domesticated servant of a woman. Although he does not live with Kay out of respect for her husband, Harold is Kay's full-time domesticated submissive.

Harold cleans Kay's house each weekend, from top to bottom, does her laundry and any other domestic chore Kay might assign. Occasionally, Kay will feminize Harold while he does his chores but that is only for variety and not the norm. For Harold, feminization is not necessary. He gets his thrill and fulfillment in serving a woman as her butler, maid and domesticated servant. Harold receives no monetary reward for his duties nor does he want to be paid, for that would take away from Harold's submissive fulfillment. He delights in being ordered to slave away for a woman.

Kay will discipline Harold if his performance is not satisfactory but other than their occasional corporal punishment sessions, the only other D&S activity they engage in is Kay controlling Harold's sexual release. Harold wears a male chastity device all of the time and Kay holds the key. As a reward for excellent domestic service (usually rendered no more than once or twice a month) Kay will unlock Harold's privates and allow him to masturbate (wearing the mandatory condom) while he kneels and kisses her feet. That is the only physical contact between them. They are never intimate on any level as Kay only shares intimacy with her husband.

Even though Harold is successful in his career, he gets his deepest personal satisfaction from being Kay's servant.

"I take pride in my housework. Kay is such a beautiful woman and it is an extreme honor to be able to serve her. I take pride in knowing that I am able to relieve Kay of the responsibility of doing the medial tasks around the house. She is free to pursue her other interests in life and I get fulfillment in knowing that I am her servant."

Kay is not the first woman whom Harold has served in such a capacity. Harold was the domesticated servant of a woman named Audrey for ten years. Harold actually lived with Audrey for the majority of that time. Audrey was not married but Harold was never intimate with her. Audrey had another submissive who was her sexual servant but Harold was her domestic servant. Audrey did engage in many D&S activities with Harold with a strong emphasis on strict discipline as she trained Harold in the ways of proper domesticated servitude. Audrey was originally from Australia and three years ago, she decided to move back to her homeland but could not take Harold with her. The desire to serve a woman consumed Harold for the following year and he is very grateful to have met Kay.

"I was intimate with a woman when I was in college but that is not important to me. My relationship with Lady Audrey was so much more satisfying than my intimate relationship with my college girlfriend. I know it is difficult for some people to comprehend but I enjoy being able to serve a woman without the sexual tension. I knew I could not be intimate with Lady Audrey and I know I will never be intimate with Ms Kay, and I like that. I enjoy serving women with no expectation of receiving sexual favors in return. Having my orgasms controlled by a woman provides me with my sexual excitement.

Truthfully, I enjoy being denied more than being allowed to masturbate. Ms Kay calls that a reward, and I am thankful that she allows me that privilege because I need it now and again, but I feel a letdown afterwards. My fulfillment is in serving a woman. I need the chastity device to keep my focus on Ms Kay's needs and away from my own gratification. There is nothing more pleasurable on this Earth than to serve a woman in a selfless way."

We will take a closer look at the practice of controlling a man's orgasms through the use of a chastity device but next we will look at another FemDom activity that is gaining in popularity among FemDom couples.

132

One element to Forced Feminization that Hillary mentioned was her use of a strap-on harness and rubber phallus to reverse the traditional sexual roles with her husband. The strap-on has become a common sex toy used in Female Domination relationships. In the next chapter, we will examine the psychology behind the strap-on.

Chapter Nine

Role Reversal in the Bedroom:
Female Domination through the Strap-On

If I take you from behind, Push myself into your mind; When you least expect it, Will you try and reject it? ...Give it up, do as I say; Give it up and let me have my way. (Madonna, "Erotica")

Cindy's rise to the head of her marriage was unconventional to say the least. She was a homemaker while her husband was the breadwinner. Cindy possesses a strong personality and she always expected excellence from her husband. Cindy will admit that patience is not one of her virtues. Cindy tried her best to be the traditional wife but inside she felt she could do a better job of heading up the marriage. Her husband's descent into servitude occurred extremely quickly. He lost his technology development job in April of 2002 and Cindy was thrust to the role of providing for her family.

"I suppose I could have been a supportive kind of wife, but I wasn't. Maybe I just don't tolerate failure well and I was worried about money and our status in the community. Or maybe I saw his trouble as an opportunity to assert myself. Whatever the reason, I began belittling and berating him for his pathetic efforts at finding a new job. The fact that he didn't fight back just made me bolder. Since he was home, I assigned him chores so that he could at least do something to help out the family. He was too sheepish to object and I was too sharp-tongued to put up with

134

any resistance, especially once I discovered that I really liked bossing him around. The day I ordered him to hand wash my lingerie, and he did, I knew that things were never going back to the way they had been."

Summer break for the kids was fast approaching and Cindy decided to go out and get a job. She also had a background in technology, although several years of child rearing had reduced her skill level somewhat. Nevertheless, she found a job quickly. Some businesses actively look for women and Cindy is not the kind of woman that easily takes no for an answer. Employers liked that kind of enthusiasm and persistence and Cindy had her pick of some good paying jobs.

"I told my husband to stop interviewing since he was going to be watching the children all summer. I told him I might allow him to start looking again in fall, not that it would do much good".

The one-two punch of her husband being thrown on the unemployment line and Cindy finding work forced a role-reversal in their marriage. Cindy had too many responsibilities to play the supportive wife. Her life was now blossoming and the re-entry into the workforce caused Cindy to develop an improved self-image.

"My responsibilities at work just increased my sense of authority and the intellectual interaction with other adults was addictive. Also, there were men! Handsome, smart, interesting men and they were flirting with me. My husband took me for granted and neglected me. This new attention made me feel desirable and good about myself. No way was I ever going back to being a housewife!"

At home, Cindy began demanding more from her husband.

"I complained about the way the house looked. Nothing was ever right for me. Although I was earning about what my husband had, I decided that we no longer had enough money to afford the weekly cleaning woman. He was just going to have to pick up the slack. I constantly reminded him that it was I who was saving the family from financial ruin and that he could at least keep up the home. My husband was working like mad to meet my increasingly difficult demands, doing much more than I ever did as a homemaker. He just took to it and I got very comfortable with giving him instructions. Any resistance from him was

met with a sharp scolding and a reminder of his failure to be a provider. He would back right down to me and I relished in my new power."

When it was time for the kids to go back to school in the fall, Cindy's husband mentioned that he was going to start his job search again. He was desperate to cease being the homemaker and he wanted to get back to the workforce.

"That was something that I could not tolerate. If he found a job, he might want to re-assert himself. He might even develop a backbone! No way, I thought. So I searched the Internet looking for ideas that would make him forget about his efforts to re-establish himself. I wanted something dramatic and decisive. I chose a strap-on dildo."

The strap-on is a harness that goes around the woman's waist or over her crotch where she can attach a rubber or silicone phallus that is shaped like the male penis. The length and thickness of the phallus can vary to short and thin to long and thick. The mere sight of a woman wearing a penis can send some men into pure panic. But to the submissive male, the image of a woman donning a strap-on can cause him to become aroused and overwhelmed with a desire to submit.

"One night, once the kids were well asleep, I brought my husband up to the bedroom. I looked sexy as hell, but definitely portrayed a no-nonsense and strict demeanor. I wore a white see-through blouse over a black bra, black leather knee-length skirt and high-heeled pumps. I ordered my husband to strip. I bet he thought we were going to have sex, something that had become a rare occurrence, but I had other ideas.

Instead, I lifted up my skirt and revealed the dildo. Before he could speak, I told him that I no longer viewed him as a man in the traditional sense. I told him that I loved him and would care for him but that if he ever failed to submit to me as a servant submits to his Master, I would throw him out and divorce him. I told him that his lot in life was to be the perfect househusband and servant. I told him that access to my body would be hard earned and that if he ever failed to please me in the bedroom, I would seek other sexual partners wherever and whenever I wanted.

While generously lubing the dildo that was strapped to my waist, I told him that he had a choice, either pack up and move out or bend over the bed and spread his legs. I said that tonight was to be a ceremony of sorts, symbolizing his new status in life. He started pleading for me to reconsider but I just said to either bend over or get out. Of course he accepted the inevitable and positioned himself over the bed and waited for me, his Mistress, to take him. I did take him and I enjoyed it immensely.

My husband is now a docile homemaker and caretaker. I believe in having weekly correction sessions. He bends over the bed naked every Thursday night and I review my list. Punishments range from a dose of the paddle to the trusty dildo."

One of the biggest advancements in the female domination lifestyle has been the invention of the strap-on dildo. This activity has done more to liberate women than perhaps the whip or paddle ever did. Why? Because of the social and psychological implications of strap-on play. Now the woman is the one wielding the former symbol of male superiority. Now the woman is the one who is the giver while the male becomes the receiver.

Strap-on play is sex of the psyches. Why do women love it so? That is a great and an important question. The rubber phallus strapped around the waist of a woman is an inanimate object. Thus, unless the woman purchases the type of harness that can stimulate her at the same time, she is feeling little to no physical pleasure during strap-on play. Yet, many women love doing it because of the mental stimulation and the mental pleasure that it provides for them. There is an incredible power exchange that takes place during this activity and the mental stimulation usually exceeds any rush that physical pleasure can provide. It makes for great sexual foreplay for the woman.

Women find this activity liberating for the social statement that it makes. Strap-on play strips the man of his masculinity and macho ways and usually causes the man to surrender his strength and his will over to his female aggressor. A woman can sense her man giving up resistance and she senses him melting into submission. This is an incredible power rush to the woman. Also, the effects of this activity usually last for some time. The man who submits to this activity has a hard time being macho around his dominant wife. He is usually meek and submissive to her outside of the bedroom after this activity.

Strap-on play is a power exchange and it has nothing to do with homosexuality or women wanting to be men. Quite the contrary, this activity is about the empowering of women as they unleash another level of their previously dormant power. Strap-on play between a woman and a man is about psychological sex as it is the mental stimulation that causes both parties to issue that all important power exchange.

The submissive man is feeling a combination of sexual stimulation, discomfort, and humiliation during strap-on sex. He now knows that what he use to place so much worth on (namely his penis) is no longer a tool to conqueror women but now the tables have been turned and the female has stripped this symbol of masculinity from him and is now using it against him. The woman is telling the man that she is not impressed with the male penis and that she can buy one that is bigger to pleasure herself and she can even use it as a tool to enslave the male gender. Strap-on play is not so much about sex as it is about mental domination. What was once a symbol of man's conquest of the female is now being used by the female to prove to the male her superiority.

The strap-on is gaining in popularity with women as they come to enjoy the societal implications. Joe discovered this first hand. Joe loved to party with his buddies and pick up girls but one night he met a woman who would forever change his attitude.

"I have had several relationships with women, have had flings, and have had one night stands. I would consider myself your typical twenty-something guy. One night, my friends and I went to a bar to flirt with some girls and see if we could get lucky. We flirted around and at some point during the night this girl approached me and we talked for a while. The girl was very nice looking, just a little shorter than I (maybe around 5'8). She had a nice fit body and was quite intelligent. I could tell she had goals and was an achiever like me. In my mind, I had already scored and my friends seemed to notice it as well. My buddies left and I told them I would stay with her. We talked until the club closed and she was the one that asked me to go to her house. I was delighted that she was totally interested in me and that it wouldn't take much for us to end up together that night."

Joe went to this young woman's home, they talked and began to make out. Joe noticed that this young lady seemed very sure of herself and very enticing. She was also somewhat aggressive, which seemed a little strange to Joe.

"I didn't mind since I was thinking I would score with her. After making out some with her, she asked me if I wanted to go to her bedroom. Of course I answered in the affirmative. Once in the bedroom, she got more aggressive. She was the one kissing, hugging, touching etc. I tried to regain the offensive and for a while both of us tried to take the lead. We spent a few minutes in a stalemate where we both were on the offensive. To me this was very new. I did not know how to react to it. A few minutes after, I found that she had somewhat taken over the lead and soon I stopped fighting. I can't really explain why but I stopped. I was tired of trying to take control and she seemed like she was not about to let go of it. Plus, she just seemed to be more intense at what we were doing which also was very strange to me. I remember thinking to myself how weird this night had become as she was kissing me all over and was holding me against the wall. I was pretty much doing what she wanted and was extremely confused and did not know how to react to the situation.

She undressed me and brought me to the bed and forced me on my back. She undressed and climbed on top of me and we made out some more, with her controlling everything. I surrendered to her and became full of passion for her. Suddenly she stopped kissing and fondling me, and she excused herself to go to the bathroom. I figured that she was taking care of birth control or something."

But that is not what this young woman had in mind.

"She came back in the bedroom wearing a strap on. I really could not tell you what I was thinking. I was confused and in shock but for some reason, I could not react to what was happening. It all happened very fast. She came to the bed, put my legs over her shoulders, lubricated my anus and she slowly began to penetrate me. I was in shock at what was happening but I just submitted to her advances. I felt pain, humiliation but most of all confusion. I was completely clueless as to how to act or what to say. She worked the dildo completely into me and she was in me for some time, thrusting her hips making it slide in and out of me. While doing this she looked straight in my eyes, which made it all even more

uncomfortable. When she was done she withdrew it and she lay down in the bed next to me. I was nervous and when I saw that she had fallen asleep, I left her house."

So what kind of an effect did this role-reversal have on Joe?

"I couldn't tell my friends what had happened since in their mind I had just scored once again. In the following days, I started looking on the Internet to see if anyone had experienced what I went through that night. I found this woman in a chat room who was familiar with strap-on play and we chatted on-line. She explained to me that this is something that was happening more and more in our society. She said as women are becoming more powerful and becoming the head of many households, it is only logical that women will become the dominant sexual partner, hence she becomes the one that penetrates while the male is slowly becoming a natural receiver. I questioned her about nature and reproduction and she said that men will only need to penetrate, if at all, when it is time for reproduction. The woman's new role will lead her to become the dominant partner. She further said that as the male falls behind in education and power positions, it will become natural for him to accept being penetrated by the stronger sex. She said this is all beginning to happen in today's society."

Much of what this woman told Joe is indeed true. Society is evolving toward a female dominated society and as women are gaining in positions of power in our society, they are becoming more aggressive in the bedroom. Granted, this young woman who seduced Joe is an exception rather than the rule. But while not all women will want to take a man to her bed and take him with a strap-on, there are an increasing number of women who prefer to be the aggressor when it comes to sex.

The concept of manhood is changing as far as women are concerned. A self assured and dominant female does not want a macho male but rather a male who knows how to respect women and who knows how to serve women. While most women still enjoy having traditional intercourse with men, many women are also choosing to introduce the strap-on into their relationship because of how it gives them a power advantage over their male partner. As Joe has discovered, the psychological effects on the male psyche is evident.

"Since that day, I am not that comfortable about flirting or picking up women. I now see women in a different light. I have a new sense of respect for them. I feel she took away my manhood that night."

The experience of being dominated by a woman will touch a major chord within the nature of most males. It has already had an effect on Joe as he no longer desires to be the sexual aggressor. If men like Joe want to live a lonely and meaningless life, then they will keep on trying to "score" by seeking short-term sexual fulfillment and one-night stands. But if a man desires to have a relationship that is meaningful, then he must learn how to treat a woman. A man needs to become a gentleman and focus his energy and attention on serving women. That is what will bring men long-term happiness and satisfaction. The strap-on experience was good for Joe because he now has a new outlook on the female gender.

Not all men are hesitant to receive the strap-on. Vickie discovered that her husband wanted her to bring role-reversal into their bedroom.

"My husband has been trying to get me to be more dominant for several years. I always thought he would get over it eventually but I think it is for real. One thing my husband mentions frequently in bed is a desire to be "used like a girl". Do you have any advice about how to go about this?"

What Vickie's husband wanted was for her to feminize him and then take him with a strap-on. That is what he meant by wanting her to use him like a girl. So just how does a woman penetrate her husband in a safe and healthy way? Once again my friend Victoria shares her expertise.

"The dominant wife or dominant woman should start out by taking her submissive man with her fingers. She should wear a latex glove, use plenty of lubrication such as KY Jelly, and "finger fuck" him before using a dildo. She must always begin dildo play by opening a man up first with her latex gloved fingers. If he has never been taken like this before, she must start out with slender butt plugs and work her way to a dildo. She should remind him to relax his muscles and set him at ease in the beginning by talking to him in whispers. And she must, she absolutely must always use lots of water based lubrication.

The rectum lining stretches so a woman needs to start out small and slender and over time, work her way to a thicker dildo when penetrating a man. After a slender butt plug, she could try a five to seven inch dildo that is on the slender side. She must use a thinner dildo before going to a thicker one.

The female could take the male from behind with him bent over the bed, a table or a chair with his legs spread wide. Or she could take him with him lying on his back with his knees spread and tucked toward his head. It depends if she wants to see his face as she is taking him. It is important that the woman communicates with her submissive as she is inserting the dildo into his rectum. She should remind him to relax and she should guide the dildo into him slowly with her hand, even if she is wearing a strap-on harness. Once the dildo slides in and the woman feels comfortable, she will probably feel powerful and will want to increase the speed and the force of the thrusts of her hips.

Some strap-on harnesses support a two-headed or dual dildo so a woman can insert the one side into her and the other into her submissive. That way she can experience physical pleasure as well as the mental satisfaction of dominating a man in this fashion. There are even vibrating harnesses that can stimulate a woman's clitoris as she takes her submissive man. As with any sexual activity, each couple must experiment to find what works best for them.

Also, use common sense. Always clean the dildo (or better yet, make your submissive clean the dildo) after each use with bleach or anti-bacteria soap. A woman should have a separate dildo for her own sexual pleasure. Any dildo she uses to penetrate her submissive male must be specifically for that use only. I would also recommend always using a condom on the dildo when engaging in strap-on play for hygienic reasons and I would replace the dildo with a new one every so often and discard the old ones. Over time, the lubrication works its way into the rubber or silicone and it needs to be replaced in order to guarantee proper hygiene. If you replace your toothbrush every couple of months, you should also get into the habit of replacing your dildos.

Once a woman becomes skilled and comfortable engaging in strap-on play, she will experience a tremendous power rush. As with any new D&S activity, the female must take it slow and experience will come with practice. After each session, it is vital that the female communicates with her man to find out what he liked and what he disliked about the strap-on experience. Also, she should afford him a safe word during the playtime, regardless of the activity.

Karen was both nervous and excited about the prospect of dominating her husband with a strap-on.

"I finally gained enough confidence to give it a try. I went ahead and bought one on line and could not wait to open the plain box when it arrived. I signed for it like it was a book of the month, knowing full well what was inside.

Well....SUCCESS! I bought a nice 6" silicone dildo that actually vibrates and is so real that when placed right next to his penis, they look exact in skin tone. Of course this one is a little longer and much thicker than his. When you squeeze this one, you have a firm handful but when I squeeze his, it collapses right down. Well last weekend, for the first time in my life, I screwed a male in the ass, not once but three times! It was even better than I expected and read about and I still can't believe that I did it myself. I am still giddy with joy. I did a lot of what I read about and went ahead and had him take two enemas ahead of time to cleanse himself for me. He sure knew what was coming but when I walked into the room with that so real penis jetting out from my hips and firmly pointed at him, he was almost in shock at the reality. I was actually quivering from being nervous and excited.

I had him watch as I rolled a condom onto my phallus as if I had been doing this forever. Then I used a good amount of lubricant on the whole shaft and the tip of the dildo. I had him bend over a short dresser and spread his legs. To see him doing this was like a complete and total surrender! I then stuck the tube up his rectum and squirted the lubrication into him, like a tube of toothpaste. I worked the head up to his tight hole and tried to just push it in using my hips, but the head keep popping out so I had to guide it in with my hand.

I took him real good for I don't know how long. My world was spinning! When I turned on the vibrator I got immense tingling near my clit that was just awesome. I honestly can say that I had a big orgasm and the thrill of doing this was more than enough for a beginner. He was moaning and writhing under me and I kept both of my hands on his hips throughout most of this experience."

Strap-on play does not necessarily have to involve anal penetration. The visual imagery of a woman donning a rubber phallus makes a powerful psychological and sociological statement to the male. Strap-on play can bring a role-reversal to the act of oral sex as the female can teach her male partner a lesson that he will not soon forget. That is what happened to James when Kathy decided to introduce strap-on play into their relationship. Kathy explains.

"I will never forget the first time I introduced James to strap-on play. I ordered the waist harness and rubber dildo from the people who published WHAP magazine. My outfit consisted of a black leather corset and soft leather gloves. I added my knee high leather boots with platform heels and of course, my new strap-on harness and seven-inch rubber phallus. I looked intimidating, powerful and sexy.

My husband was waiting on me in the bedroom in his required submissive position of on his knees with his head to the floor. I entered into the bedroom and gave him permission to view me with his eyes. When he looked up, he almost fainted from his excitement. I am a big woman of about five feet, ten inches tall with a large frame and an athletic build. I have powerful legs and thighs, a large but firm ass and I am a "C" cup in my bra. The corset had accented my large breasts as the corset left my breasts exposed and pushed up. My hourglass shape was greatly enhanced by the corset, making my hips even more powerful looking. As my husband scanned my body with his eyes, he about fell over when he noticed the seven-inch black rubber penis strapped around my waist.

I began by ordering him to perform his usual opening act of worshipping my body from toe to head with his tongue. He started out by licking my leather boots. He prefers the thigh high ones with the spiked heels but I prefer these knee high boots with the platform heels when I am going to be doing a lot of moving around. It is an interesting experience to watch a man lick your boots. I know that it sounds weird but I get excited at the sight of my husband groveling on the floor, licking my boots in a worshipful fashion. I ordered my husband to lick harder because I like to feel his tongue against my foot and calves when he is licking my boots. I enjoy the tingling sensation of having my husband licking my feet and calves through the boots. Add that pleasurable feeling with the erotic sight of a man humbling himself before me, and I was becoming quite wet between my legs.

Once I gave my husband permission to move beyond my boots, he worked his way to kissing my upper legs, my thighs and ultimately my buttocks. This is another wonderful benefit to the female domination lifestyle. I love foreplay but most men are only interested in screwing or receiving oral sex. Female Domination is the perfect sexuality for a woman because women need foreplay. What better foreplay than having a man slowly make love to every inch of your body with his lips and tongue?

After an extended amount of body worship, I forced James back to his knees, facing me. Confronting him was the strap-on dildo. I hadn't planned on doing this but the urge came over me. I wanted to watch him suck it. I know that my husband has absolutely zero homosexual desires. As a matter of fact, he is a real homophobe. The urge came upon me out of nowhere. I wanted to force my husband to do to me what I had done to him a number of times.

Going down on a man was never my favorite sexual activity. I found it to be rather humiliating and degrading. Men have no idea how degrading that act can be. It is not the same as when a man goes down on a woman. When a woman goes down on a man, she is often gagging from his tool being thrust into her throat while all the man cares about is getting off. I have heard men make the crude joke about how the perfect woman would stand waist high and have a flat head so the man can place his beer can on her head while she sucks him. How sick is that? But that is the male mind. We women have put up with such crude humor for years and many women have been deceived into believing that sucking a man's penis is her wifely duty. Young girls have been taught this from movies and rock music. What was it Monica Lewinski said to her girlfriend about going to work in Washington? Something like, "I am going to need my kneepads as I climb the political ladder." How sad is that? Do young women really believe that is how they will get ahead in a man's world?

So here I am, towering over my husband with my very own artificial penis and all of these thoughts are running through my mind. My dominant nature was stirring and I wanted to humiliate him. He represented all men to me at that moment. He was standing in proxy for the male gender and I wanted to dominate him in a way I had never done before. He wanted to be married to a dominant wife, well than he had to submit to my dominant whims.

I calmly whispered for my husband to "suck my cock." He looked at me in total disbelief, so this time I said it more firmly "James, Suck My Cock and Do It Now!" To my amazement and delight, my husband obeyed me and he placed his lips around my rubber phallus. I grabbed him by the hair and I slowly guided the dildo into his mouth. As he began to suck it, I became overwhelmed with power. I cannot describe the power and liberation I felt at that moment. I felt like a bird cage had opened and I was flying around the house totally free. I began to forcefully move my hips and I delighted in his gagging sounds as he continued to suck. He tried to pull away a few times but I held his head there tightly with my hands. I knew what to do because other men had done this to me before. This was so sweet. I began to verbally tear into my husband. I asked my husband how he liked sucking cock. I kept banging the dildo in and out of his mouth as I interrogated him about such a degrading act. Finally, I released my grip and he released his oral grip on the dildo.

He was panting and gasping for his breath and he was slightly coughing from choking on the rubber penis. It was then that I informed my husband that I had made the decision that I would never perform oral sex on him again. From now on, he was going to be the only giver of oral sex in our house. He would perform oral sex on me as much as I desired and he would also have to suck my dildo on occasion to remind him of his place. However, I would never suck him again. My husband nodded his agreement to my new rule. I had broken him down and I never felt more powerful in my life.

I took off the strap-on harness and I ordered my loving husband between my legs. He orally pleasured me until I had multiple orgasms. It didn't take long because I was so turned on. After I was satisfied, we laid together and embraced. He looked so at peace. You would have thought he was the one who had just had the orgasms but the fact is that my dominance had taken him to a place of submissive fulfillment. I could tell that he would not trade that for any kind of orgasm."

By submitting to strap-on play, a man is surrendering his will over to the female and he is acknowledging her dominance and her supremacy in the relationship. This activity can transport a man to subspace and he may find fulfillment on a higher plain than just the sexual realm. That is what Kathy discovered when she introduced strap-on play into her marriage.

By dominating her husband this completely, she had struck a chord within him. The submissive male desires to be dominated and disciplined by a woman. Most men long for this inside and spend a good portion of their lives searching for this void to be filled within them. Once they experience the strong yet loving hand of a dominant female that they trust and love, it fulfills them and it brings to them tranquility and contentment. The strap-on is merely one tool in the dominant woman's arsenal. Male orgasm denial is another.

Chapter Ten

Sex is for the Woman's Pleasure:
Male Orgasm Denial and Enforced Male Chastity

"I must not be denied, I can't be denied"; and with that he fell to kissing me so violently, I could not get rid of him. (Daniel Defoe, "The Fortunes and Misfortunes of the famous Moll Flanders", 1722)

Woman's power lies in man's passion (Leopold von Sacher-Masoch, "Venus in Furs", 1869)

Women who embrace Female Domination have discovered that if they will dominate their man in the bedroom, he is usually easy to control outside the bedroom. Most women no more enjoy nagging their husbands to get chores done around the house than husbands enjoy being nagged. But the man who has been dominated in the bedroom, usually develops a "yes, dear" mentality and is eager to serve. Thus there is no need to nag but simply to request (or order) with loving female authority. Why are dominated men so eager to please? In a word, Passion!

The dominated male feels a special bond to his female dominator and feels romantic toward her. The dominated man becomes a passionate man and he usually wants to touch, fondle and caress his Queen. His submissive nature unleashes sexual energy and the wise wife will channel that energy into getting her needs (sexual and domestic) met.

However, there is a potential stumbling block to this gateway to passion and servitude and that is the male orgasm.

Women have come to discover that a denied and sexually frustrated male is a passionate and productive man but a sexually fulfilled male is a lazy man. So some women have embraced the practice of male orgasm denial to limit the amount of orgasms their man has. This keeps him in a heightened submissive state. Men love to be sexually dominated by a woman and men love to be taken to subspace. The mental stimulation and mental pleasure a man encounters from being dominated by a woman has been described as "heaven on earth". When a woman "tames the beast", the lasting fruit is a loving, passionate and eager to serve male.

Male orgasm denial may vary depending on what works best in the training and controlling of each individual male. Orgasm denial means different things to different couples. If a man would have his way, he would be allowed sexual release multiple times a day. That is not a good idea if a woman wants him to be attentive to her needs. So if a man wants to have an orgasm every night but his wife denies him what he wants and limits him to say one orgasm per week, then that is considered orgasm denial. There are women who deny their men longer and limit them to only one orgasm every ten days to two weeks. Then there are women who think one or two orgasms a month is sufficient for a man in order to keep his plumbing cleaned and his desire to serve at a maximum level.

The male orgasm is a biological function that causes a sexual release, which relaxes both the body and the mind. The body wants to relax or even sleep after orgasm and the last thing it wants to do is to be forced to do a physical activity. This is why men lose the desire to pleasure a woman after they have climaxed and that is why so many women are unfulfilled sexually. This is especially true if the male achieves more than one orgasm. The woman that performs oral sex on a man and follows that up with intercourse should not be surprised by her lack of sexual fulfillment. If a woman decides that she is indeed going to allow her man sexual release she would be wise to forbid it until after she has been sexually satisfied. It takes women more time to orgasm but the payoff is well worth the wait.

The female orgasm is like the waves of the ocean whereas the male orgasm is like the eruption of a volcano. The female orgasm is the gift that keeps on giving but the male orgasm is Wham, Bam, Thank you, Ma'am. Keeping a man aroused and denied is the greatest technique a woman can employ for her own sexual fulfillment. As a man becomes full of passion, his energy level goes beyond his normal physical endurance. This sexual energy under the control of a woman can be channeled into her being pleasured. Then once she has been satisfied, she may permit her man sexual release. Or she can keep him denied and he will be much more attentive to her needs both that night and in the days to follow.

Men are less inclined to be obedient after orgasm because physically they are relaxed and they become lazy. They are not as easily aroused and thus their sexual drive is not as high. This is particularly true as men age. The male reaches his sexual peak years in his late teens and early twenties. The female does not reach her sexual peak years until her late thirties and well into her forties. The younger male is easier to get excited again after orgasm due to his testosterone level. However, as a man ages, his testosterone level decreases and it will take him longer to become excited again. But the denied man is easily excited and aroused and thus he is easier to control by a female.

The fastest way to a man's will is his penis and it is through the will of a man that a woman will achieve obedience. To be obedient or rebellious requires a decision and that decision is made within the human mind. The sexually satisfied man cannot be as easily controlled through his sex drive but the easily aroused man who is denied is eager to obey as his sex drive is at the forefront of his psyche.

An interesting aspect to the FemDom practice of male orgasm denial is the sexual impact it has on women. Few things rival the sexual intensity that a woman will experience when she denies her husband sexual orgasms while she enjoys as much pleasure as she desires. It is a psychological power exchange that releases more of a woman's dominant nature and sexual desires. Women begin to not only enjoy the benefits of male orgasm denial outside of the bedroom but also the benefits inside of the bedroom. Male orgasm denial is all about control and the woman who controls her man's orgasms ultimately controls her man.

A man being kept denied while pleasuring a woman is an incredible experience. The intensity of sex for a woman that is being orally serviced by a denied and passionate man will surpass most sexual experiences for the female. Likewise, few things rival the mental pleasure that the denied man experiences when he is being denied while required to sexually satisfy his Mistress. Those who have never experienced this power dynamic do not understand the power and intensity of male orgasm denial.

Priscilla discovered the advantages of orgasm denial when she began to control her husband's sexual release.

"When I found out that my Ted had a problem with habitual masturbation, I felt hurt and betrayed. I figured that men did this but I had no conception of how frequently some men masturbate. I caught him one night masturbating while he was watching a sexually provocative music video on television and I just about lost it. We had been married for eight years and I had no indication about his masturbation problem. He apologized and promised to never do it again and being the naïve wife that I was, I took him at his word.

It wasn't long before I found more evidence of his dirty little habit, like the stained hand towels in the laundry, and I caught him doing it again, this time in the shower. He was embarrassed and he confessed to me that he could not control himself. That is also when he admitted to me that he had been masturbating multiple times a day since he was a teenager, including most days since we were married. I knew that men were different than women when it came to self-control but I felt betrayed and hurt by his confession. Our sex life was not the greatest and now I knew why. He preferred to pleasure himself.

To his credit, Ted felt ashamed and he wanted to please me by going cold turkey with his masturbation habit. I made it clear to him that I did not trust him and I saw no way he could ever convince me that he could control himself. Ted could see the disappointment in my eyes and that is when he suggested the implementation of a chastity device.

I never knew such devices existed but Ted had been reading about them on the Internet. He showed me a site dedicated to a device known as "The CB-2000". It was a plastic cage that went over the male penis with a ring that went around his testicles. This device prevented the male from touching himself. The cage had gaps in the top so a man could still urinate and clean the head of his penis while wearing the device. As I read the testimonials about this device, I became enthused about the possibilities and I told Ted to order me a CB-2000.

When it arrived, Ted shaved his pubic hair and installed the chastity device. It took him a little time to get use to it and he had some discomfort from the ring pinching the skin of his ball sac, but I liked the concept of my husband being under my control. The CB-2000 came with a little pad lock and once it was locked in place, I kept the key in my possession. Ted's penis was completely at my mercy.

He wore it for twelve straight hours that first day before I let him out. The next day I made him wear it for twenty-four hours. It was a Saturday so he stayed near the house. The third time he wore the device, I made him go three days, which included wearing it to work under his slacks. The CB-2000 is a little bulky so he had to wear dark slacks and he was worried that people would notice, but they didn't. Ted had his mental struggles with the device and he began to change his mind about giving me this much control. He wanted me to forget about having him wear a chastity device and he promised me that he would never masturbate again. His pleading to be released only made me more determined to keep him locked in the chastity device.

After the third day, I let him out for a day or two but the next time, I kept him locked in it for an entire week. Ted finally became resolved to the fact that I was not about to change my mind so he got use to the device. It would pinch him at times when he was exercising or doing physical activities but he learned how to adapt. He had to wear dark slacks to work and dark colored shorts out in the yard to hide the slight bulge in his pants from the chastity device, but he eventually became more comfortable.

Our relationship began to change due to Ted's chastity. Ted was always the dominant partner in our marriage but with me controlling his orgasms through the use of a chastity device, I began to develop a dominant attitude toward him. The first thing that changed was our sex life. I released Ted from the CB-2000 once a week in which he would clean both himself and the device and shave his pubic hair. I would allow him a few hours out of the device before requiring that he re-install it. During his few free hours, I would allow him to have sex with me. He would spring to erection and his passion toward me was the best since we were newlyweds. But there was one minor problem. Ted was so sexually frustrated from being confined in that cage all week without being able to touch himself, that when I permitted him to have sex with me, he would have a pre-mature ejaculation, which left me frustrated. An even bigger problem was that after his quickie orgasm, he seemed to revert back to his old self, meaning a loss in passion and a short temper toward me. This was not good so I had to make some adjustments to our sex life.

I began to only have sex with Ted while he was wearing the CB-2000. In fact, I only permitted him out of the device about once every other week and then only for a few hours to allow him to shave, to clean himself and clean the device. If we were going to engage in sex, he had to be wearing the CB-2000. The results were that for the first time in our marriage, our sex life became all about my pleasure. Ted orally pleasured me for as long as I wanted and I pleasured myself with a dildo or a vibrator. Ted was so full of passion that he began to perform oral sex on me for hours at a time. Before, he never liked to go down on me but now, he was doing me with passion and an incredible endurance. I would also make him pleasure me with my sex-toys. I took great pleasure in pointing out to Ted how my dildo was much bigger than his penis and how my dildo never went limp.

Ted had to remain in the CB-2000 during sex, which caused him some discomfort from his penis fighting to become erect but being rebutted by the tight cage of the chastity device. Ted began to beg me for sexual relief and I loved having this control over him. My urge to dominate him began to expand into other areas outside the bedroom. I made Ted earn the privilege of an orgasm. I began to assign him chores around the house each night and he had to do a satisfactory performance in his housework in order for me to allow him an orgasm the next time I released his penis from its cage. When I would let him out of his cage, intercourse was not an option because of his problem with pre-mature ejaculations. So I began to have him masturbate for me, in front of me. This lead to all kinds of exercises in Ted's humiliation as I would invent creative ways for him to entertain me while he masturbated for me. I found myself getting on the Internet to research ways a woman could dominate a man sexually and this fueled my sexual arousal and provided me with new ways to dominate Ted.

Ted was soon doing all the household chores, including the cooking. I enrolled Ted in cooking classes and in massage therapy classes. Ted began to be my personal servant. I took charge of almost every aspect of his life and he was so horny all the time from being sexually denied that he obeyed practically all of my demands. He became rather docile and submissive toward me and I kept growing more dominant toward him.

On the weekends, Ted is no longer allowed to play golf or watch sports. He has to attend to my needs. I began to make him fast from sundown Friday to sundown Saturday. During Saturday, he is required to read books on female care, hair care, nail care, skin care and such. Before his fast ends, I will administer to him an enema to promote health as well as incorporating another method in dominating him. Once again, this has made Ted more submissive toward me.

On Sunday, Ted must utilize what he has learned by pampering me. He will do my hair, my nails, give me a massage and of course, he will orally service my body and bring me to multiple orgasms. Every other Sunday, I will free him from the CB-2000 and allow him to masturbate in a way that I find to be entertaining. I might make him dance for me as if he was a Chippendale dancer and he must masturbate for me as part of his performance. Or I might make him lay across my lap and hump my leg while I spank him until he climaxes. Or I may have him lay across the bed and hump a pillow while I paddle his behind. It depends on my mood and what interesting new way I have found on the Internet. I correspond with other women who have purchased a CB-2000 for their husbands and we share stories and ideas.

Another advantage to this new arrangement is how I was able to motivate Ted to live a healthier lifestyle. Ted had a terrible eating habit and he rarely exercised. Now that I have gained control over him, I make him exercise and eat right. He gets up early each morning and goes to the gym before work. After work, he performs his domestic duties and has dinner ready when I get home. I took charge of our finances and I only give him a small allowance for lunch each day. Therefore, Ted now eats less and eats healthier. He lost weight, toned up and looks amazing in the nude. I am so proud of him as he is now my trophy husband.

None of this would have been possible had I not confronted him about his masturbation habit. Ted now lives a disciplined life and he tells me that he has never felt better and has never been happier. I can honestly say the same. It took the chastity device to reverse the roles in our marriage but now that I am in control, our lives are more fulfilled."

There is an evolution that takes place within most women as they experiment with this lifestyle. Most women start out timid and unsure about this lifestyle. Then once they begin to overcome their inhibitions and embrace the dominant side of their personality, they begin to love being dominant and controlling. Over time, the Dominant Female's appetite grows and she hungers for more control and more power. Denying a man orgasms is a real power rush. Women who practice this lifestyle will eventually learn that a sexually satisfied man is a selfish man but a denied man is an obedient man. Like Priscilla, Pamela discovered the benefits when she began to deny her husband.

"I was quite shocked at some of the things my husband had been reading on the Internet. From searching the history of our web browser, I discovered that he was interested in Female Domination. Most of it really turned me off but some of what I read began to get me excited about the possibilities. I decided that I would love to have the upper hand in my marriage. My husband had hinted at having submissive fantasies before, and I was eager to see how far he would go in a dominant/submissive relationship.

The first thing I did was to take charge in the bedroom. I required my husband to please me orally and I set up a schedule where he had to satisfy me four times to be allowed an orgasm of his own. I found him to be very submissive and soon I assigned household chores to him. It became clear to me very quickly that the more dominant I acted towards him, the more subservient he became to me. There was little or no resistance when I took over the finances. I ran into my first problem when I ordered my husband to stop surfing porn sites on the Internet. I found more web sites in our history file. I also suspected that he was masturbating while looking at these sites.

When confronted with the evidence he confessed to both, begged for forgiveness and admitted to a lack of self-control. At this time I started spanking him for any shortcomings and I ordered a chastity device which I hold the key! Having him in chastity 24/7 has helped increase my power in the relationship to the point that my husband is completely submissive to me. He is also completely dependent on me for any sexual relief, and this is a very powerful weapon when wielded by a woman who is not afraid to use it.

He does most of the housework and all the yard work. He not only cooks for me, but also caters to my personal needs. In the last year, I have trained him to shave my legs, help me with my bath routine, and to serve me in the bathroom. He cleans me with tissue, sponge, and powder when I finish. I feel that his service keeps his attention where it belongs; and that is on me. Failure to please will result in punishment, usually a spanking or longer length of time to release from his chastity belt.

I allow him to orgasm only about once per month. This has forced some changes in our sex life. I take my pleasure from his tongue usually three or four times a week. I have become hooked on oral sex, and I have very strong orgasms when he tongues both my vagina and my anus. It makes him more submissive after he has spent the evening servicing me orally. A few months ago my husband complained that we did not engage in enough penetrative sex. I ordered a strap-on dildo and now use it on my husband regularly. I also ordered a chinstrap dildo, when he wears it he can penetrate me and lick my anus at the same time.

The natural growth in our marriage has been toward a female dominated union. My husband is not only my lover and friend, but also a complete servant. He obeys me at all times, though in public we act very much like the couple next door."

Men are much easier to control and dominate when they are denied orgasms. Plus, it makes the entire FemDom lifestyle more pleasurable for the man if he is denied and sexually frustrated. Once a man climaxes, he experiences a letdown and his enthusiasm to serve the female is greatly diminished. To many submissive men, they love the power exchange of being denied while being forced to pleasure the superior female as often as she demands. The thought of having such total control over a husband that even his orgasms can be under her authority, excites many wives.

It would be difficult to deny a man that wasn't excited about some aspects of Female Supremacy or Female Domination. The woman feeds off of the submissive male's excitement and submission. The submissive husband desires to surrender to his wife and the dominant wife seizes upon his desire and thus she begins to desire more submission from him. Some women love the thrill of knowing that their husband would rather give them pleasure than receive pleasure himself. It makes the female feel very powerful and sexual. The man has been trained so that his fulfillment is in knowing that his Queen is being fulfilled. To the submissive male, he is troubled if the moans of his wife's ecstasy do not convey intense pleasure and sexual satisfaction. The submissive male gets much personal fulfillment in pleasing his Queen, which is how it should be within a FemDom marriage.

Kari discovered the power of orgasm denial and enforced male chastity in her relationship with her husband Kenneth.

"My husband and I are both college educated, professional, have an active social life, go to church and share many interests together. A couple of years ago, my husband (a more adventurous person than I) revealed to me his desire to become a submissive husband. I didn't understand what he meant. I love my husband very much, however at first I was convinced he needed psychological help. I did listen though and I did investigate. I realize now he didn't need psychological help at all and I am glad he shared his desires with me.

I keep him denied most of the time and our life now is so much better (especially for me). Each day he tells me he falls more in love with me and thanks me for allowing him to serve me. He thanks me for allowing his submissive nature to be revealed, actualized and nurtured. Each day he submits his will to mine and puts my needs and wants ahead of his. I too love him more and more. I sometimes feel selfish but then I realize we are doing what hubby wants and what makes him happy.

Our marriage is based on mutual respect and understanding. We both are committed to making our relationship not just successful but joyful. As with any relationship, even a female dominant one, it takes effort from both of us to achieve our desires. I am learning how to be the decision maker in our relationship. I was raised to be a traditional submissive wife, but in the last several years I have become the opposite. Hubby is still very much apart of my decision making process. I am learning submissive does not equal stupid or weak. Hubby is very smart and wise. I always seek his counsel before making a decision. I want him to feel he has a role in our relationship. It's just not the dominant role. He will give his thoughts when asked and accepts the decision. I also know no matter what crisis may pop up, hubby will not run and hide. He is there next to me supporting me. It's wonderful knowing I have such a helpmate.

As wonderful as hubby is, he is still a man. I have also learned men generally are not the equal of women and will mature only so far. Fortunately hubby understands this and accepts his diminished role in our relationship. I know what's best for us (and him) and set rules for him to follow. Hubby tells me he appreciates me doing this. He tells me just because he was born with "balls" does not make him as mature as me and he needs rules and guidelines and discipline. While he hates spankings, corner time, punitive enemas, mouth washing, being put to bed without dinner (he really hates that one), and being denied, he knows as a man he needs corrective discipline. He thanks me for loving him enough to not allow disobedient behavior on his part. He thanks me for putting forth the effort to discipline him."

So how did Kari go from complete novice to such a believer in Female Domination?

"Through an alternative newspaper here in my home town, I discovered a FemDom club. I was curious, but I didn't want to go alone so my best girlfriend (my husband is my best friend) went with me. At first I thought no way could I become a dominant woman but with encouragement from the other women I was meeting and my husband, I began what I consider a transformation.

At the FemDom club, I met a woman who was also a therapist. I took my husband to see her to explore why he wanted to become submissive and if he was really willing to submit to me or was his feelings merely a fantasy being expressed. My husband was adamant that he wanted to be submissive to me and would obey me and not try to top me from below. We attended several counseling sessions and expressed our thoughts and expectations.

With the help of this woman therapist and our openness with each other, we decided on new living arrangements. I would control the sex. This was difficult at first. I generally am not an aggressive woman, nor controlling one, but I am learning to be both. My husband though submissive still had a strong sex drive, sometimes he would revert to his old ways and try to initiate and that created tension. While it was uncomfortable, I had to learn how to discipline him. One of the female dominant friends I met at the FemDom club came over the first time and took me through my first bare bottom over the knee spanking of my husband. He was then sent to time out and to bed without super. He had to learn, and so did I, that I am in charge and I say when and where for everything now. I was finding this very liberating.

Inside our home and around female dominant friends, my husband must address me as Ms Kari and my lady friends as Miss or Ma'am. He must sit at my feet and unless I tell him otherwise, in only a tee shirt and chastity device. To control his habit of masturbating and to constantly remind him of his submission to me in all areas, I purchased a CB-2000 chastity device. I am the key holder and he wears it 24/7. He is also now my houseboy. It is such a joy to be relieved of household chores. Hubby is learning to be good at doing domestic chores. On those rare occasions when he has been a little lazy on housework, I find a teaspoon or two of castor oil, punitive enema and an over the knee spanking works wonders."

There are a number of quality chastity devices on the market, ranging from affordable to quite expensive. There is the Access Denied, the Chastity Tube, the Tollyboy belt, the Carrara belt, the Neosteel belt and the ever popular CB-2000 (just to name a few).

Why a chastity device? Some men have a problem with self-control when being denied and other men (like Priscilla's husband) have a habitual habit of frequent masturbation. Within most FemDom marriages, masturbation is forbidden as once again, the depleted male is a lazy male. In cases where the male is having problems resisting the temptation to pleasure himself, a chastity device is an option for the dominant female to ensure obedience in the area of male sexual self-control.

While most dominant women like to incorporate male orgasm denial on some level (be it allowing male orgasms only once a week, twice a month or once a month), a few women go even a step further with their men. There are relationships where the dominant woman has incorporated permanent denial and permanent male chastity. Eva enjoys such an advanced FemDom relationship with her husband.

"I am a practicing female supremacist and am enjoying this life more than I could have imagined. I am having the most incredible orgasms of my life. I have been married to my husband for five years now and he has not had an orgasm for the entirety of our marriage. I am heavily into orgasm denial and his frustration keeps my libido high.

Our honeymoon night was his last orgasm because he knew what we had planned as a couple and our "pre-arrangement" to be a D/s couple. His last orgasm was onto a copy of the contract that we had prepared out in detail. I let it dry and he framed it so he could see what he was never going to get again as long as we were married. We have a loving relationship and even though his frustration grows rapidly, I handle him with true superiority.

Is such a relationship possible? Can a man really be denied permanently? Some women claim that they have such a relationship with a submissive male and there are permanent chastity devices on the market that come with break-off screws and can be installed in accordance with a Prince Albert piercing or a Frenum piercing in the male's penis. From my research, it is important for health reasons that a man is allowed to have his plumbing cleaned out periodically. So how does a woman achieve permanent denial in the training of her husband and at the same time ensure his proper health and mental well-being? The key seems to be with a practice known as "prostate milkings".

Some dominant women milk their husbands' prostates to clean out his plumbing without allowing him the pleasure of an orgasm. A prostate milking is where the female inserts her latex covered finger in his anus, finds his prostate gland and massages it. Done correctly, this will cause the male to release built up semen out of his penis, only it is not intense like an orgasm but rather the semen kind of flows out in a long, continuous stream. An erection is not necessary for a prostate milking so a chastity device can be worn during this process. The end result of the milking is to relieve the male of stored up semen without giving him a pleasurable orgasm.

Another unusual and rare FemDom practice that I have encountered a few times is the enforced virginity of the male within a FemDom relationship. This usually involves an older woman and a younger man. Lydia is in such a relationship and her story is quite interesting.

"I have been in a Female dominated marriage with a younger man for the past eight years. I am Forty-one and my husband is Twenty-nine. I was married once before but got divorced. That marriage only lasted five years and I was pretty hurt.

When I was thirty-two, I began to date a twenty year old man. He was actually the son of a woman I use to work with. It is a long story about how I ended up going out with this boy but to make it short, I found myself in a relationship with a man that was twelve years younger. Not only was he only twenty years old but he was also still a virgin. We went out just as friends in the beginning and as we became attracted to each other, I made up my mind that I was not about to sleep with him. I figured that this relationship would never last and since I knew his Mother, I did not want to be the one who took his virginity. His Mother was Ok with us dating because I told her we were only going to movies and dinner as friends.

This young man fell for me and I enjoyed being the dominant partner in a relationship. My maturity automatically made me the dominant one. I was attracted to him and the sexual temptations began to become strong. We began to kiss and make out passionately but I told him that I was not about to have sex with him unless we were married. I did not want to take his virginity.

He would beg me for sex and I came to enjoy denying him. That is when something totally unexpected happened to me. I developed a bit of a fetish in teasing and denying this young man. We would kiss and he would get rock hard and I would take him to the edge and then make him back off. The problem was that I was getting so excited, after my dates with him, I found myself masturbating at home alone with my vibrator. I started to desire to have sex with him but I also was enjoying this power

I had in teasing and tempting this virgin boy. I thought something was wrong with me and I kept my self-perceived perverted fetish to myself.

I could not seem to contain my desires and my arousal when I teased this virgin boy. I began to dress more provocative for our dates and I loved to make out with him. I would rub his hard penis through his jeans, take his hands and allow him to fondle my breasts through my bra, get him to the edge and then tell him that we must stop because he must remain a virgin until marriage. I would then go home and pleasure myself with my vibrator as I fantasized about my virgin boy.

Our dates grew to the place where not only did I allow him to fondle my breasts, but I began to allow him to suck my nipples and eventually, I even allowed him to orally pleasure me. My fetish could not be contained within the recesses of my mind and I became so excited that I needed sexual relief and I desired his touch and tongue. I taught him how to orally please a woman and how to bring me to orgasms but I stayed true to my commitment and did not permit him intercourse. My original motives in keeping him a virgin were pure, as I was doing this because of my relationship with his Mother. But it developed into this strong fetish. I literally got off in denying him sex while he had to pleasure me.

He did not know the pleasure I was getting within my mind by denying him and he thought I was making him stop short of intercourse for morality reasons. We continued to date and eventually we became engaged. I stayed true to my commitment even after we became engaged. His mother was surprised at our engagement but she saw how happy her son was so she actually gave us her blessing for our marriage. She assumed her son and I were in a traditional and vanilla relationship.

My goal was to keep him a virgin until our wedding night. Somehow my fetish and sexuality became so strong that I almost needed for him to be a virgin. I can't explain it but I felt so in control and so powerful making him pleasure me while I denied him. He had accidents and climaxed a few times as we were making out. I even stroked him to orgasm on a few occasions but I would not permit him to penetrate me.

I became so turned on about the thought of a virgin boy performing cunnilingus and worshipping my body. I experienced many orgasms as he would eat me and I would often pleasure myself with my vibrator when I was by myself as I pondered this power dynamic in my mind. I enjoyed this intense mental stimulation so much that I realized that as soon as he lost his virginity, this power dynamic would be gone forever and I worried if I would still enjoy sex with him. Strange, I know, but I could not help what was occurring with my sexuality.

A few weeks before our wedding, I asked him if he would be willing to remain a virgin after our wedding. He said 'No' but I was so use to being the dominant partner and I was so accustomed to getting my way, that I threatened him by saying that perhaps he should find someone else to marry. He was stunned and devastated so he begged me to marry him and he agreed to abide by any terms and conditions I decided to set. This excited me even further.

I found myself researching feminism and female domination. I began to desire to really control and dominate my soon to be new husband. I tried to learn about my fetish but could not find anything on this type of desire. Eventually, I discovered material about female domination and D&S. I went to a fetish store and talked to the female owner. I told her about my fetish and my situation. She gave me some books about Leather sex and S&M and she told me about chastity devices. I really became excited.

I gave my soon to be young husband my terms for our marriage and he reluctantly agreed to those terms. He became excited about Leather sex and Female Domination and he agreed to remain a virgin as long as I wanted. We agreed not to engage in intercourse until our fifth wedding anniversary and if it went well, it would then become a regular part of our sex life. He agreed and we were wed as planned.

Shortly after we were married, I had him fitted for a chastity device. Our marriage has become a totally FemDom marriage and I incorporated spankings, discipline, strap-on play and other D&S sex into our marriage. My young husband orally pleases me as much as I demand and his orgasms are supervised and determined by me. I love being married to a young virgin and denying him. I knew what intercourse was all about from my first marriage and my past dating experiences but I was not tempted to have it with my new husband. When I want penetration, I make him pleasure me with my dildo.

Due to our D&S lifestyle and the power I have by keeping him a virgin, he has become even more submissive toward me with each passing year. Once our fifth year anniversary approached, I asked him if he still wanted to lose his virginity or could we expand it for five additional years. He wanted to lose it but I still was not ready to surrender this power. My control over him is so complete that I convinced him to go five additional years. So the plan now is for me to allow him intercourse two years from now on our tenth wedding anniversary. I plan on staying true to my promise because a part of me does want him to experience what intercourse with a woman is like. He will be thirty-one when it finally happens. But I know it will change things some. I still get wet thinking about being married and denying a thirty-year old virgin. It drives my sexuality and makes me horny every time I think about it, which is often."

Dating a younger man placed Lydia in the dominant role with a man and this interaction released her dominant desires and true nature. It found its expression in her mind in the form of sexual excitement by being an experienced woman in the dominant role with an inexperienced man. This actual experience triggered sexual stimulation in her mind for some unknown reason. She loved having power over this younger man and to her, that power comes from keeping him a virgin. This gives her an incredible amount of control and power over him and it is that power that arouses her and unleashes her dominant energy. It makes sense that they eventually came into D&S because the controlling of a man's sexuality is D&S and Female Domination. At its most basic point, her desire is a desire to control and sexually dominate a man. This fills her with power and that power makes her aroused and sexually excited.

Lydia is not alone in this kind of relationship. Some friends of mine (June and Jim) are active in a FemDom support group that has a couple in their group where the woman keeps her submissive male partner a virgin (and intends to continue down this path once they are married). I will allow June to tell this story.

"We are members of a FemDom support group that meets about ninety miles from our home. This group meets twice a month and is made up of a half dozen couples at the present time. Our FemDom group meets in the home of the founding couple of the group. They have a "secret" room in their basement that has D&S equipment and that is where our group

meets and plays. Due to the limited space in their home, they have to keep the membership to no more than six couples at a time. Whenever a couple must drop out for whatever reason, then they allow another couple to join.

A few months ago, a new couple joined our FemDom group. The woman is forty-one years old and very attractive and her submissive boyfriend is only twenty-two and is as cute as can be. He has a boyish looking face, blonde hair and all the women in our group just love this young man.

As is a custom when someone new joins, the Female introduced herself and talked about her experience in FemDom and her philosophy as it relates to Female Supremacy. She then had her young submissive introduce himself and he was rather shy but did a fine job in speaking to the group about why he likes being in submission to women. Then his Mistress made him confess to the group his rather interesting secret. He blushed a little as he told the group that he is still a virgin.

You should have seen the reaction of the women in our group. We were so taken and excited about his revelation. His Mistress then told the group more of their little secret. She proclaimed that she and her young submissive are engaged to be married and that she is going to keep him chaste and a virgin. As long as he is married to her, this young man will never know what it is like to have intercourse with a woman.

They proceeded to tell our group the rest of their story. He has to orally pleasure his Mistress but she will never perform oral sex on him or permit him intercourse. She then had him pull down his pants and he showed our group the custom fit chastity belt he was wearing, complete with an attachment for a butt plug. This young man is not only a virgin in the traditional sense but he is also a virgin when it comes to strap-on play. His Mistress is having him wear a butt plug to open him up for their wedding night, when she plans to take him with a strap-on.

We later learned the details about how they met. He grew up in a religious family and that is why he was still a virgin. His parents and his church programmed him ever since he was a teen the importance of saving himself for marriage. However, he had these submissive desires and he always fantasized and masturbated to FemDom fantasies. These two conflicting values pulled on him and he finally decided that he needed to explore his submissive nature.

He met this woman over the Internet through a Kinky contact service. She did not know anything about him being a virgin when they started their FemDom relationship. They were compatible on a number of other areas and began to date. But once he told her that he was still a virgin, that is when she made up her mind that this opportunity needed to be seized upon. They mutually decided (with her leading the discussion and decision making) that their marriage could make a major statement when it came to Female Domination and Female Supremacy. So he will remain a virgin and have his orgasms monitored and controlled by her while he must orally provide her with as many orgasms as she desires."

This is definitely an advanced and some would say extreme form of Female Domination but they are both legal adults and there is no law that says they must engage in intercourse. The women of June's FemDom group think it is sexy that an attractive older woman is marrying a cute younger man whom she is going to keep chaste and a virgin in order to make a social statement. The women I talked with about this subject think it is romantic that this young man would be willing to live such a selfless life in order to be married to a dominant woman. I would imagine each time this young man orally services his dominant wife, she will think to herself that he is still a virgin and that will add to her an extra ingredient of arousal and excitement.

This young man has a freewill and obviously this power dynamic is as exciting to him as it is to her. In a way, they are having sex of the minds and that is more powerful and fulfilling to the submissive nature than actual physical sex. Physical sex can never touch the intensity or pleasure as the mental stimulation of D&S of the minds. After all, the brain is the greatest sex organ. Not only is their sexual dynamic providing intense stimulation to them but also to those whom they share their story with. This young man will get to serve a woman in a way few submissive men ever will. Such a relationship is not for most but as we have discovered, certainly not totally unique.

Female Domination and D&S is about a sexuality of the minds. It takes on many forms but the reason those who practice a FemDom lifestyle are so passionate about it is the amount of intense mental and physical pleasure they experience when compared to traditional or vanilla sex. Since the mind is the greatest sex organ, sex can become so much more than the mere exchange of bodily fluids. Arousal begins in the mind and arousal's intensity is developed in the mind. The body follows the mind so relationships which make a social statement to the couples involved can increase the intensity of sex because living their daily lives becomes a form of fore-play and sex becomes an act not so much between two bodies but between two psyches.

One controversial FemDom activity that usually incorporates both orgasm denial and sex between the psyches of the dominant wife and the submissive husband is the sexual practice known as cuckolding.

Chapter Eleven

Cuckolding: Female Liberation or Promiscuity?

To be the slave of a woman, a beautiful woman whom I love, whom I worship...who binds me and whips me, treads me underfoot, while she gives herself to another. (Leopold von Sacher-Masoch, "Venus in Furs")

As women become more liberated and gain in power, there is another societal role reversal that is occurring and that is for the female to seek extra-marital affairs. It was common for the man to have both a wife and a mistress on the side during a patriarchal marriage. Most of the time the wife was powerless since she had no financial means of support. Today, some women are turning the tables and they have both a husband and a lover. However, there is a fascinating element to this within the lifestyle of Female Domination. It is the husband who is encouraging his wife to seek other sexual partners. This practice is known as cuckolding.

The words cuckold and cuckolding are derived from the cuckoo bird. The cuckoo is a European tree bird that migrates from Africa each spring. The female cuckoo bird lays its eggs in the nests of other birds leaving them to be cared for by these other birds. The French equated this female cuckoo to a woman who is unfaithful and who "sleeps around". The husband of such a woman is know as being cuckolded or married to an unfaithful wife.

In Female Domination this term has come to mean a liberated wife who has other lovers for the sole purpose of humiliating her husband and using that humiliation to drive the husband into deeper submission to her. The dominant wife claims that she is free to do whatever she pleases, including having sex with whomever she desires. The husband must be monogamous to her and must suffer the shame of being cuckolded. In Female Domination, often orgasm denial and control of the husband accompanies cuckolding. The dominant wife enjoys having sex with another man while denying her own husband the right of having sex with her. It is a mind game and a power exchange.

To couples who embrace this flavor of the FemDom lifestyle, cuckolding becomes a form of sex between the psyches of the dominant wife and her cuckolded husband. Denise and Gary are a FemDom couple who claim that cuckolding has enhanced their marriage. How is that possible? Denise explains.

"My husband and I discussed cuckolding probably twenty years ago. We fantasized together about my bringing home a total stranger to have sex with. This was as foreign to me as skydiving and something I knew I would never really do. But I played along with the fantasy. I had only had sex with two men in my life and I was married to both of them. I'm not a flirt nor the least bit impulsive in my actions. I am very down to earth and practical minded - a realist through and through. However, cuckolding became a reality for us back in 1998.

My husband introduced me to the FemDom lifestyle over our many years of marriage. He was wise to begin by stressing the male servitude aspects of the FemDom lifestyle and not the D&S activities. Over time, I learned all about FemDom and D&S and came to love this lifestyle. I especially enjoyed the power I felt over men.

We have a great marriage but I resented the fact that there were activities that I enjoyed but my husband didn't want to participate in with me. I especially like to dance and go out to listen to music. I saw single women enjoying themselves with single men and going out to do things they enjoyed. When friends invited my husband and I to go to a nightclub with them on New Years' Eve to dance, I really wanted to go. But I didn't want to have to beg and plead with Gary to go with me. And even if he agreed to go, he would not have fun and it would affect my enjoyment also. So, I casually said "maybe I will get another man to take me". Just testing the water.

To my surprise, my husband actually seemed excited about that possibility. We have a dungeon in our home where I dominate him. In the dungeon, we have a cage that I lock my husband in when I want to discipline him. I teased my husband about how I might ask out this handsome, eligible bachelor that we knew to accompany me on New Years Eve, while I locked my hubby in his cage all night. Again, I could tell that this thought excited him. So, I called up this single submissive man who knew we were in the FemDom lifestyle (he was a member of the same D&S group that we are) and I asked him if he would escort me on New Year's Eve. He accepted. This was my first date in almost nineteen years so I went to the beauty shop and had my hair and my nails done to perfection. I bought a lovely and sexy dress and wore heels, and stockings with garters.

My date showed up at my door all dressed up and looking really nice, handed me a beautiful bouquet of flowers and told me how lovely I looked! I made my husband greet him at the door, wearing only a pair of feminine frilly panties. I could tell that my husband was as excited about this date as I was. He went happily into the cage and we left. Before we left, I laid the cordless phone in the cage with him so I could call him throughout the night to let him know how my date was going. I love my husband and I wanted to include him in on what I was experiencing, as I knew this had been a fantasy of his for a long time. I guess I wanted to both include him and humiliate him about what he was missing.

I had no romantic feelings toward my date, as we were just friends as far as I was concerned. But, when we got on the dance floor, he was nothing but smooth and attentive to me. After a couple of slow dances, I was feeling very attracted to him. Suffice it to say, he made me feel very special and beautiful. I had a wonderful night with my date and it developed into more than I had originally planned. I want my husband to describe what happened, as this was a night either of us will ever forget."

Gary continues the story.

"Our dungeon has a cage in it and that is where I spent the evening. My Mistress/Wife Denise gave me our cordless phone and she took her cell phone with her. She planned to call me now and then throughout the evening to let me know how things were progressing. When she had me

in the cage, she put the padlock on the door and locked me securely in for the night. (We do have an emergency escape system in case of fire or other problem, by the way.) She also took the trouble to throw her panties she had worn that day in the cage with me. Ms Denise said goodbye and then she turned out the light and closed the door. I was plunged into darkness as I heard them open the back door and leave for their date.

After about two hours the cordless phone rang and I fumbled for it in the darkness and finally answered it. My wife was telling me they had met the other couples in the motel suite and had a few drinks and some snacks and were now at the club where the party was held. She said her and her date had a few slow dances and they were both feeling quite comfortable. She asked how I was doing and I said fine and then she said goodbye and hung up.

After about another hour the phone rang again and Mistress Denise was sounding quite mellow. She told me she was in the lounge of the women's rest room so it would be a bit more quiet to talk. She teased me how there had been several slow dances and her date's hands were roaming around her body rather freely and she was really enjoying it. My heart and respiratory rate went up by several points and my excitement began to grow.

Midnight came and went and it was now 1999. About 12:30 AM my wife called to tell me they were headed for the motel suite to meet the other couples who had left already. Then there was silence until about 3 AM when I heard the back door to the house open and my wife and her date had arrived back home.

After some conversation in the living room they moved to the dungeon, opened the door, turned the red light on, and entered. Ms Denise didn't even bother taking the cover off the cage. Since her date is a sub male, she had him take most of his clothes off and then she attached him to the St. Andrew's cross, facing out. I could not see what was going on with my cage still covered but I could hear some very erotic sounds coming from both of them.

Eventually my beautiful wife pulled up the cover on my cage, unlocked the door, and crawled in a short distance. She was looking so very turned on as she told me the plans had changed. I was going to remain locked in the cage for the rest of the night and her date was going to bed with her. She then studied me very closely and asked if I was okay. The alternate state of consciousness I was experiencing (variously known as being in sub space) must have been obvious. All I had to say was "yes, I am okay" and she kissed me and backed out of the cage. She then locked the cage door, pulled down the cover, and turned off the room light. In a second they were out of the dungeon and the door was being closed.

I heard them head for our bedroom and soon there was silence. During the night I heard the sounds of them having sex with lots of moans and groans of pleasure coming from my wife of almost twenty years. It was official . . . I was a cuckolded husband/slave."

Denise further explains the evolution of their new marriage.

"Our marriage would never be the same from that night. Actually, it is better than ever. Since that night, I have had a number of boyfriends and lovers. I include my husband, as I like us to act out other scenarios together. Sometimes my husband chauffeurs my lover and I to a restaurant, etc. We sit in the back of the car and make out while my husband drives us around. Sometimes, my hubby is my coffee table in front of the couch to hold drinks for my lover and I while we make out. Other times, my lover and I will go out for dinner and I will lock slave Gary in the cage while we are gone. I always give him the cordless phone so I can call him while we're out and let him know what we are doing or just to check on him and say hello. Sometimes Gary makes dinner for my lover and I and serves it to us. There are other scenarios but I just wanted to let you know that it's more than just sex in our cuckold lifestyle.

When I have sex with my lover, my husband is probably in the bedroom with us about 1/3 of the time. At first, I prefer for my lover and I to spend time alone so we can get comfortable with each other. During these times, slave Gary might be in his cage in the room next to us (the dungeon) or he might just go on to bed. In the cage, he can hear most of the sounds of our lovemaking and/or talk. Other times I have him sit by the side of the bed or in the corner and watch us. I let him lick me clean afterwards sometimes. When he is in the room with us, I can make comments to humiliate him. Sometimes I allow him to jerk off after we are through having sex and then he goes right back to the cage. There's no one way to do this and it's more fun changing the scenario around so that he never knows where he will be.

My husband loves being cuckolded. He goes deep into sub space and he experiences a kind of euphoric high. He loves it when I place him in a chastity device and deny him sexual pleasure for long periods of time (I've denied him for months at a time), while I am being sexually pleased by my lover. Yes, I am still intimate with my husband and I let him kiss me, hold me, give me pleasure orally and even have intercourse if the mood strikes me. Sometimes I use his penis as my dildo but with the chastity device still on him. It causes pain for him but gives me pleasure at the same time.

We go out together and hold hands just like other married couples. I consider Gary to be my closest friend in the whole world and know that he is always there for me. I think we have deep, companionship feelings about each other. I am not always in a relationship with a lover as I have time in between boyfriends but I can honestly say that we are both happiest when I have a lover. I know it is hard for others to understand and I definitely do not recommend cuckolding for all couples. It works for us but it takes a lot of work on my part to make sure that the cuckolding experience is fulfilling for all parties."

So what does Gary get out of the cuckolding experience?

"I am put into immediate sub space when my Wife is with her lover and locks me in my cage and denies me sex and release. I don't think I even have any conscious thoughts about it. When my Mistress/Wife has me crawl into the cage, throws in Her worn panties and proceeds to click the padlock closed, I look at Her with total love and awe and I am consumed with Her. When She pulls the cage cover down, shuts off the room lights, and closes the door, I am left in the dark with my thoughts. But I am not really aware of what those thoughts are. It's all feelings. Feelings of floating in space with nothing but total pleasurable sensations around me. When I hear Her moans of ecstasy and pleasure, I am transported even deeper into that place where endorphins rule."

The desire to be cuckolded is certainly not new within the psyche of the submissive male. Leopold von Sacher-Masoch (the author of the classic

FemDom novel "Venus in Furs") tried to pressure his wife into cuckolding him back in the late 1800's. In her book "The Confessions of Wanda von Sacher-Masoch", the wife of the man from whom the word "Masochist" was coined, claimed that her husband continually tried to set up liaisons for her with other men. She asserts that she managed to evade following through on her husband's fantasy but according to Wanda, her husband was obsessed with the desire to be cuckolded. While the urge to be cuckolded may not be a new desire within the psyche of the submissive male, the frequency of that desire and the volume of men who have that desire seems to becoming more prevalent in today's society now that women are liberated.

Many of my male clients in recent years have confessed a strong desire to be cuckolded. I do not recall hearing much about cuckolding in the 1980's and early 1990's. There seems to be a major sociological event happening here and a new leap for the entire Female Domination/Female Supremacy movement as far as what submissive men desire within a female/male relationship. To be physically dominated is no longer enough. Men also desire to be psychologically dominated. That is where the cuckolding desire comes into play.

Some men desire ultimate and complete submission to the ultimate female authority figure in their lives, namely their wife. What is the worse thing that a husband can fathom (other than the death of his spouse) in the most important relationship in this life (the marriage)? It is the fear that his wife will be unfaithful and become an adulteress. What shame and humiliation a man suffers when this happens. His entire world is shattered and his self-image is sunken to as low as it can go. To a man, that is the ultimate form of rejection. A wife who has sex with another man is saying to her husband that he is not man enough to satisfy her and that she prefers another man sexually over him.

Now take this shameful and hurtful event over into the world of female domination and we can gain an insight into the mind of a submissive man. How much more dominant and liberated can a wife be, than a wife who openly and brazenly has sex with other men, with her husband's full knowledge no less? How weak and how far into submission is a husband who's wife gets in his face and proclaims that he is not worthy enough or man enough to have sex with her? How inferior is a husband who is enslaved by his wife, made to be her total servant, is physically dominated by her for her entertainment, and is humiliated by her having sex with whomever she desires, while he is denied any sexual relief? That mental image is so powerful that it unlocks the door to a deeper world of submission for the male.

Orgasm denial almost always accompanies cuckolding in these men's fantasies. That is the ultimate form of humiliation and slavery. What a sociological statement that makes in his mind. The wife forbids her husband any sexual pleasure, while she is ravished in erotic pleasures with her many lovers. Not only must he bear the physical and emotional pain of being constantly sexually frustrated while being married to a beautiful woman, but he must also bear the shame and humiliation of his wife taking other lovers. He must bear the emotional pain of being cuckolded.

To the submissive male, this mental image can be so powerful that it shakes him to his core and unlocks more of his desire to submit to the superior female. The wife that society proclaims to be the weak and submissive spouse, rules the submissive husband, controls the submissive husband, enslaves the submissive husband, and humiliates the submissive husband. She ascends in power and authority while the husband sinks to new depths of submission. This signals to society that the new woman is not only superior to the man but she is far superior. She will not only rule but she will crush the male so that he can never rule again.

That is why this fantasy is so powerful to some men. The submissive male wants the female to own all of him. Cuckolding and such intense mental domination takes him to a new submissive zone. It is a place that is even more intense, more exciting and thus more tranquil than his previous submissive zones. He desires his wife to be the most bitchy and dominant wife that ever lived because he desires to be the most submissive and controlled husband that ever lived.

Even though the wife is the one experiencing the physical sex, the cuckolded husband seems to be the one having the most mental pleasure. Brandon shared with me why he enjoys being cuckolded.

"My wife is in my eyes the most beautiful woman in the world. I love her with all my heart and I love her more today than ever before. We are

both in our mid-forties, we have been married for almost twenty years, we are both professionals and we have no children (although we tried to have one early in our marriage). I introduced my wife to Female Domination ten years ago. Like a lot of men, I tried to suppress my submissive feelings from her and I visited a Pro Domme behind her back. I felt guilty about this so I finally decided that I needed to come clean with her and tell her about my submissive desires.

She did not understand where I was coming from in the beginning and she was confused, but to her credit she stayed open to the idea and was willing to explore FemDom with me out of her love for me. We had a healthy and active sex life but FemDom made everything fresh and new again. I was by no means an expert but I taught her what little I knew and we visited a Pro Domme together so she could learn. As I look back to those days, I must say that my wife was a good sport about it all. She was primarily humoring me in the beginning.

I can't recall exactly what it was and neither can she, but about five years ago, my wife had a conversion. Where as before she was merely playing D&S games with me, all of a sudden, something clicked with her and she became a believer in this lifestyle and she became a believer in Female Supremacy. I guess it was all of our playtime and all the FemDom literature she had read over the previous years. It kind of kicked in and she stopped going through the motions and became a dominant woman. As you would say, she embraced her dominant nature and her dominant energy was unleashed.

It was wonderful and fulfilling to watch her blossom into such a lovely and confident woman. I know it was difficult for her to go from being dependent on me for everything to becoming the decision maker and dominant partner in our marriage. But once she embraced it, she flourished in the dominant role. I then melted into submission to her authority. Not over night, as I had some adjustments to work through as well, since I was use to being the decision maker. But eventually, my wife got me to surrender to her full female authority."

So just how did cuckolding make its way into Brandon's marriage?

"We attended a D&S weekend function and there my wife met a Canadian woman who worked one of the vendor booths. She was a

stunning brunette, wearing a tight rubber dress and my wife and her hit it off. We were visiting her booth looking to buy some more D&S toys and before long, my wife and her became instant friends. We invited this woman to dinner with us that night and the evening ended up back at our hotel, with this woman teaching my wife some D&S skills, like rope bondage and how to use a single tail whip. I was the more than willing subject of these educational sessions.

We live in the southern part of the US but my wife kept in contact with this woman through e-mail. This woman (her scene name is Alexandra) is married and her husband is her 24/7 submissive. Alex mentored my wife through e-mail and the phone on how to take me deeper into submission. Eventually the topic of cuckolding came up. Alex regularly cuckolds her husband and she mentioned that to my wife. My wife was not familiar with the term or the lifestyle so she had a million questions. Alex explained it all to my wife and my wife became excited about it.

My wife and I openly talk about everything. Even though I am my wife's 24/7 submissive, my wife still discusses all things with me and gets my opinion before making her decision. My wife felt me out on cuckolding and I told her that I was familiar with the term and that in fact, the thought kind of excited me. I did not know how it would play out in real life but my wife could read me and she decided that this was something she wanted to explore.

My wife had her eye on a man that she was attracted to sexually. He worked with her but he switched jobs and moved out of her building. My wife had kept in contact with him as friends and they e-mail each other. I did not know it back when they worked with each other, but once my wife had me in submission to her, she confessed to me that she found this man to be sexually attractive and she often flirted with him. It took everything within her to resist his sexual advances when they worked together and they eventually became just friends. My wife decided that he was the one she wanted to cuckold me with.

She e-mailed him and asked him out on a date. He accepted and they went out a few times before they finally became intimate. Each time she went out with him, I had to prepare my wife for her dates. I can't explain what a submissive rush that is to a submissive husband. Words cannot describe what was going through my mind and my body as I bathed my wife, shaved her legs, helped her pick out a sexy outfit, and helped to dress her for her dates. The sexual energy between my wife and I was incredible. We fondled each other the whole time I was preparing her for her dates and she was afraid that I would masturbate once she left. We did not own a chastity device at that time, so what my wife did was she took Saran Wrap and wrapped my penis to the inside of my left thigh. Then she wrapped another piece around my waist and had me put on a pair of her panties, and wrapped my crotch area three or four times with the Saran Wrap.

She took the Saran Wrap with her and put it in her car. That way, she would know that I had not removed her homemade chastity device while she was on her date. My wife drove her car to meet her new boyfriend and I was left at home alone with my thoughts. The hours she was gone were incredible. My mind raced back and forth with all kinds of submissive thoughts. I fell deep into subspace. I was able to touch my penis through the Saran Wrap but it was wrapped in a way that I could not feel any sensation. I dared not remove any of it for it would have been obvious to her on her return.

My wife would call me about once an hour when she was on her dates. She made the experience special for me, as she would tease me over the phone about how much she enjoyed being a liberated wife with a submissive husband and a new boyfriend. This drove me wild with passion for her. Finally, she would come home to me. The first couple of dates, nothing occurred between her and her new boyfriend. But that didn't matter. Just the fact that she as a married woman had gone on a date was enough to fuel both of our passions. My wife teased me mercilessly when she returned home from her dates and she was full of sexual energy and a desire to dominate me. We had incredible D&S play sessions. I can't describe how I felt other than to say I felt weak, helpless and inferior to my wife. But it was a good feeling, almost euphoric. She felt powerful, sexual, and dominant. She felt good about herself, like the desirable woman that she is.

She dated about once a week but the whole week leading up to her next date was incredible. She would tease me about my situation, taunting me and humiliating me in a fun and playful way. Then when her date night came, we would repeat our pre-date routine, complete with my homemade chastity device."

Brandon and his wife came to the discovery that done correctly and with the proper motivation, the cuckolding fantasy can be exciting. For the wife, she gets to exert her female authority and female liberation. This allows her an incredible power advantage over her cuckolded husband and this added dynamic usually carries over into all other D&S activities within the marriage relationship. Cuckolding within female domination is not so much about the physical sex as it is about power and it is that female power and female liberation that gives the wife the ability to use intense humiliation on her husband. That intense humiliation may transport him to subspace as he yields to her authority.

Brandon describes how the humiliation became more intense and powerful as cuckolding moved from a fantasy to reality.

"On her third date with her new boyfriend, my wife called me and told me that she was bringing him home. My heart began to race and I began to breathe heavy. I was nervous, scared but excited. I had met this man in the past (when my wife worked with him) but I had not seen him in a number of years. I was not sure how I could face him. I felt embarrassed and ashamed. My wife called me to tell me that she wanted me to dress in a shirt and tie with dress slacks. I obeyed and I dressed as sharp as I could.

They came in and I greeted him. It was awkward to say the least. My wife had told him everything on their first date and he was Ok with it. This added to my humiliation. They sat in our living room, arm in arm and I had to serve them drinks and food. My wife talked to me as if I were her butler and not her husband. She barked out orders to me when she wanted something and she would dismiss me when I was done serving them. I would stand in the kitchen and listen to them talking and laughing like they were best of friends. I was full of mixed emotions. My wife was smart enough to deny me during the week so I was horny, aroused, and deep into subspace. She looked beautiful and desirable so I was also feeling jealous. I think above all, I was in heavy anticipation. I knew what was about to take place and my pulse was racing with excitement.

After socializing in our living room, my wife dismissed herself and came to me in the kitchen. She took me by my hand and ordered me to follow her. She led me to our spare bedroom and closed the door behind us. She then teased and taunted me mercilessly as she undressed me and applied my Saran Wrap chastity device. She fondled my body and teased me about what was about to occur. She tied me to the spare bed (face up) and she placed a blindfold over my eyes. Other than the blindfold, all I had on was the homemade chastity device and her panties. After I was secure, she told me that our relationship was about to change forever. With that, she gave me a kiss, turned out the light and she left the room but left the door slightly open so I could hear. I was left in the dark, helpless and swimming in submission.

A short time later, I heard them enter our bedroom across the hall. She left that door wide open and I could hear everything. The next couple of hours my ears were filled with the sounds of my wife fucking another man. It was the most erotic night of my life. I was floating in subspace. I was so excited and overcome with such passion and submission, that I thought I would climax any minute from the light pressure of the Saran Wrap against my bulging penis. My wife was very verbal as she had sex with her boyfriend and I felt like I was in her room in spirit, watching. I felt like I was strapped to her wall, or was under her bed as she flaunted her sexual power and liberation in front of me. My wife was mind fucking me while she was physically fucking her boyfriend. It was incredible.

After they were done, I heard them leave. My wife did not even talk to me, although she later would tell me that she checked in on me before she left. She drove him back to his car and shortly returned to me. I was still swimming in submission and was lightly brought out of my trance when she flicked the light on in my room. She removed my blindfold and she was dressed in a wild leather outfit. She had this outfit for weeks but was waiting for a special occasion to wear it for me. She was also wearing a strap-on harness with a new dildo strapped around her waist. She looked very intimidating and dominant.

My wife untied me and massaged my arms and legs that had fallen asleep from being bound that long. Then my wife began to dominate me. She was bitchy and authoritative and more aggressive than I had ever seen her. She dominated the hell out of me that night. She practically raped me with her dildo and she humiliated me unrelentingly about me being a cuckolded husband. I climaxed as she took me with her strap-on and that orgasm ranks up there with my all time most intense orgasms. It was incredible."

Brandon and Gary were transported to subspace by the cuckolding experience. Subspace is that special place for a submissive male. Different activities will transfer a man into that submissive zone, based on his own unique submissive nature and desires. Being transported to subspace is being transported to a world where the Female rules supreme. It is a place in the submissive male's mind that is tranquil and peaceful. In subspace, a man can surrender to his submissive desires in totality and he is at peace with his submission. Most men struggle with their submissive nature their entire life. They feel guilty and ashamed about it because society frowns upon it. In subspace, a man surrenders to those submissive desires and that surrender brings peace.

So how did this cuckolding experience alter Brandon's relationship with his wife?

"Our relationship changed that night but it was a positive change. My wife continued to date her boyfriend for the next six months (about once a week) and most dates ended in sex, either back at our house or over at his house. Yet, my wife made sure to include me always in some fashion. Be it a replay of being tied up in the spare bedroom and forced to listen or being called on her cell phone and teased before and after she had sex with her lover. I always prepared her for her dates in some manner and she always returned to me to dominate and humiliate me about being cuckolded.

I have always been allowed to worship her body and have occasional intercourse with my wife. However, I have now been cut off from intercourse. Once again, this adds to my submission to her and her power over me. I must say that so far, I am enjoying these new power dynamics. I am more motivated to submit to her and I cannot get enough of my wife. I long to be in her presence and to serve her in some capacity. I actually ache to touch her but I am no longer allowed the freedom of a husband to touch her whenever I want. I am only allowed to touch her if she gives me permission, and that is rare. Touching her is now a privilege and a reward for obedient behavior. The cuckolding experience has elevated my wife to almost Goddess status in my eyes. I find that our sexuality is more on a mental sphere than a physical one and I worship her in spirit. She now wields enormous power over me and she is able to take me to subspace with ease, sometimes with only a few spoken and teasing words. It also excites me that other men find my wife to be so desirable.

My wife has developed into such a sexual woman and she loves to flaunt her sexuality in front of me. She likes to buy sexy lingerie and underwear as well as plenty of fetish outfits. She walks with a self-confidence and sexuality that I never noticed prior to her blossoming into a dominant woman. My wife radiates sexuality and dominance and I find this irresistible. It is frustrating to live with such a sexual woman but be denied access to her body. Yet, on those occasions that she allows me the privilege to worship her body or orally service her body, it is so intense and special. I feel like I have just been granted permission to touch and pleasure a supermodel or a movie starlet. Think about it? How many husbands take their wives and sex with their wives for granted? I never do because it is now rare that I get to touch my Goddess and each time is like the first time I have ever been with her. That is what cuckolding has done for our relationship."

It is the mental stimulation and mental domination that transports the submissive to a new level in his submissive nature. The act of cuckolding is about giving the wife the experience that she can than use as a mental image to dominate her husband's thoughts. It is not so much about sexual fulfillment. There may indeed be some physical sexual fulfillment but the sexual act is only temporary whereas the using of the act as a tool for mental domination can be on going. With cuckolding within a loving female domination marriage, the wife uses the mental image of the cuckolding to repeatedly tease and humiliate her husband, which triggers his submissive nature and causes him mental pleasure and thus submissive fulfillment.

I do not endorse cuckolding but I certainly do not discourage couples from exploring all aspects of their sexual natures. Women are discovering their sexual power and are using that power to take control of their marriages. As the female gains in power, men will become more submissive and will desire to submit to her both physically and mentally. Cuckolding is all about intent and motive. Unfortunately, there are women who take advantage of their husband's submissive nature in order to live a promiscuous life. Some get away with it but most do not.

Somewhere along the line the act of cheating will come back to haunt those that engage in this destructive behavior.

Having said that, there are couples that have been able to successfully incorporate cuckolding into their female domination marriage. Cuckolding means different things to different people but within female domination, cuckolding is an activity that a wife engages in to take her husband into a deeper level of submission to her through intense humiliation.

Denise and Brandon's wife do a wonderful job in making sure that all parties are fulfilled in their cuckoldry marriage. That is no simple task. A man does not realize how emotionally difficult it can be on his wife if he were to encourage her to cuckold him. Being intimate with another man besides her husband can be exciting for a woman but it also can be emotionally painful as she can become attached to her lover. Sex builds intimacy and sex with a boyfriend will build some intimacy between the wife and her lover. However, because the lover knows that the wife's heart belongs to her husband, after awhile he will probably end the relationship because he does not feel comfortable being a woman's number two or he feels guilty about having sex with another man's wife. Therefore, women who cuckold their husbands usually end up going from boyfriend to boyfriend because it is hard to maintain a relationship with the same lover. This can cause the woman to experience some emotional pain.

It is difficult to gauge how often cuckolding actually takes place in our society since the couples who practice this lifestyle are naturally hesitant to admit their involvement. Cuckolding is not an open marriage, or wife swapping or a swinger lifestyle since the husband must remain monogamous to his wife. True cuckolding is an open act of female domination where the wife is sexually liberated and openly informs her husband about her affairs, down to the most graphic details. Within cuckolding, the wife includes her submissive husband in some manner, be it pre-date preparation, post-date domination or the actual involvement by requiring the husband to either watch or listen in on the actual sexual exploits of his wife. One thing is for certain, based on my research, cuckolding occurs far more frequently in our society than one would imagine. An unsuspecting person would no doubt be shocked if they were to encounter someone who practices cuckolding. That was the case for Adam.

"I had to attend a conference for my job in Denver, Colorado. I usually attend this conference each year with one of my co-workers but due to some budget cuts, I was the only one who was sent this past year. During the conference I met a woman in her mid forties. Her name was Gwen and I found her to be very intelligent and very attractive. I noticed her beautiful diamond wedding ring so I knew she was a married woman. Still we struck up a conversation and when she found out that I was alone at this conference, she invited me to dinner. We had some common business interests so I accepted.

I really hit it off with this woman and we had a wonderful time at dinner. I noticed something else as well. I found myself becoming aroused as she was a confident woman and there was something about her personality that was attractive to me. We both were staying in the same hotel so she asked me if I would meet her in the hotel lounge for a nightcap. I was a little hesitant since she was married but I was so taken by her that I accepted. After a few drinks and some more laughs, she invited me up to her room. Once again I hesitated but my attraction to her caused me to go against my better judgment.

When we got to her room, she started to kiss on me and undress me. I felt guilty so I stopped her and asked her about her husband. She pulled away from me and she told me that she and her husband have an understanding and she is allowed to have sex with whomever she desires. I was a bit shocked so I asked her if he was also allowed to have sex with other women. She surprised me by saying, "Absolutely not. He is not allowed to even look at another woman without my permission and I would never authorize him to touch another woman." I couldn't believe my ears but for some reason, I grew an immediate erection.

She walked over to the phone and dialed her husband. I was worried and I begged her not to call him. She ignored me and she got him on the phone and she informed her husband that she had picked up a nice young man that she was attracted to and that she was going to "fuck my brains out". She asked him if he had a problem with that? I couldn't believe how aggressive and brazen this woman was with her husband. She ordered her husband to tell me that it was Ok with him and that I had his blessing. She handed me the phone and this intelligent sounding man told me that he and his wife have a FemDom marriage and thus she can do whatever she desires. I could hardly answer him but I squeaked out something like, "thank you" or something lame like that.

Gwen grabbed the phone from me and proceeded to tell her husband that he had five minutes to get into "position" and that she was going to leave the phone receiver on the night stand so he could listen to our sexual activities. She set the receiver on the stand and turned it to face the king sized bed. I asked her what the "position" was and she informed me that her husband had to insert a large butt plug, dress in feminine lingerie, lay on her bed and listen to the sexual exploits that were about to take place. I asked her if her husband would be masturbating while we had sex and she laughed and said, "No Way! He is locked up in a chastity device and he is unable to touch himself."

Gwen undressed, stripped me naked, jumped on top of me and she told me to relax, as she would do all the work. She became very aggressive with me, almost like a wild woman. She was very forceful and very vocal to make sure that her husband was hearing and understanding everything that she was doing. We had wild sex that night and it was the best sex of my life. Gwen was always on top and always in control. She had her way with me and after a long session of intercourse, she pinned my face between her legs and I orally serviced her for what seemed like an hour. All the time she moaned loudly to make sure that her husband was humiliated by the proceedings. When we were finally done, she picked up the phone and made her husband confess to her that he accepted her right to have other lovers and then she kissed the receiver and told him that she loved him and she would be home in a couple of days."

Was Gwen having sex with Adam or her husband? I think the answer is obvious that Gwen was having physical intimacy with Adam but she was also having mental sex with her husband. If Gwen wanted to be a promiscuous wife, then why even bother to call her husband? Why allow him to listen in on her sexual escapades with Adam if Gwen merely wanted to get laid? Gwen and her husband no doubt have a FemDom marriage and I am sure that Gwen used her one night fling with Adam to tease, humiliate and mentally excite her husband for weeks and months to follow. For Adam, it was a memorable one night only event. For

Gwen's husband, it was an exercise in FemDom that she used on him over and over again by reminding him of what she did that night in Denver.

Cuckolding is a very controversial topic. I have interviewed couples who claim to have wonderful experiences with cuckolding and I have had people tell me about their terrible experiences with cuckolding. I have heard tales of unwanted pregnancies, STD's, and great emotional pain all caused by cuckolding. A friend of mine who has successfully cuckolded her husband for fifteen years says cuckolding is like dynamite. If used properly it can be a very useful tool in dominating a husband but used incorrectly, it will blow your hand off. She goes by the name of Ms Lilly and her philosophy is that the husband must be an active part of the entire cuckolding process and the wife must be focused on how the cuckolding will affect her husband at all times.

The overall consensus among those who enjoy this alternative lifestyle is that cuckolding should only be attempted within a healthy and strong marriage. It may seem like the opposite would be true but cuckolding in a weak marriage will destroy the marriage. Only where the husband and wife are secure in their love for each other and only where the husband trusts his wife's judgment and character, can cuckolding be done successfully. There has to be a strong marital foundation to withstand the potential emotional stress and intense power exchange that can come from cuckolding.

It has also been my observation that the marriages that successfully incorporate cuckolding are the ones that first enjoyed many years of mutual monogamous sex. Denise and Gary were married for almost twenty years before they engaged in cuckolding. Anna has a similar story to tell.

"I have been living a FemDom lifestyle with my husband for over twenty years. He introduced it to me about five years into our marriage and I embraced it and have been practicing it ever since. We have had our challenges, like raising three children while we kept our lifestyle a secret from them, but overall this lifestyle has been a tremendous amount of fun and sexual fulfillment for the both of us. I think it is fair to say that we have tried almost everything as it relates to FemDom and D&S over these past twenty years.

Lately, however, I felt that we had gotten into a bit of a FemDom rut. The kids are grown and on their own and it is just the two of us. It was liberating to have the entire house to ourselves at first and believe me we took full advantage of it. Nevertheless, after twenty years I felt we needed something extra to take us to a new level in our FemDom marriage.

The one FemDom activity that we never pursued but I was reading about was cuckolding. The thought of cuckolding my husband both excited me and made me feel uneasy at the same time. After all, I had not been with another man other than my husband for going on twenty-eight years. I was nineteen the last time I had sex with someone other than my husband. I really had no desire to ever bring another person into our sex lives but the more I thought about it, the more I knew that this is what we needed.

My husband is a good submissive but after twenty-five years of marriage, he takes me for granted. He knows me inside and out and he is very good at topping me from below by pushing my buttons. I needed to do something that shook his world and at the same time displayed my ultimate authority over him. I researched a number of activities and I came to the conclusion that I needed to make him a cuckolded husband.

With a renewed goal and vision for our relationship, I began to dominate my husband on a more frequent basis. All things became new and fresh just as they were in the beginning of our D&S lifestyle. The spankings, the discipline, the forced feminization, his domestic and sexual service of me all became more intense and exciting due to my new goal. Each time I dominated him I probed his mind about cuckolding, telling him that I was going to pursue it and that there was nothing he could do about it.

What I found out was that he became erect when I discussed it within a D&S scene. I probed his mind and his submissive desires and I was able to uncover exactly what would excite him about me cuckolding him. He was threatened by a man around our age due to a fear of me leaving him but he was excited about the thought of me seducing and having sex with a younger man. To him that represented Female Domination and Female Conquest and he was not threatened by it. He was jealous and humiliated by it but this only added to his submissive desires. Once I learned this, I had what I needed to pursue the cuckolding. At forty-seven, I decided that I would cuckold my husband with a twenty something year old man. This excited me as well but how could I seduce a twenty something male?

I enrolled at the local college and took a few classes. This enabled me to pursue a personal interest that I had for a long time and it also placed me around lots of young men. With my goal firmly in mind, it didn't take me long to fulfill it. Men are so easy to seduce and young men are really easy. I was surrounded by lots of young and beautiful girls so what odds would a forty-seven year old woman have? I found the odds were greatly in my favor if I would use my wisdom and my dominance.

I was very selective but I finally found a young single man who was twenty-two. He was cute, had a nice body but most important, I could tell he was submissive. I wore leather to class a couple of times (leather pants one time, a leather skirt another) and this young man would stare at me. One day after class, I struck a conversation with him and asked him if he would mind if we studied together for an upcoming test in the library. He agreed and the rest is history.

I learned much about his personality from our study times and I could tell he was the one. I liked his personality and his submissive nature. I was also attracted to him, which was a must. We had little in common as far as pop culture and intellectual interests, so he was never a threat to my husband. Our age difference made it a sure thing that our relationship could only be physical. We did not connect intellectually but I was not looking for that.

Our study times turned into a few social lunches together and then I made my move. One day during our studying, I flirted big time with him and I took his hand and placed it on my leg. I could tell he had an immediate erection. I told him that I was an aggressive and dominant woman who took in life what she wanted. I explained to him that I was happily married but that I dominate my husband and that I was looking for a young lover. I gave him his chance to back out but he yielded to my advancements.

I planned for our big date night. I had my husband prepare me for my date and it was the most exciting evening for the both of us. My husband was rock hard as he bathed me and helped to dress me for my date. He objected slightly but I kept teasing him and he melted into submission and total obedience.

The date was nothing to write home about, as my twenty-two year old stud was nervous being with such an older woman who acted so dominant. I wore leather and he was like a puppy dog around me. I asked him if he was still a virgin and he said No but he had not had a girlfriend for over a year. He was not a virgin but he was still young and inexperienced. After our date, I took him home. I borrowed something I had read on the Internet and I tied my husband up in the spare bedroom and left the door open so he could hear everything. I was just as nervous as this shy young man but it didn't take me long to take him to bed.

The sex that night was great. He may have been shy and inexperienced but he was a fast learner and an eager pupil. I was reserved at first but I became quite aggressive once I got comfortable. Once I relaxed and allowed myself, I basked in much sexual pleasure. I taught him how to properly orally service a woman and we had intercourse using a condom. He was a good lover and I had accomplished my goal. I had cuckolded my husband.

After the young man left, I dominated my husband with an energy and a dominance that I had never known. I was extra bitchy and forceful with him. I had such a power surging through my body. He was a little upset but he quickly yielded to my power and I took him deep into subspace. We had a marathon strap-on session that night. I broke him to a new level of submission.

I date my young lover once a week and we usually end our date back at my house for a night of sex. My husband has yielded to this totally. We have ground rules and the majority of my time and focus is on my husband. I have not cut him off from sex or orgasms like some of the women who cuckold their husbands do. I feel that intimacy with my husband is more important now than ever. But of course I tease and humiliate him about how he doesn't measure up to my young lover. My husband no longer takes me for granted. He has doubled his efforts in serving me. Our D&S sessions are more intense than ever and we have found our new level.

I am encouraging my young lover to find a dominant girlfriend of his own. I care for him but I know he has no future with me. But until he meets someone else, I am more than happy to be his lover and his teacher. I even spank him and dominate him as I am teaching him about Female Domination."

Much like Denise, Gwen and Brandon's wife, Anna has made cuckolding an exercise in mental domination and mental sex between the liberated wife and her cuckolded husband. To the novice, it would appear that the wife who cuckolds her husband is selfish and promiscuous but that is not necessarily the case. When you talk with couples who practice cuckolding, you discover that their lifestyle is an agreed upon lifestyle and in fact, most of the time it is the husband who initially encourages the wife to pursue this lifestyle. When a woman humiliates her husband to this degree, it actually becomes a form of mental sex between her and her husband. Her abusive and cruel ways might excite him and touch his submissive nature in ways that most would not understand. The psyche of the submissive male is a fascinating study and it can be complex.

My personal feeling on cuckolding based on my research is that a woman who will use cuckolding as an excuse for cheating and being promiscuous, is hurting her marriage and risks permanent damage to her marriage. Cheating is never right and having sex with another man behind the husband's back is infidelity. However, as long as the husband is also excited by and agrees to the cuckolding, than it is not cheating.

The bottom line is that Female Domination should enhance the marriage. If either partner has a real problem with any FemDom activity (especially cuckolding) then they should not engage in it. If an activity will not strengthen the bond of the marriage and the level of intimacy and trust between that husband and the wife, then the activity is not worth it. Like all things, cuckolding needs to be discussed openly and honestly between the husband and the wife to see how they both feel about this subject and the wife must ultimately make the final judgment.

Chapter Twelve

Mental Domination: Humiliation Play

Some of them want to use you, Some of them want to be used by you; Some of them want to abuse you, Some of them want to be abused. (The Eurythmics, "Sweet Dreams")

Roxanne works as a phone counselor for a popular phone domination service. She has spoken to over three hundred male clients seeking to be dominated by a woman over the telephone. Her clients are men from all walks of life; business executives, physicians, lawyers, truck drivers, and the whole rich spectrum. A common request that Roxanne receives from her phone clients is the request to be verbally humiliated. When Roxanne first stated out as a phone counselor, she could not believe how many men wanted to be humiliated by a woman. This surprised her in the beginning of her phone career but now she is experienced in the art of humiliating men and she has verbally humiliated hundreds of paying clients over the telephone. What do these men seek?

"Virtually every call involves, in one form or another, extensive verbal humiliation. These men desperately need an assertive Woman to verbally reinforce their submissive status and sense of inferiority to Women. They are weary of pretending to be the stereotypical "real man," and find great solace – if only temporary – in surrendering their macho pretensions and "manhood".

The degree of verbal humiliation sought by each male varies, but one thing the majority seems to have in common is the need to feel loved or cared for – even as they are debased and degraded by the superior Woman. This seems like a contradiction, but it isn't. Like a Boot Camp drill instructor, I understand that verbal humiliation is a necessary training technique, employed both for the benefit of the recipient, and the greater good. In my case, the goal is a more rational, less violent society – one governed, of course, by the Feminine.

Before genuine character reformation of the male is possible, old attitudes and internal defenses must be stripped away. This is the high purpose of verbal humiliation. Yes, the male is seeking his immediate sexual gratification (what else?), but the process can also help men accept their true self and fundamental need to serve Women. Verbal humiliation overrides their machismo, and, eventually (if training is successful), strips away those last vestiges of "traditional" masculinity to which they cling. Once the subject is torn down, the essential re-building can begin in earnest, and both the man and Woman are happier.

It is rather sad that many submissive males spend an inordinate amount of time searching in vain for a superior Woman who will bring them to their knees, and take control by calling them "sissy," "panty boy," "slave," and "slut" – the names most commonly requested. While it seems the majority of men that I speak with prefer soft verbal humiliation, (i.e., being called the aforementioned names), there is a smaller group of men who prefer what I consider harsher treatment, such as being called "worthless worm," "dick wad," "pussy-whipped" or " bitch boy."

Many of my callers so desperately want to serve a superior Female that they are willing to go to great lengths to prove themselves worthy to serve. Upon my command, they become puppy dogs, who bark, walk on a leash on all fours, pee on a newspaper, and eat out of a dog dish. Heterosexual men are trained to wear panties, garter-belts and stockings, and taught to become skilled and eager "cock-suckers" (with the prop of a dildo), all at my direction.

They spank themselves, painfully pinch their own nipples, and fuck themselves with dildos. There is truly no end to the list of things men want to do to prove themselves worthy to serve the strong Woman."

Any woman who works in the field of professional domination will substantiate the fact that a lot of men desire to be humiliated by a female. One of the many services the professional Dominatrix offers to her clientele is what is known in D&S as Humiliation Play. This is where the woman will humiliate a man both verbally and physically in order to fulfill some sort of psychological need within him. The humiliation triggers something within the male psyche based on the equation of his submissive nature plus his life experiences. As was the case with cuckolding, it is the mental stimulation that triggers the submissive and sexual desires within the male and this trigger can cause mental pleasure and sexual arousal. What to one person may seem as being mean spirited and abusive, to the submissive man within the safe confines of a D&S scene, it is pleasurable and even therapeutic.

Humiliation Play will transport some men to subspace, and the more intense the humiliation, the deeper level of sexual excitement and mental fulfillment. For the most part, the professional Dominatrix is not there to counsel a client about the root cause of why he wants to be abused and humiliated. All she knows is that the man requests this activity and he is willing to pay a woman to humiliate him. A large number of men crave to be humiliated and certain men can only become sexually aroused if they are humiliated by a woman in some manner.

These are not isolated cases of only men who were seriously abused as children. From my experiences in counseling with men who desire to be humiliated, most males who desire humiliation play do not know why they like it. All they know is that something on the inside of them enjoys it when a woman humiliates them and even abuses them within a D&S or sexual setting.

Some men who desire humiliation play may have been abused but these are the exceptions and not the status quo. To those males who were abused or mistreated in their childhood, humiliation play can be pleasurable as it touches a psychological trigger that stimulates them mentally which produces an intense sexual arousal. When a person has a physical wound in their flesh, it is both pleasurable and painful for it to be touched. Scabs tend to itch and the desire is there for it to be scratched. The same goes with an emotional wound or hurt. Many times a man who has been mentally abused as a child can only get aroused through being verbally abused or humiliated. What may seem cruel to most people is actually pleasurable for him, if done within a sexual setting. A man may seek Humiliation Play because he desires for those emotional scars to be touched. This is what fulfills him sexually. Within a loving FemDom relationship, the dominant woman who has had an intense "humiliation scene" with her husband can bring emotional healing to him by afterwards holding him, kissing him and loving him.

Nevertheless, from my experience and my observations, the vast majority of men who desire Humiliation Play were never abused. The male desire to submit to a woman is so strong that the act of being humiliated helps the submissive male to feel inferior to the female and this inferior feeling transports him to subspace. That is the main appeal of Humiliation Play.

The key to humiliation play between loving couples is that the humiliation must be within a sexual, D&S or FemDom setting. If a wife would verbally humiliate her husband within their everyday lives, chances are he will become either angry or hurt. The woman who calls her husband stupid or worthless outside of their D&S playtime is being mean-spirited and risks driving her husband emotionally away from her. But the woman who verbally humiliates her husband within a sexual setting, might touch a chord within him that drives him to subspace and thus will cause him to bond with his wife emotionally. As with any D&S activity, the man must enjoy humiliation play on some level in order for it to be effective.

Humiliation play will not work on every man, as it will only be productive on those males that respond to such an expression of D&S. If a man were to become emotionally hurt or were to withdraw inwardly, those would be signals that the man is not responding to the humiliation. But if the man were to become erect and excited while being humiliated, that is a sign that he finds this activity enjoyable.

I love my husband and I would never want to hurt his self-esteem but we do enjoy intense humiliation play. I am a master (or should I say Mistress) at verbal humiliation. I can reduce a man down to nothing in a matter of seconds. When I humiliate my husband about being an inferior male or about the inadequacy of his penis, I am attacking his male ego. I am wounding his male pride, which causes his submissive nature to come forth. This is much different than attacking his self worth. I never humiliate him about his physical looks or his career choice or his performance on a task that I have assigned. I find I can get my husband to perform better outside the bedroom by complimenting him and showing him genuine love, respect and affection. But inside the bedroom, that is a different story. I like to humiliate him about being of the male gender and thus inferior to me. My goal with humiliation play is to shatter his male ego and the best way I've found to do this, is to attack his manhood (especially the ultimate symbol of his manhood, the penis). He gets excited about this kind of humiliation play and this transports him to subspace.

I totally agree with Roxanne's evaluation of humiliation play. The purpose of shattering a man's ego and stripping him of unhealthy male pride is so I can build him up again in such a way that he will respect and yield to the feminine. Most men have been programmed by a male dominant society and thus they may have some wrong perceptions about women. I may use verbal humiliation in the bedroom or during a D&S scene to break my husband of unhealthy macho attitudes but I am also quick to praise him outside the bedroom for being such an obedient and loving husband.

Do I feel unladylike when I utilize verbal humiliation? My philosophy is that if you can't let your hair down around your husband, than whom can you be free around? I like to talk erotic and sexy around my husband when playing with him. I call him names in the bedroom that I would never call him in our everyday life. I rarely use foul or vulgar language outside the bedroom. I try to be a lady and I don't appreciate people using obsccnc language around me. There is a time and a place for everything. I don't use obscene language around my husband during our everyday living, but when we "play", I feel free to talk very "dirty". This turns us both on.

As far as verbal humiliation goes, some women humiliate their men by teasing them, rather than being a Bitch. Some women tease their men about having a small penis in a playful and sexy way. Other women do it in a loud, bitchy way. Each woman must find what works best for her and than she should just relax and have fun with it. Some of the best Dominant women I know never raise their voices. They dominate men with their sexuality and their dominant aura. They talk in seductive whispers and dominate with their seductive stares and their dominant body language. Domination does not always have to be brazen and forceful. It can also be mysterious and sensual. Either approach can touch a man's submissive nature and either approach can be used in humiliation play.

Some women struggle with humiliation play and I have counseled with couples where the husband wanted the wife to humiliate him within the bedroom but the wife just could not get herself to treat him in such a manner. This is perfectly understandable but I try to encourage couples to find a balance and to at least experiment with humiliation play if the man has this desire. A number of women, who were dead set against such play, later told me that once they overcame their initial inhibitions, they absolutely loved humiliation play. It caused them to feel powerful and helped them to become bolder in the bedroom. A lot of women have a low self-image due to how they view their gender when compared to the male gender. Humiliation play gives the female an opportunity to release her dominant nature and express an aggressive side to her personality within the safe confines of her marriage or personal relationship. The woman who humiliates her husband at home may not be so intimidated by men in the workplace. The woman who is accustomed to seeing her husband grovel before her at home, will no doubt begin to view all men as less threatening.

Humiliation Play can be about much more than just verbal humiliation. Some of the FemDom practices we have already examined could be classified as a form of humiliation play. Forced feminization and cuckolding are definite exercises in male humiliation with the objective to use that humiliation for a greater good. Roxanne not only utilizes humiliation play professionally as a phone counselor but she also incorporates it within her own marriage. As a part of her humiliation techniques, Roxanne employs the practices of forced feminization and cuckolding.

"Besides my professional interests, I am very much also a lifestyle Dominatrix, who relishes the many and varied benefits of a FemDom marriage and household. I've been married to my wonderful submissive

man for over ten years – and naturally, consistent and incremental humiliation techniques have been essential to hubby's ongoing progress.

Hubby and I are closer – more emotionally attached and "in synch," than before I took control. As the scope of my power increases it just gets better for us both. I should mention that although we had a loving marriage before I seized the reins, I didn't hesitate when Tommy hinted at his submissive desires. I seized the chance to take our relationship to a new, higher level. I gave Tommy one last chance to back out, warning him that perhaps he didn't really want what he thought he wanted. To his credit, he was steadfast in his need and desire to submit to Female authority.

It was only a short time before I had him wearing panties under his clothes - first one day a week, then everyday. That readied him for nylons, also worn everyday to work. Soon (at my command) he was shaving his legs so they would look and feel better with his stockings. At that point, I knew my handsome, ex-naval officer hubby was emotionally ready to become my willing cuckold. We had a long talk and hubby readily agreed that I should enjoy the pleasures of other lovers. I assured him that, as my "sissy slave" hubby, he would always be cherished by me.

Very selectively then, and taking all appropriate precautions, I proceeded to take a small number of lovers over the past few years. I always make sure Tommy is informed and aware, in order to enhance his humiliation – a training essential (in his case, at least.) On occasion Tommy has been privileged to watch his Mistress being "ravished" by a well-endowed stud. If hubby is not physically present to observe, he is sure to receive a phone call from me either shortly before, during, or after "the act."

Over the past few years, Tommy's cuckold training has evolved to the point where I take occasional vacations with certain lovers. They delight in flying me to Florida, Las Vegas, and other destinations for a brief holiday of fine dining, sight-seeing, and lots and lots of hot sex. Meanwhile, I have left hubby at home with detailed instructions and chores to complete during my absence. He will be "dressed" at all times (when away from the office), and he loves to wear his maid's uniform *while performing household tasks. To ensure he's not "naughty," I require him to wear a chastity device.*

I require hubby to keep a slave journal, which I review often. He is progressing quite wonderfully, and is happier and more content than ever. If he is a good sissy, I allow him supervised masturbation usually 1 to 2 times a month. In addition, he has learned to crave my strap-on, and believe me, I relish giving it to him. He knows better than to ever ask for sexual release (of any sort) – the right to initiate sex belongs only to Me.

Tommy hand washes all my lingerie, in addition to his own. He has learned to love this task, and is taking on more and more of the household chores. (If he didn't have a demanding job, he'd be responsible for everything). As you would expect, his macho attitude is diminishing rapidly, though he still has a way to go. Tommy knows that I have also revealed his special status to a few of my trusted girlfriends, several of whom are younger, in their 20's. These women are completely supportive (and at least a little envious). I admit that I'm more than a little proud of the example I'm setting.

In short, as a result of his training, Tommy has become more communicative, thoughtful and loving. He knows that I adore him and would never leave him."

As Roxanne has demonstrated in her marriage, humiliation play can encompass a variety of FemDom practices. Besides verbal humiliation, there is physical humiliation, public humiliation, and activities such as Objectification, Trampling, Queening and Water Sports.

Public humiliation seems to be a favorite for some couples. I created an exercise that I share with couples who want to explore public humiliation. It basically involves a public outing where the submissive man accompanies his dominant wife or girlfriend on a shopping trip. The woman is dressed in leather but looks classy and not sleazy. The submissive man is dressed in shirt and tie and he treats his Dominant woman with respect in public. He is to walk behind her, not to talk until given permission, pay for her purchases, and carry her purchases for her. He is to open doors for her and be her servant out in public. The woman may use the shopping trip for some public humiliation by making little remarks when her submissive is paying for her purchases. Things like,

"Charles, be a good husband and pay for my purchases". Or, "Hurray up, Charles, I don't have all day. Obedient men are so hard to train."

Debra enjoyed her shopping trip with her husband and it led to a most unexpected event.

"I loved going out shopping in my leather outfit and new boots, while my husband followed behind me and carried my purchases. I got a lot of stares from both men and women. I was able to really humiliate my husband a couple of times in front of other women. However, the most memorable thing that happened was when a young man was staring at my boots during dinner at a restaurant. He was seated across from me, and through the mirror that was hanging on the wall next to our booth, I could see him taking many peaks at both me and my sexy, leather boots. Where he was sitting, he had a great view of them.

I humiliated my husband through dinner by whispering to him about the nice looking young man that was staring at me, and how I might have to invite him home to get a better look. Well, I was just teasing my husband about it, not expecting anything to actually happen. But when we left the restaurant, this young man left at the same time and he happened to be parked right next to our vehicle. As I was getting in our vehicle, I noticed again how he was staring at me, so I said something to him like "Do you like my new boots? I got them as a present from my husband."

This young man's face turned all red and he nervously squeaked out how he thought my boots were very nice. I can't believe that I did it, but a burst of boldness and dominance came over me, so I told this young man that I was wearing them because my husband was submissive and he gets weak just from seeing me in my boots. Now my husband's face turned red.

I than asked the young man if he had a boot fetish, because I noticed him staring at my boots inside the restaurant. Again, he was embarrassed and nervous, but he admitted to me that he also gets weak seeing a woman wearing leather boots. Needless to say, I capitalized on this opportunity. I asked the young man where he lived, and it turned out that he didn't live far from us. I then ordered my husband to give this young man our telephone number, and I told this young man that if he wanted to get a much closer look at me and my boots, to give me a call sometime.

The next day, he called me up. I talked to him for about a half-hour on the telephone just to make sure that he wasn't a weirdo. He wasn't as he told me where he worked and a lot of other personal information. Once I felt comfortable with him, I invited him over to our house. Before he arrived, I tied up my husband's genitals real tight with a pair of my stockings, I inserted a butt plug into him, and I made him stand in our closet with the door cracked slightly, so he could see out a little.

When the young man showed up, I was wearing a very sexy and a very intimidating looking leather outfit complete with my boots, of course. I explained to him that this was going to be a one time only treat for him. I was going to allow him to kiss, lick, and worship my boots, but first he had to totally get undressed. He had quite the erection when he took off his clothes and I got lucky in that he was a little larger than my husband, which added to my husband's humiliation. I ordered this nice looking young man to worship my boots, and he went right to it.

He was nervous and a little awkward at first, but I could tell that he had a strong leather and boot fetish, so it didn't take him long to really get into it. I got so excited watching this young man lick my boots, that I allowed him to also kiss my hose covered thighs as well as lick my leather clad ass. I even sat on his face and smothered him a little while he licked the leather from my min-skirt. I also stroked his throbbing penis with the heels of my boots. This was both pleasurable and painful to him, as he squirmed from the touch of my sharp heels. I brought him right to the edge of climax, but I didn't want him to soil my new boots. Therefore, I ordered him to lie on his back and to masturbate, while he sucked my boot heels clean of the few drops of his male juice that had seeped from him. He climaxed on my command.

I made him wipe himself off with a towel and I ordered him to get dressed. I sat and talked with him a little and I explained to him again that this was a one time only event. He was very sweet and he said that he understood and he thanked me for fulfilling his fantasy, than he left. I brought my husband out of the closet and humiliated him the rest of the night about my handsome, young boot slave. My husband was able to see most of the action and he was excited, humiliated, and even a little jealous. I really humiliated him about the fact that my young boot slave had a larger penis than he did. I proceeded to dominate my husband and we had quite an evening, as we both were very turned on."

For Debra and her husband, Humiliation Play was sexual foreplay that led to a night of intimacy and romance. Humiliation Play can also take a negative and turn it into a positive from the potential D&S implications. That is what happened for Charles.

"I have been able to draw on the masochistic side of my personality to enable me to accommodate and cope with what for many men would probably be a crippling and very depressing burden. I refer to male impotence or erectile dysfunction. There can be few humiliating experiences to deflate a man's ego than to find he can no longer serve his wife's needs physically, even with all the help of modern medicines such as Viagra. A woman can never lose her ability when she chooses to please her man, but the poor inferior man has to perform to please, and (oh boy!) he can't half fail in that department.

In my case, though I am in splendid health for a man of my age and still have all the old urges towards my wife, I can no longer perform my manly duty in the conventional way to my wife's satisfaction. No physical cause can be found, though it is probably a malfunction in my veins and definitely not primarily psychological in origin. I am sure of this, as from past experience I know that the humiliation of having my wife demanding a more adequate performance when witnessing my sluggishness would have given me a real 'hard one', instead I now get only a partial erection for as long as my wife is willing to let me try to give her pleasure.

Without ever condoning my failures, or pretending she is not insulted by them and displeased with me, my wife has graciously conceded that there are some benefits in my impotence for her. That is, provided it makes me more aware of the gulf between her superiority and my inferiority and provided this awareness drives me yet more diligently to seek to serve her better in other ways so that I compensate by becoming the best house slave I can be. I must admit to feeling completely inadequate as a man, but so grateful to my wife for so generously taking advantage of this fact and exploiting it to her advantage.

It makes me feel so much better about my impotence knowing that at least my wife enjoys having me trying to compensate her by more diligent service in other ways, especially doing all the household chores. I am so grateful to her and pleased to be married to such a wonderful, superior and considerate woman. Indeed, because of my wife's wonderfully generous response to my impotence, I feel I have fallen in love with her all over again, but this time I am totally in debt to her. Of course my wife has quite explicitly made it crystal clear that she can quite happily live without my feeble efforts to make love to her, but just occasionally, when she is in the mood, she is gracious enough still to let me try to please her, when I have earned enough points to deserve a treat. Almost always this ends in failure and humiliation for me. The frustration of sexual denial is probably far greater than that of any chastity device as there is no chance of ultimate relief. My wife is very subtle as she leaves me to make all the running, asking for opportunities for intimacy; she then strings me along, sometimes from one week to the next, never knowing when she will oblige. When I then fail as a man, I guess I end up feeling even worse about letting my wife down, as it was I that asked to try and give her pleasure, only to fail yet again.

My wife is actually using my impotence to manipulate me to her advantage. Perhaps this is why she has always implied I should just accept my lot in life and that I am making a mountain out of a molehill by seeking medical treatment for my impotence. The idea of any sort of medical consultation together is something she has firmly rejected; it is my problem as an inferior male and that is the end of it. It is not worth spending money on treatment for something so trivial in her eyes, "think of all the real illnesses other people have to put up with." My wife really does welcome my impotence as a weapon she can use to make me behave towards her, as she wants.

I also know my wife benefits from knowing I have unwittingly given her a new powerful weapon of humiliating me in front of our friends. If ever I really upset her, she would expose for their amusement true stories about my failures in bed. I have not forgotten how one year, when overseas, I forgot my wife's birthday and the fun this allowed her to have telling all her friends about my omission. This all helps keep me on my toes and striving to serve her in every way I can. Her dominance of me is instead so subtle and mental, but that is how my wife seems to want it, frustrating though it is for me. She is dominant but avoids any explicitly dominant behavior but rather enjoys the mind games. The uncertainty where I stand keeps me on my toes. Her greatest compliment is 'not bad'.

I am proud that my wife has lots of independent interests inside and outside the home and she is often out enjoying her hobby, singing in choirs, relaxing at her gym and leisure club or going away for weekends with her friends. I fit in by having her meals ready according to her schedule; helping her pack and unpack and ensuring her gym kit is clean and ready for when she needs it. I am trying to feel less jealous and threatened when other men who are not sexually impotent seek to have ostensibly platonic friendships with my wife. I am sure they must find her immensely attractive as I do. Though I know my wife loves only me, nevertheless, I feel vulnerable knowing that I am a spent force if it ever became a competition with another man for her favors. At least this keeps me on my toes and vigilant in my efforts to please her and maintain her approval and well-being. My wife has me under her thumb, just where she wants me, loving and adoring her and striving ever more to please her as her servant."

Charles' wife has tapped into the power of using mind games and humiliation play as it relates to her husband's impotency. This form of Humiliation Play and Charles' excitement from these games is satisfying to him and his submissive and masochistic nature. Her subtle domination stirs his submission to the place where it gives him the energy and motivation to do all those chores for her. While he is serving her by being her house slave, this gives him submissive fulfillment and to him that is as good (if not better) than sex. The brain is the greatest sex organ and even if it is unable to send the necessary signals to his penis due to physical problems, the mind is still stimulated by her dominance and his submissive nature reacts to her dominance, and thus it sends off pleasurable sensations and that takes him to a place of both sexual arousal and inner peace and harmony. Charles' penis may not be able to receive the message but his soul receives the message and this is pleasurable to him on an emotional level.

Objectification is another form of Humiliation Play. Nancy's husband Greg has the submissive desire that revolves around him wanting her to use him as a piece of furniture. He likes to be her footstool, or her chair or her rug, or even her clothes rack. He shows her pictures off the Internet where women use men as inanimate objects and he asks her to do this to him. She incorporates this activity within their play sessions and even some within their everyday life. Nancy enjoys Objectification because it gives her a powerful feeling of control over her husband and this satisfies a part of her dominant nature. She also enjoys the fact that this activity takes very little effort on her part.

Treating a man like an inanimate object has been known to do wonders in fulfilling submissive desires within some men. Plus this activity is a great way to dominate a man when the woman is not in the mood or does not have the energy to engage in a D&S session with her submissive man. She can just order him to be her coffee table, footstool or clothes rack while she relaxes and reads or watches television. In doing this, the woman is dominating the man's psyche without too much effort on her part.

To understand why some men enjoy this activity one must look at it from the submissive male's psyche. To a submissive male, the mental image of a woman using a man as a piece of furniture is a powerful mental picture. It sends the symbolic image that women don't need men and that to a dominant woman, a man is no more important than an inanimate piece of furniture. Such an image causes the submissive desires within a man to stir and he becomes excited by the thought of a woman treating him with such little regard. To the submissive male, this image makes the statement that women are so far superior to men, that a man is only worthy to be used by a woman in such a humiliating and degrading manner. It elevates the woman to Royalty and even to Goddess status in the mind of the submissive male. How can he ever be the equal of a woman who treats him this way? This causes him to feel humble and subservient. The psychological effect stays with him for a period of time after the objectification so he is primed to serve his Goddess in more practical ways.

There are also some bondage elements to Objectification. A man that enjoys being helpless and likes the feeling of being in bondage, may enjoy being an inanimate object. Especially a clothes rack or a similar object where fetish clothing is placed over him. This may cause a man to be transferred to subspace much the same way restrictive bondage does to some men. Regardless of why a man enjoys this activity, a smart woman learns how to use this fetish or desire within her man for her benefit. The dominant woman should consider what is going through the mind of her submissive and view his unusual requests from how the activity will affect his submissive nature.

Objectification causes the man to view the woman who humiliates him in this manner as being superior to him. It elevates her to Goddess status in his mind. Like any D&S activity, objectification must be kept in proper balance. A man that desires to be an inanimate object 24/7 is out of balance and needs to become rooted in realty. However, it is perfectly Ok for a woman to explore this desire within a man from the safe and intimate confines of a relationship and then build upon it for her own benefit and advantage. That way both parties end up winning and being satisfied.

Another form of Humiliation play is Trampling. Beth's husband Trey enjoys this form of being dominated. Trey slips into subspace when he is helpless under Beth's feet as she uses him as her rug, doormat, bathmat or footstool. Whenever Beth wants to dominate her husband, she will order Trey to lay prostrate on the floor as she stands and walks on his backside. Beth's favorite method of trampling Trey is to stand on his naked backside with her bare feet.

"I love the feeling of Trey's naked skin against my bare feet. He tightens up at first but then I can feel him relaxing as he loses himself in submission. I will walk back and forth over his backside, from his upper back to his firm ass cheeks to the back of his upper legs. Sometimes I will add a different sensation for him by wearing a pair of shoes or boots. I've been known to trample him in high-heel shoes. He really has to focus as my sharp heels dig into his flesh. Much like the martial arts, Trey must use mind over matter to overcome the pain in order to relax so he can slip into subspace."

Beth weighs fifty pounds less than Trey and she has educated herself on the male anatomy so she understands where she can and cannot apply her entire weight as she tramples her husband. She also watches out for her own safety by placing her hand on a rail, a piece of furniture or she will even use a walking stick to maintain her balance as she walks on Trey.

"In the beginning of our relationship, I though he was strange for wanting me to walk on him but once I began to do it, I found that it was erotic and fun. I feel powerful and sexy as I walk on my husband. It

makes me want to dominate him in other ways. The trampling is usually our foreplay to other D&S activities. Once he slips into subspace from the trampling, I am able to do just about anything I want to him and he eagerly obeys my every command."

There is more to the Trampling activity than just walking on a man's backside. Beth and her husband enjoy it when she puts her bare feet on him while she talks on the phone to one of her girlfriends, totally ignoring him.

"I will be seated in my easy-chair or on the edge of my bed while I place my feet on Trey's face or maybe on his genitals. I will move my feet all around his body, stroking his penis lightly with my feet and then grinding them hard into his groin. I have been known to do this with the spiked heels from my shoes or boots. It takes very little effort on my part but he becomes very docile and submissive from being used as my footstool or my carpet. He seems to slip off into another world when I do this to him.

Sometimes as part of a romantic evening, Trey bathes me and when I am finished with my bath, I use him as a bathmat when I get out of the tub. I stand on his back or his buttocks while I towel off. I might even make him roll over so I can trample his front side. I like to stare into his eyes when I stand (partial weight only) on his chest or grind my heel into his groin"

A woman must be cautious about the practice of trampling. She needs to know the male anatomy and skeleton structure to understand where she can and cannot apply her full weight. The laws of physics do apply here so the woman's weight and size and the man's physical build do play a factor. The bones in the face are fragile and can be crushed easily so a woman should never place her full weight on his face.

Beth stands with one foot firmly planted on the ground with her other foot pressed to Trey's chest or crotch but she never stands on his face, chest, stomach or crotch with her full weight. She is extra careful about his stomach area, as this is where most organs are located.

When she uses him as a bathmat, she is careful not to jump up and down on him. Her husband is a bit of a masochist and he likes to be trampled with high heel shoes or stiletto boots. When doing this, Beth begins by only applying light pressure as she either sits or stands with her other leg planted next to him. Then she experiments with degrees of pressure from her shoes or boots to gauge his reaction and pain threshold.

Why do men desire to be trampled or used as a doormat or bathmat? It has to do with desiring that feeling of helplessness. There is a form of bondage in being used as a footstool or a bathmat. There is also mental stimulation as to what this activity represents. It represents to the submissive man that he is indeed under his wife's feet. She is the conqueror and he is the conquered. It goes back to ancient times when on the battle field the victor would place his foot upon the head of the vanquished as he decided if he would kill his enemy or allow him to exist as his slave. To the submissive male, the female that tramples him has conquered him and he is now her slave. The act of being trampled reinforces that to him and mentally transports him to subspace. The submissive male likes to just lie there under her feet and bask in his weakness as she flaunts her superiority over him.

This activity also appeals to the woman's dominant nature. She enjoys seeing her husband helpless under her power and her will. She enjoys feeling his flesh under her feet or even under her tush. The sociological statement this makes to her is profound and satisfying.

Queening is a form of trampling only the man is under the woman's tush, instead of her feet. Queening is basically where the dominant female sits her butt on the face of a submissive male and has him orally service her bottom. This is an erotic and pleasurable experience for the woman, and a very humiliating and submissive act for the male. Most submissive men are extremely turned on by the female bottom, its shape, appearance and softness. To a submissive man, the female tush also represents power to him. Not only does the submissive man crave to kiss and orally worship the feminine bottom but he also desires to be crushed by it. He desires to be held captive and helpless through the act of face sitting so that he is conquered and at the mercy of his female captor.

Queening can be done with a device known as a Queening Stool. This is a short stool or a box with a large padded hole in the middle and an opening in the bottom for the male's face to slide in. The dominant sits on the seat of the stool (or box) and the submissive male's face is tight against the other side of the seat, and he adores and services his Queen's bottom, thus the terms Queening and Queening Stool.

The Queening stool adds an element of bondage to this activity but you don't need a Queening stool to engage in it. Sitting on a man's face can be just as effective. However, the woman must make sure that she affords him the proper amount of air that he needs to breathe. A man should have at least one hand free so he can give a hand signal if he is having any difficulty in breathing. Few Female Domination activities will transport a man into the deep and submissive state known as subspace as fast as Queening. I earlier discussed how I can defuse an argument between my husband and I by incorporating Queening. No matter how upset he may be, if I order him to lay on my bed and I proceed to sit my bare bottom on his face while commanding that he kiss it or rim it, he will melt into submission and his anger and temper will quickly recede.

A woman can also Queen submissive men in a non-sexual way. A woman can play with other men that she does not wish to be intimate with. She can sit on a man's face wearing a pair of tight leather pants, for example. A submissive man with a strong leather fetish will enjoy being Queened by a woman in this manner. If the woman wants to feel some pleasure but not allow a submissive man to have direct access to her crotch or bottom, she can Queen a man by wearing a pair of panty-hose. That way the woman can still feel the pleasurable sensations of the submissive man's tongue but the nylon material prevents the submissive from direct contact with her flesh while he is being Queened.

Ambrosia enjoys a more sensual form of Female Domination and Queening works for her and her husband since he likes to be humiliated in this fashion.

"The Female Domination activity that I enjoy is face sitting. I am a very sensual female and I love to have my butt and my crotch licked for prolonged periods of time. Before we were married and my husband was still my boyfriend, he told me how performing oral sex on me made him feel submissive. I never paid a whole lot of attention to what he meant by that, all I knew was the pleasure I got from oral sex.

I am a laid back and rather passive woman but I do have a selfish and aggressive side when it comes to sex. My husband wanted to introduce me to the Female Domination lifestyle but he knew me well enough not to push me toward S&M or physical D&S. My personality would not have adapted to that and I am sure I would have rejected the whole lifestyle. My husband was smart and he sold me on the benefits of the Female Domination lifestyle by submitting to me through female body worship, and in particular face sitting.

I enjoy placing him in bondage and sitting on his face for long intervals of time, while he performs cunnilingus and analingus. I learned about the practice of Queening a man and about a device known as a Queening stool. I got very excited when I read of this and I told my husband to make me one. The first model of the Queening stool was very crude, as it was basically a small padded wooden box with no bottom and an opening in the seat. He would sit on the floor, lie his head face up on the couch or a chair. I would place the Queening stool over his face and sit on the padded area with the open seat. He would then perform analingus. It worked but it really wasn't very comfortable for me or for him.

My husband kept at it and he has since built some wonderful pieces of furniture for Queening. He took one of our barstools and he removed the seat and replaced it with a very comfortable padded open seat, complete with a backrest for me. He attached strong rubber elastic strips about six inches under the hole in the seat and he made himself a sturdy and comfortable headrest. It also has hooks in the top of the legs of the stool so I can attach his collar to the hooks and keep him in bondage as his head rests on the rubber harness, just under the opening in the seat of the stool. Once I secure him in the head harness, I can take my place on the stool and have him perform analingus for as long as I desire. If I sit with my face toward the backrest, I can have him perform cunnilingus, again for as long as I want. Both positions are very comfortable for me. My husband struggles with air at times and we have hand signals that he uses if he needs me to stand up in order to help him to catch his breath.

Another piece of furniture he made was what we call the Queening couch. He took an old leather couch that he got at an auction and he raised it by replacing the short legs with legs that are around two feet in length. Then he cut a hole in the middle of the couch, just large enough for his head. He cut the same size hole in the middle cushion. Now I can lay on our Queening couch and watch television or read and my husband lays under the couch, with his head inserted up into the hole. If I lay on my back, I can straddle his face with my crotch tight against his face.

This is a wonderful way to receive prolonged oral sex. If I want him to perform analingus, I can sit on his face directly or I can lay on my stomach and spread my legs so his face can snuggle up to my bottom.

We have both of these pieces of furniture in our family room in our finished basement. We have an extra cushion for the Queening couch (without the hole) and we replace that middle cushion when company visits. We put the Queening stool in a closet. But most of the time, no one visits our family room so I like to keep my Queening furniture ready for my use.

My next project for him is to create a Queening bed. I saw a picture on the Internet of a woman lying on a large bed and there was a man's face trapped in the middle of her bed. You could only see his face, as the rest of his body must have been bound under the bed. In the next picture on this site, the woman straddled his face and had a look of ecstasy on her face. I have challenged my husband to make us such a bed. I tease him that I really only need his face for sex, so why allow the rest of his body on my bed?"

Creativity sure seems to find its expression within the Female Domination lifestyle. Again, all safety and health precautions must be taken when practicing Queening. The dominant female must maintain proper hygiene for the wellbeing of her submissive and she must be careful not to engage in any kind of prolonged suffocation. The brain needs oxygen so air is always needed when engaging in Queening. Therefore, all Queening devices must afford the submissive male the required amount of air.

Water sports are still another form of Humiliation Play. Water Sports is usually comprised of Enemas and Golden Showers. A Golden shower is where the woman urinates on her submissive male in order to humiliate him. Some couples find water sports to be fun because the sensation of warm water on the skin or filling the body via an enema, is erotic and sensual. That is the big appeal of golden showers. Besides the obvious dominant implications, urine leaving a woman's body is wet, warm and sensual as it makes contact with the male's body. Water Sports are perfect for Female Domination because it combines domination and humiliation with sensuality. The pleasure to a submissive male is both physical and mental. The warm water is pleasurable to the body and the domination and humiliation of being peed on is pleasurable to the submissive mind.

Some men get excited about golden showers because to them it is the ultimate in servitude and the depths of submission. To them, there is nothing so degrading and humiliating, yet exciting. To some submissive men, it is the moment right before the golden shower that is the most exciting. To have his Queen positioned over his body, perhaps seated on a Queening stool with him bound below her, awaiting to be degraded. It is that moment of anticipation that submissive men have confessed that they felt unbelievably submissive, as if they had indeed been conquered by their Queen. Then as they felt the warmth of the woman's urine against their body they knew there was no doubt that they could never be her equal.

Enema's can be very erotic when administered by a dominant woman. A number of men over the years have told me an enema story from their childhood. It usually involves a boy's Mother, Female Guardian or a Nurse being a bit forceful when administering the enema and this has been known to trigger submissive desires within males. In Corey's case, it was his Aunt.

"When I was a boy, probably around eight or nine, I was staying with my Aunt Jane for a few weeks this one summer. My Aunt was my Mother's older sister by five years and she was probably in her mid thirties. Like my Mother, my Aunt Jane was a beautiful woman with long black hair, dark skin and lovely brown eyes. When I was staying with her, I had a constipation problem for some reason and was not going to the bathroom. I can't recall why, maybe it was an emotional thing from being away from my Mom for two weeks or maybe it was eating too much junk food at my Aunt's house. Whatever the cause, I was not going to the bathroom and my Aunt knew this so she wanted to rectify it and she told me that I needed an enema.

My Mom gave me an enema a few years earlier and I remembered that I did not enjoy it at all, so I told my Aunt, "no way". She insisted and I got rebellious toward her and refused. This only made her the more determined. She told me that I had to have one for my own good and that she was going to give me one, whether I cooperated or not. We were the only two in the house that day, as my Uncle was either working or somewhere else.

My Aunt went into the bathroom and got the enema bag all ready to go and called for me. I refused and I ran from her and she chased me around the house. Her dining room, kitchen and living room formed a circle and she finally caught me going the other way. She was a rather large and strong woman and she dragged me into the bathroom where the enema bag awaited me. Once she had me inside the bathroom, she locked the door so I could not escape. She forcefully undressed me and I was screaming and resisting her. She finally got my clothes off and she forced me on my stomach and ordered me to hold still. She lubricated the nozzle and she sat on me as she started to insert the lubricated nozzle up my butt.

I freaked and I jerked away from her, splashing the warm water all over her clothes. My Aunt Jane took off her wet clothes right there and stripped down to just her bra and panties. I had never seen a woman in bra and panties like this before and I remember that I got sexually aroused for the first time in my life. I just froze staring at her large breasts sticking slightly out of her bra. My Aunt Jane than re-filled the enema bag and she grabbed me and once again forced me to the bathroom floor and sat on me to hold me still as she inserted the nozzle into my butt. This time, I gave up and surrendered. I just relaxed as she filled me with the warm water and I found myself loving the sensation. Feeling the soft skin of my Aunt against my back and feeling helpless as she sat on me and filled me with the water from the enema, was my first sexual moment in my life. A special bond was formed between me and my Aunt Jane at that moment.

Once she was done with the enema, she unlocked the door and gave me my privacy to relieve myself. It worked, as I was no longer constipated. I was very obedient toward my Aunt from that moment on. I think she took an extra liking to me as well as she would always ask my Mom for permission to take me places like the Zoo and to amusement parks, just me and her. Nothing sexual ever happened again between us but I was always very loving and docile towards her and I know that she loved me being so well behaved. I was always attracted to her from that day and my early sexual fantasies almost always involved my Aunt Jane."

If Mothers or Female Guardians only knew how harmless everyday events in rearing a little boy affected their son's sexuality. I sometimes wish I could share with every Mother the stories their dear grown up sons share with me about how their submissive desires were unlocked due to an innocent Mother/son event, that to the son was sexual. Mothers, Aunts, Teachers and other female authority figures help develop and trigger a boy's submissive nature through no more than just being a woman. That is all it takes because that is how boys are wired. One glimpse at a woman's beautiful anatomy and one stern word or forceful act, and the male is instantly under the woman's power (a power most women do not even know they possess).

Corey's childhood experience caused him to develop a fetish for enemas. Now he and his wife make them a regular part of their sexuality.

"Now I am happily married and my wife has just begun to embrace her dominant persona. My wife also enjoys water sports and she administers enemas to me on a regular basis. She is always trying to come up with creative ways to humiliate me as I hold in the enema waters and I always must worship her body before she allows me to relieve myself."

As we have seen, there are many variations to Humiliation Play. Some are more intense than others but they all center around the male desire to be in submission to a Dominant Woman and his need for Loving Female Authority.

Chapter Thirteen

The Three Faces of Eve:
Goddess, Mistress and Queen

She answers him as if she knew his mind; ...She puts on outward strangeness, seems unkind; Spurns at his love and scorns the heat he feels, Beating his kind embracements with her heels. (William Shakespeare, "Venus and Adonis")

Your beauty and dominance transports me to another world; A world that has no worries, no cares, no strife. There you are all that matters; My Queen, my Goddess, my Superior Wife. (From "Another World", a poem by James dedicated to Kathy, 1998)

Female Domination can take on an almost spiritual dimension. Some men go beyond mere submission and enter a world of actually worshipping a woman. Female Domination and D&S can transport a man to a place within his psyche where he views the woman in his life as more than a life partner. The word Romantic does not begin to describe the beauty of some Female Domination relationships. The deep love that a man develops for a woman who dominates him transcends the mind and the physical world.

The Dominant Female takes on many roles within the psyche of a man. She can be the strict and demanding Mistress who disciplines and trains her submissive in the ways of servitude. She can be a Queen who is

214

majestic and superior in the eyes of her submissive man. She can even be elevated to the status of Goddess in the heart and mind of a submissive male.

Karl is a twenty-three year old male with a very worshipful and respectful attitude toward women. He met Andrea, a thirty-nine year old Female Supremacist. Andrea's mother is Helga, a blonde Swedish lady who was a professional Dominatrix in the Netherlands during the 1970's. Andrea was born within a Female Supremacist marriage and she was herself a Pro Dom during college. Now Andrea has a boutique and Karl is her shop-assistant and her house husband. Andrea could have married numerous men since she believes in Female Supremacy and draws submissive men with her dominant attitude and aura. She chose Karl because of his worshipful attitude toward the female gender. Andrea saw in Karl a pure heart and an eagerness to serve. Karl describes their untraditional but pure FemDom relationship.

"Our marriage is a female supremacist one. We married eighteen months ago and from our wedding night, I wear a chastity device and the only form of sex for us is with me tonguing Andrea, usually twice a day. She is dead set against vanilla intercourse and she says the tongue is the real sex organ of males. Nothing wrong in this, she is a woman and knows the facts of life better than me. On the other side, I empty myself twice a week, on Saturday and Sunday night if I'm a very good boy during week. This happens almost every weekend because I do my very best to pamper her. The way this is done is a routine and a ritual.

Before bedtime she emerges dressed in only her panties, bra and high heel shoes. Believe me, her feminine power is unbelievable. I drop to my knees at once and hurry to kiss her feet. Andrea is so beautiful and powerful I can't resist from dropping to my knees. If she's in a good mood, Andrea lets me kiss and lick her feet for a while and then she blindfolds me before taking off her panties. I'm always blindfolded when I worship Andrea because we've learned from the early time of our marriage that the sight of her naked body is enough for me to have a wet accident.

Next, she ties my legs together and my arms firmly in place behind my back. Of course I'm always naked for this ritual. When my hands are secured, she unlocks the chastity device and I get an erection ready to be used for sex. Andrea lightly slaps my balls to get rid of my swelling and to cool me down to avoid wet accidents. Two or three painful slaps are usually enough to soften me down. At this point, Andrea slips my penis inside one of her shoes still warm from her foot. Then, she fixes it firmly in place with one of her stockings. This done, she has me lay on her bed, on my belly, while my penis grows erect, filling her shoe. Then she begins to spank me.

She uses a large belt or her slipper as her spanking instruments. A belt is a lethal weapon in her hands. She doesn't like to use her hands and she's very experienced as a spanker. To tell you the truth she doesn't call these "spankings", but instead: "lessons in humility and respect". During the spanking I have to hump her warm shoe, pumping it as quickly as it rests on her bed. A few hits from her on my ass are enough to make me beg her for mercy. She spanks me without fury or anger, but with method and regularity like she's doing some fitness exercise. I'm in tears in seconds but believe me, I cry like a baby not for pain but for the joy to be spanked by Andrea. I don't know how to explain what I feel. I'm very proud of her, and I feel a deep happiness to be her husband. These feelings are rising in me week by week.

Since we've been married, her shoes are as close to making love to her as she has permitted. In the beginning, I wanted to make love with Andrea, but I've learned to accept her rule. I learned quickly to thank her with all my heart for the opportunity to make love to her shoes. In spite of the sexual pleasure rising from my member encased inside her warm shoe, the spanking is hard enough to reduce my sexual pleasure and so I can go on like this for a long time. It's hard to explain my feelings during those moments. I'm both in heaven and hell. The spanking ends when I come in her shoe and during the entire spanking she scolds me. After coming she lets me cool down for a few minutes, during which she goes on lecturing me about respect for females. Then I have to thank her politely and if I'm not respectful enough she gives me another round of blows. As you can imagine, to avoid it I'm very submissive and very respectful. When she's ok about my behavior, she releases my penis and I have to lick her shoe clean. Ended this task, she cleans me using a wet and cold towel before locking my chastity device in place again. Once I'm safe, Andrea unties my arms and legs and lets me kiss and lick her feet as reward. Then, it's my duty to tongue her vagina urgently until she obtains two or three orgasms.

With a few laps of my tongue, I lose myself. The world is cut away from my mind and I only exist to worship Andrea. Blindfolded and on my knees, smelling her scent and tasting her, my thoughts run miles away and I am lost in my mind, in subspace. If she doesn't stop me by patting my head with her hand saying "it's enough, boy!", I'm able to lick her for hours and I am in heaven. How can the female sex be so powerful? A wave of profound happiness rises in me when I worship my Goddess."

It is a beautiful thing when a man worships a woman in such a selfless and humble manner. Karl is a beautiful man and one can see why Andrea chose him as her husband. Given her background, she could have chosen hundreds of men but she was looking for that male who would worship her with a humble and eager heart. I am sure her mother taught her in the ways of Female Supremacy and Andrea was looking for a man who would not only be trainable but also eager to be the best servant in the world. Nothing is more pleasurable for a woman than a man who orally pleasures her with an attitude of humility and worship.

Jody describes his love and devotion to his Wife, his Mistress and his Goddess.

"I am a 33 year old man, previously married, and with previous experience in a full time D/s relationship (although not in my marriage). From a very young age I can recall fantasizing about 'Amazon' like women holding me as their slave and doing their bidding. Not much has changed. I am currently living with the Woman that I will spend the rest of my life with. She is 29, with beautiful long red hair, a wonderfully curvy body, and a smile that has the ability to make me melt, or get aroused (often both). When we first moved in together, we talked very openly and honestly about everything, including our sexuality.

The relationship continued, but the honeymoon seemed to be fading. I realized that being dominant was the last thing I wanted, as I truly believe in Female Dominance and Female Superiority. I was miserable, and because of that, all of the servile things I had been doing ceased. When that stopped, she became miserable too, neither of us were happy whatsoever. We both agree that our love for each other is nothing like either of us has ever experienced before, however something was wrong. I have no idea how the topic came up, but we found ourselves talking about how a role reversal needed to be in play. And so it began.

My daily routine involves waking my Mistress up to breakfast in bed each morning, making Her a healthy lunch while She is showering and getting ready for work, greeting Her with worship and praise when She returns home from work, as well as a hot dinner. I paint Her toenails, and pamper Her feet. I am becoming a much more positive, happy, and healthy person, and I owe it all to Her. To me, she is my Mistress, and my Goddess. I truly do love, admire, and worship Her. The natural ease that She has settled into Her role as a Dominant Woman is almost frightening. I have never felt so completely in awe of confidence and power. I am the happiest and luckiest man on the planet. I have the privilege of serving the most beautiful, powerful, sensual Woman I have ever met."

Pure submission cannot be faked. A woman will spot and sense an act of selfishness and a woman will spot and sense an act of genuine submission. Give the female what she needs and a true submissive male will experience fulfillment. Alex discovered this with his wife Lynne.

"I have had submissive tendencies since I was about ten or eleven. At the time, I knew nothing about Femdom. I remember that there was a twenty-year old girl who worked at our local movie theater. She had the shapeliest legs. I used to fantasize about her kidnapping me. I don't recall any more details about my fantasies about her beyond that. As I grew older, my fantasies about being enslaved by women continued. After puberty, they became more sexual in nature. I fantasized about being a sexual slave. Being a Christian, I felt I should suppress those fantasies. That only worked for weeks or months at a time.

When I met Lynne, my future wife, I thought that I could control my fantasies. For the first few years, I did quite well, but eventually my desire to be submissive kept resurfacing. Now I desired to submit to my wife. After about seven years of marriage I finally worked up enough courage to confess my desires to Lynne. I told her I fantasized about being her sex slave, etc. She was willing, though reluctantly, to fulfill some, but not all of my fantasies. Over the next few years we both experienced a series of frustrating experiences because Lynne felt reluctant to dominate me. She didn't want a FemDom relationship because she didn't think Christian husbands and wives engaged in such relationships.

I tried to persuade her by submitting to her by doing the laundry and washing dishes, etc. without being asked. I would occasionally kneel at her feet and give her foot massages. This seemed to put her in a more receptive frame of mind. She confessed that she liked the idea of me submitting to her. Her dominant nature started to grow all by itself. I used to joke with her (but really wished) that she should collar me. To my surprise, one day she brought home a dog collar and produced it from under the sheets when we went to bed. She commanded me to get on my hands and knees on the bed, then she put it around the back of my neck. Grabbing each end of the collar, she pulled my head forward roughly and announced "You are now my property. You will serve me as my slave.

She put the collar on me and commanded me to strip naked. I was then required to lay at her feet and be her footstool while she laid back and read. She would occasionally fondle my hard penis with her bare foot. From time to time, she would look down and tell me that I was in my proper place at her feet, or she told me I must submit to her and obey her without question. Another desire of mine, which I often confessed to Lynne, was for her to play with my body, using clamps on my nipples and a riding crop on my body. Since BDSM and porn sites turned her off, I didn't think she would ever get any of those items. I underestimated her creativity, though. One night after she collared me, Lynne produced an oversized serving spoon from under the sheets. It was about a foot long, with the scoop and neck made of metal and the handle made of plastic.

The scoop was weighted. Lynne explained that she had been thinking I should be disciplined because I have been taking my Mistress for granted. She also stated that she decided that this spoon would be more effective and quieter than a riding crop since we have two kids that know nothing of our lifestyle. She commanded me to lay on my stomach and proceeded to strike my bare butt, alternating cheeks with every blow. Within a few strokes my cheeks were on fire! Lynne did not stop until long after I started to beg her to do so.

Fast forward to the present. I am now required to sleep naked, except for a newer and thicker collar secured snugly around my neck. I am forbidden to touch it. Only my Mistress can remove it. She often comments how she hates to take my collar off in the morning. In addition to the household chores I must perform, I am also required to be my

Mistress' personal servant. I give her regular foot massages and put lotion on her feet. When she wants me to, I serve her as her footstool. I also kneel at her feet in our tub and shave her legs every other night. I am required to caress her whenever she demands it, and of course, I sexually serve her on command. When my Mistress allows my penis inside her vagina, it must be with me lying on my back with my legs spread wide apart for her in submissive invitation to her to take me. I love the feel of her naked thighs pressing the back of my own thighs when she rides me. Mistress says that as her slave, my place is underneath her, therefore I am forbidden to climax inside of her in any other position."

Alex's approach is the best when trying to introduce a woman to this lifestyle. The man needs to focus on submitting to the woman in a way that is pleasing and beneficial to her. Not to him but to her. Lynne had misgivings at first, as do most women, but as Alex continued to serve her, Lynne's dominant nature came forth and she overcame her inhibitions. Lynne discovered that this lifestyle is wonderful for women and the sex is out of this world.

Jessica likes for her husband to view her as his Queen. They view their roles as not only Wife and husband but also Queen and servant. Jessica uses her creativity to make the most mundane tasks fresh and exciting within their marriage.

"My husband and I recently have come to a unique arrangement regarding our finances. The underlying thesis of our plan is that all of our marital assets belong to me. First, we have a joint checking account (with my name appearing first, as in the phone book) and my husband is responsible for making sure all bills are paid. The trick is that he prepares all the checks, but I am the only one who signs them. My husband is not allowed access to our checkbook except when he does bills and I take it after he's finished with check preparation and balancing, and lock it in a lock box, of which I hold the only key. I also keep the only credit card, which also has his name on it and he's only allowed to carry it when supervised or traveling alone and then for emergency purposes only.

My husband is allowed only $20.00 per week cash allowance, which I give him each Friday at the bank, and this also allows for some *delightfully subtle public domination (my new hobby). On the Fridays he gets paid, I take him to the bank, have him sign the check in front of the teller, and then he hands me the check for deposit. I take out one twenty and hand it to him and several more for myself, which I put in my purse. On the Fridays he doesn't get paid I take him to the bank, withdraw only a twenty from the teller and hand it to him. The point is that he is not allowed to take money directly from the teller (even in the drive-thru I make him hand the cylinder to me first), and he's never allowed to go to the bank alone. I always try and go to female tellers and I'm sure they've caught on. Many of the female tellers are young and I like to think I'm educating them as to how men should treat women.*

In addition to paying bills he has to prepare a "Queen's Yearly Budget" which is on hardcopy and different pages examine Her Majesty's Assets, Liabilities, and Monthly Expenses. I will review each bank statement as it comes in to monitor hubby's work, and he is to give me a quarterly report in which we will discuss the condition of the Queen's Treasury and Her long-term financial goals. I like this arrangement because it leaves the burden of managing for our future on him but leaves all the power with me.

If hubby wants more than his allowance, I allow him to have a special hearing before the Queen, which is held in our bedroom. I wear a long black satin robe, and black garter belt with stockings, and nothing else and sit on the bed. He will knock at the door and after I say "Enter" he will come in and kneel before me totally nude. I then say "Yes" and he bends down and kisses the top of each foot and says, "My Mistress, I have come to petition your Highness to allow me to have additional funds from Her Majesty's Treasury." I will then listen to his request and grant or deny it. If I deny it he is stood in the corner and whipped with a riding crop for wasting my time, and then made to kneel in a corner for thirty minutes to think about why he was punished. If I grant it he is required to kiss the top and bottom of each of my feet, and say "Thank you my Queen." Sometimes I'll condition my grant upon his putting his head between Her Majesty's legs and licking her to orgasm within fifteen minutes, and failure will be punished as mentioned above.

Family budgeting can be fun, especially in a Female Supremacist Household. The last day of the year he'll be up for review to see if he deserves a raise, which will depend on how well he's served me over the year, which will be measured by his performance at work and at home. This lifestyle is such fun!"

The finances are usually the hardest area for a man to surrender over to his wife. Finances represent a man's time and talents. When the wife takes over the finances, she is indeed taking over the last area of resistance. A man works at his occupation and earns a paycheck and that paycheck represents much to a man. For him to surrender total control over to his wife and allow her to make the financial decisions, it is true female domination and male submission. A woman who owns a man's paycheck, owns that man's time, talents and career. From here on out, Jessica's husband works for her. He will now experience more and more dependence on her and he will become more and more submissive toward her.

Our Mothers, Grandmothers and the women of those generations were accustomed to being held captive by their husbands holding all the money. Women had to always ask for money and give an account for what they needed it for and why. In most homes, the wife was no different than the children, as she had to try to catch her husband in a good mood before she made her financial requests. Well, now the tables are turning and women are keeping control of their finances and even gaining control over their husband's finances. Men are now required to grovel to their wives to beg for a few bucks and to give an account of why they need the money. At least Jessica makes it fun and creative for her husband. It wasn't fun for our Mothers and our Grandmothers when men controlled the money. All women should remember the Golden Rule. Whoever controls the Gold, will Rule. In a Female Domination marriage, the Woman Rules.

Mistress, Queen and Goddess. These are three of the multiple faces of a wife within a Female Domination marriage. The pure humility and devotion of a man can seduce a woman's dominant nature and cause her to expect and even demand worship and reverence.

Some men would prefer to be a woman's slave rather than her traditional husband. Some men seem more fulfilled in the role of slave than of traditional husband. Not every submissive man is the same and not every woman is the same. In the final analysis, each couple (primarily the woman) must decide what will work best. It may take years of trial and error to find that which works best but life is a journey and a relationship is a journey. Darren's marriage went from traditional to part-time FemDom to 24/7 Mistress/slave.

"My wife and I have enjoyed a D/s relationship since we were in our early twenties. It had been a part time lifestyle as we both were busy with our careers and the other responsibilities of life. We tried to play when possible and about four times a year we had week-long sessions where I would be my wife's slave. She enjoyed these times when I was her slave so much, that my wife often told me that she wanted it to be a full time arrangement. The Internet opened my wife up to new ideas about D/s and the more she learned, the deeper she wanted to take our lifestyle. I was the one resisting the idea of being her full time slave.

In July 2001, I was informed that I would be facing forced retirement at the end of the year. I was offered an attractive package that would allow me financial freedom. My wife immediately wanted to have me as a 24/7 slave as soon as my retirement was settled. I knew she would continue to work, so again I resisted. My wife is in her mid-fifties and is still a knockout. So she used her sexy ways to convince me to try it. Since I always enjoyed our D/s sessions, she convinced me I would enjoy full time slavery.

The date was set---Jan.1, 2002, the date my life would change. I kept asking questions but was told not to worry and that she would take care of everything. On Dec.31st we dressed up and began making our rounds at several New Years Eve parties. At midnight, my Wife gave me a long sexy kiss and took me by surprise when she told me to enjoy it, for it would be my last kiss.

We immediately went home. She took my wallet, cut up each credit card along with my driver's license. I was ordered to strip and kneel. She took a long chain and locked it around my left ankle. She grabbed my hair and pulled me into the garage, took the other end of the chain and locked it to the bar holding the door in place. It was impossible to remove the chain. I was in this position before during some of our playtimes but this time, there was no escape. My wife then shocked me by giving me a couple of backhands across my face. I became terrified. My wife had a look of determination that I had never seen in her before. She had wanted to do this to me for a long time and now her fantasy was becoming a reality, and her enthusiasm and excitement were obvious.

I was told to stand and not to move until she returned. She told me that she was going back out for more partying but this time by herself, as a single woman. I think two or three hours passed when the door opened. She appeared looking sexy and as desirable as I had ever seen her. She also had a riding crop in her hand. I knew I was in for it. She began to whip me harder than at any time during our previous D/s play. This time her whipping was not erotic, this time it was not play. This time it was real and she was breaking me and I was quickly submitting to her dominance.

Over the weeks and months to follow, my wife continued to break me and transform me from being her husband into being her slave. I loved her as much as ever but I now also feared her. I now clean, cook, do the laundry, iron, answer my Mistress's mail and e-mail. I work a 12 to 18 hour day every day of my life. Do I enjoy it? Yes! I am disciplined daily and punished when necessary. I have lost 35 needed pounds and increased my muscle structure. I follow these simple rules:

1-Obey at once.
2-Mind your business.
3-Stay on your knees with your eyes down.
4-Answer Yes Ma'am or No Ma'am.
5-Speak only when spoken to.
6-Never ever expect sex.
7-There are rewards and punishments-so never complain.

I am now only allowed to kiss her feet as a sign of respect. Anytime she enters or leaves a room in which I am working, I must kneel and wait. She may approach and place her feet under my bowed head, this is a signal to kiss her feet. At times when I've worked extremely hard, she might kiss my head. We are no longer intimate. Yet, I have never been more attracted to her. I see her in a new light, with a fresh adoration and a new respect. In my eyes, she is the sexiest woman alive.

To those who wish for a 24/7 life, it is hard work. You must love your Mistress as well as have lust for her. Lust is all you can have and deserve. Once you are there, there is no getting out. I have no money, no credit cards, no car and have very little clothing. My hair is cut by my Mistress when it's necessary. This lifestyle is hard, frustrating, and at times, painful, but I love it. I get to live what many men only fantasize about. I am truly the slave of a beautiful woman. My wife loves me like this and I love pleasing her."

This is a most interesting story and one of the more extreme FemDom marriages I have encountered. Here you have a happily married man, who introduced his wife to the female domination lifestyle when they were in their twenties. They played D&S games for close to thirty years, which over time caused his wife's previously dormant dominant nature to become aroused and unleashed. She grew in her dominance to have this hunger where she wanted to take her husband from being her part-time submissive to being her full-time slave. Her D&S fantasies and desires surpassed his D&S fantasies and desires. She was the one who wanted to experience having a full-time male slave and she wanted that slave to be her husband. Then once he was retired and had no reason to live in the so-called outside world, his wife seized upon this and made him into the fulfillment of her fantasy. I find this fascinating.

A lot of men do fantasize about being the permanent slave of a beautiful woman but in Darren's case, his wife was the one who had the fantasy of being the owner of a male slave. She had been harboring this desire for over twenty years and their occasional D&S sessions only fueled her desire to make this a reality. His wife obviously has a sadistic side to her dominant nature and she wanted to have a slave whom she could be severe and no nonsense with. And she didn't want just any man to be this slave, she wanted the man that she loved to be this slave. She didn't want to play games with this lifestyle, she wanted it to be a present reality. Now it has become just that. She made her desires a reality and in the process, has made a life for her husband that he finds to be challenging and yet, also fulfilling.

What must run through his mind when she leaves him alone to do chores? Where does she go? He knows that she still has a career but she no longer shares with him the details of her life. He is now her slave and a slave does not have the right to question his Mistress. Where does she go and what does she do when she is not home? Since she is no longer intimate with Darren, does she have a lover? Is he a young lover? Darren must wonder if she is intimate with someone but he does not know and she loves keeping him in the dark. She was intimate with him for thirty years but now no more, for he has become her slave.

Darren is her husband in legality but not in reality. He has surrendered everything over to his wife and she comes and goes as she pleases. His life is not one of leisure. He does not spend his retirement on the golf course. No, his life is about the serving of his Mistress. He must do chores for her, to tend to her house, to spend hours being bound while he reflects on what she may be doing with her liberation.

I find all of this to be fascinating. By being her slave and working for her, Darren actually has a sense of self-worth. He has found contentment and this life is a challenge for him and this life is fulfilling for him. His wife knew the kind of structured life he needed to be content and fulfilled. He is freed from mental responsibility and can focus his energy on pleasing his Mistress. Darren's sexuality is now in worshipping his Mistress and serving her. No more intimacy but his sexual fulfillment comes in submitting to her. His is a life of giving and not getting, yet it is fulfilling because he loves giving of himself in such a pure manner to a woman.

Darren's situation is extreme but not unique. Over my many years of participating in this lifestyle, I have on occasion encountered these types of FemDom arrangements. Such an arrangement obviously leaves the man open to an abusive situation, yet what makes this arrangement work for Darren and his wife is the fact that they first enjoyed many years of marriage and intimacy. They deeply know each other and they first established a relationship of trust. Darren's wife seems harsh and cruel but their track record together allows Darren to trust his wife with this much power and control over him.

Slavery is to lose that position of partnership. Obviously no man loses his free will and in a free society, a man can always walk away from a relationship. Darren is free to walk away from his situation. But to the man who wants to give up his free will to a woman and who can endure a life of total servitude, the thought of walking away will not be an option because the life of being a woman's free-will slave is fulfilling. It is rare but it does exist. Most men never descend to such a depth in their submission but Darren finds his current position to be satisfying and fulfilling. Most men fantasize about being a true 24/7 slave of a woman but the reality is that few men could live it.

Mistress, Queen and Goddess. The nature of a woman is complex, as she is the giver of life, the Nurturer, the Mother, the Wife, and the Matriarch. A woman is kind, tenderhearted, merciful, beautiful and sexual. Society has labeled women as the fairer sex and the weaker sex. But women are also strong, manipulative, selfish, powerful, dominant, aggressive, and authoritative. The submissive male worships a woman for her many moods and submits to her many moods. The male gender craves to submit to loving female authority, no matter how it is expressed.

Chapter Fourteen

Age Regression and Female Authority Figures

When I was a young boy, Said put away those young boy ways; Now that I'm gettin' older, so much older, I love all those young boy days. (John Cougar Mellencamp and G.M. Green, "Hurts So Good")

I'm a Bitch, I'm a Lover, I'm a Child, I'm a Mother! (Meredith Brooks, "Bitch")

One of the questions I ask a male client who has submissive desires is "Can you recall the first time you realized that you wanted to be sexually dominated by a woman?" Quite often, the male's answer will be an experience from his childhood that involved an adult female authority figure. Briefly, here are few responses:

From Brian: *"When I was ten years old, I was sick in a hospital. There was this one nurse who was absolutely beautiful. I remember that as she was taking my temperature and performing basic medical procedures on me while I was passive in the hospital bed, I became attracted to her. I desired to be dominated by her. She was the first woman that I recall having sexual fantasies about. Even after I was discharged from the hospital, I would lay awake at home and fantasize about her as I played with my body. In my fantasies, she would dominate me and have sex with me. I have no idea why I had such desires about her but I guess it was because I was so helpless to her when I was in the hospital. I never saw her again but I loved her from afar for the next year."*

From John: *"I had this teacher in junior high school. She was a brunette and she was incredibly sexy. She'd wear tight blouses, tight skirts and sexy high-heel shoes. I remember one day when she wore a leather skirt to class and it drove me crazy. I think she dressed this way to tease the boys in her class. I had such a crush on her. I use to stay after class and volunteer to do things for her because I just wanted to be near her. I felt weak and very submissive toward her. I would fantasize about her all the time and she was the object of my thoughts the first time I ever masturbated."*

From Richard: *"I had this sister who was six years older than me. My parents would assign each of us chores but my sister would make me do hers when my parents were not home, and she would take the credit. When I was eleven, she was a senior in high school. She was very bossy toward me and I loved it. Most little brothers would fight with their older sisters but not me. I would do anything for her. I was attracted to her and the meaner she treated me, the more I loved her.*

I remember when she would sunbathe in our driveway. She would lie on a chase-lounge right under my bedroom window. I would stand on my bed and peek out the window and stare at her beautiful body. As I look back, I feel ashamed about it now but back then, it seemed like the natural thing to do. She was a Goddess in my eyes. Now that we are older and both have families, we enjoy a very close brother/sister relationship. She has no idea that I once fantasized about her. I would hang around her just to be near her. I loved it when she bossed me around and ordered me to do chores for her. Those are some of the best memories from my childhood."

From Darrell: *"I had this Aunt who was really built. She was a very dominant woman and she would boss my Uncle around. My father would make jokes behind their backs about how my Aunt had his brother by the nose. It bothered my father but I loved being near my Aunt. Our families would camp together every summer and I would love spending time with my Aunt. As I came into puberty, I loved watching her swim in the river as she wore this tight one-piece bathing suit and I remember seeing her nipples through the swimsuit. She often displayed quite a bit of cleavage. I remember that I would lie in my tent at night and hump the air mattress, pretending that my Aunt was sitting on top of me in her one-piece bathing suit, bossing me around like she did my Uncle."*

I have counseled many males over the years that had some variance of the Adult Woman/young boy fantasy. Probably the most common ones are the Babysitter/little boy and the Teacher/pupil fantasies. The Aunt/nephew, Mommy/son, and Governess/teenager are also popular among submissive men.

This fantasy revolves around female authority and it usually involves some sexual elements. When a male is an adolescent and is coming of age sexually, his first sexual fantasies are usually geared toward the adult females in his life. Some boys become sexually attracted to their Babysitters, Teachers, Aunts, older Sisters and even their Mothers. A boy's first orgasm might be through masturbating at the fantasy of having sex with one of the female authority figures in his life. It might even be with an article of the Female Guardian's clothing, such as a bra, panties or pantyhose.

Besides the sexual aspects of this fantasy, there is almost always domination and discipline involved. The submissive male that has this fantasy wants to submit to the adult woman's authority. Some submissive men enjoy travelling back in time in their minds to become a boy again, and they want to be spanked by the babysitter, smacked with a ruler by the teacher, paddled by his mother or female guardian and possibly caned by his Governess. The discipline by his female authority figure adds to his submissive and sexual desires toward her.

There is usually a form of the desire to submit mixed in with the sexuality. A young boy is accustomed to being bossed around and dominated by the adult female authority figures in his life. Then when he begins to enter puberty, his sexual fantasies often involve being the helpless victim to an adult female authority figure. He fantasizes that she has her way with him and thus teaches him the facts of life from her experienced and skillful authority position. Not all boys start out their sexual exploration with these types of fantasies but it is surprising how many boys do.

When these boys grow up to be men with submissive desires, they often still maintain the fantasy of being an innocent and helpless boy that is being dominated and sexually used by an adult female authority figure. They recall that their first submissive desires were toward their Teacher, Babysitter or Mother and they remember how pleasurable and exciting it was to have these fantasies and sexual dreams. As these males discover sexually oriented Adult magazines and videos, it is the stories and scenes where an older women dominates a young boy or younger man that causes them the most intense sexual arousal.

Roxanne receives numerous calls from submissive men looking to role-play an Adult Woman/young boy scenario. Roxanne's phone clients tell her which Female Authority Figure they wish for her to role-play and she takes on the role of Teacher, Mother, Aunt or Babysitter while her callers take on the role of themselves when they were a young boy. Then she pretends to sexually dominate these men while they pretend to be boys.

"In my experience, it seems that a substantial percentage of my clients who want age play sessions are seeking to satisfy a need that has been unfulfilled since they were young. They are usually seeking one or any combination of the following -- nurturing, approval, sex, and/or discipline. Their favorite scenarios are Mother/son, Aunt/nephew, and Teacher/student, and their "fantasy" ages range from 6 to 18 years of age.

Interestingly, a small number of the men I speak with tell me that their fantasies are based on events they experienced in their youth. One gentleman was sent to stay with his Aunt one summer when he was 15, and his Aunt was very attractive. She had shapely legs and she would always wear shorts and sandals. He developed a juvenile crush on her and began fantasizing about her when he masturbated. While nothing every came of it in reality, he still fantasizes about her and feels the need to play it out with me over the phone.

A similar Aunt/nephew scenario turns more incestuous. My client reverts back to about 17 years of age and he visits his attractive Aunt while his Uncle is at work. The Aunt tells him to wait in the living room while she goes upstairs and changes her clothes. He disobeys her instructions, climbs the stairs, peeks into his Aunt's bedroom, and sees her in her nylons and slip. He sneaks into the room and ultimately his Aunt seduces him.

Another client of mine prefers the teacher/student scenario in which I am his attractive teacher and he is about 12 years of age. We are alone in a classroom and I take down his pants and put him over my lap. His need is for extreme corporal punishment, and he is looking for permission to cry and exorcise the guilt he is feeling. This would seem an impossible scenario via the telephone, but his need is so strong that he actually punishes himself with a large wooden paddle during our phone session.

Age play is complex and fascinating, and men have myriad reasons that compel them to act out in this fashion. Whether it is nurturing, approval, sex or punishment they are seeking, many men will use age play to search their own souls until some semblance of satisfaction is attained."

Roxanne asked me once if I could explain why so many men request this service for she was blown away at how common this desire was within the male gender. To be perfectly honest and blunt about it, most of these men wish that an older woman would have had sex with them when they were boys. They often fantasize that it was an experienced older woman who taught them how to sexually please a woman. Some of these men never felt comfortable being the aggressor that society dictates they be when it comes to the opposite sex. They prefer to be passive and helpless when having sex. The Adult Woman/young boy fantasy is a place where they can be innocent and passive while worshipping and discovering the mystery that is the female in all her beauty and authority.

Unfortunately, a lot of the erotic literature that deals with these fantasies has been censored by our society under the rightful concern and need to protect children from child pornography and child molestation. The fear of these very strict laws prevent most new adult erotic literature that deals with the Adult woman/young boy fantasy from being created. That is too bad because this particular fantasy is not about a little boy being molested but rather an adult man hearkening back to when women were in authority over him and his coming of age sexually. It is sad that society does not wish to understand this common male desire and draw the clear distinctions. Most of these men wish that they were the helpless victims of a loving and authoritative woman. Such erotica needs to be free from censorship as it might assist men in discovering more about their submissive desires.

Of course, this common male fantasy is still expressed in some tastefully written mainstream books and movies. Men have told me about their sexual arousal when reading about or watching the Older woman/younger man scenes in "The Boys of Summer", "The Graduate",

"The Summer of 42", "My Tutor" and other such books and films. While such scenes primarily deal with teenager and young adult male encounters with older and more experienced women, some literature does push the envelope. The purpose of such erotica is not intended to encourage a premature sexual encounter between an adult woman and an under-aged boy, but rather for the purpose of expressing this common submissive desire, which is within most red-blooded males.

Society never learns that when something is taboo or forbidden, it only makes the forbidden fruit more desirable. Of course all child pornography must be banned and never produced as society needs to protect children from being exploited but adult erotica that deals with this natural and common part of a boy's adolescence needs to be uncensored and better understood. The censorship that is taking place today is only fanning this fantasy within men, as one cannot censor the submissive male's mind. That is why men seek out an understanding and caring woman to assist them in exploring this fantasy within a safe environment. It is actually a healthy thing for this fantasy to be role played between two consenting adults. The male never got to experience this taboo fantasy as a boy but he can live it through role-playing it with an Adult woman. That is why Age Play is commonly requested by submissive men when they call a Female Domination phone service or when they visit a professional Dominatrix.

Victoria has role-played the Adult Female/young boy fantasy with a number of her paying clients. When one thinks of the professional Dominatrix, the mental image of leather, whips and elaborate bondage equipment comes to mind. However, Victoria conducts just as many domination sessions in a softer, more eloquent atmosphere. Every man has a unique submissive nature and that nature is expressed differently within each man's sexuality. Victoria is skilled in all explorations of the male submissive nature and Age Play is a rather common request from her Adult male clients.

"I would have to say that the Female Teacher/male pupil and the Female Babysitter/little boy are the two most requested role-playing scenarios that men request when it comes to age play. First, I get into character. I might be Britney, a twenty-one year old college student who has been hired to baby-sit young Billy. Most men want to regress back to being

somewhere between the ages of ten and sixteen. I like for the male to go back in his mind to the time he was coming into puberty.

I might pull my hair back in a ponytail to look like a young college student. I might dress in a tee-shirt and tight, form fitting shorts to further look the part. I pretend to be an out going, aggressive young woman who at this early age, has already realized that females are superior to men. I am going to find young Billy to be very cute. I pretend that Britney is attracted to little Billy but Britney doesn't really care for boys. They treated her bad when she was their age and now that she is older and has dated, Britney has come to really dislike the way boys and men are always bossing her around. Britney is attracted to men physically but she doesn't like their attitudes or mannerisms. I explain this to my client to set up my character.

I then begin to role-play with William as he pretends to be young Billy. I strike up a conversation with him like any babysitter would to a new boy whom she is responsible in overseeing. I tell him that I think he's cute and I pinch his cheeks. Then I tell him that he's been bad. I tell him that all boys are bad and should be punished. I ask him if his mother ever spanks him. He might say Yes or he might say No. It doesn't matter. I tell him that I think he deserves to be punished and that I am going to give him a spanking. I will order him to undress for me and once he is naked, I will laugh at how small his little penis is. I might tease,

"My little Billy, how will you ever please a woman with such a little wee-wee. You had better hope it grows as you do."

Grown men will turn beet-red from embarrassment as I humiliate them in this way. I might next tell young Billy that it feels hot in his room and I need to get comfortable before I spank him. I will then remove my shirt to reveal my bra. I will grab William (young Billy) and pull him over my lap. I might take my hairbrush or just use my hand and I will proceed to give Billy a spanking. I tell young Billy how bad he is and I give him a good, hard, old-fashioned spanking while I lecture him. I tell him how much stronger I am than he is and how I enjoy paddling his dear little butt. After I feel William has been spanked long enough, I release him and I might stand before him, with my hands on my hips. I may say to him something like,

"What are you staring at, you little pervert? Haven't you ever seen a girl in her bra before?"

Once again, such talk will cause a grown man to become embarrassed, almost as if he were a little boy. Most of the time the mature male will turn his head in shame or stare at the floor from his embarrassment. This is part of the role-playing process as he begins to travel back to the innocent days of being a little boy who is discovering his sexuality. There is guilt mixed in with his excitement. He recalls feeling guilty about desiring his babysitter but he is also sexually excited. Most men will become erect as I talk to them as if they were little boys. Then I will take the role-playing from the discipline over to the sexual. I might say,

"This is why I am superior to you, Billy. I have a masterpiece for a body, don't I? Would you like to touch me, Billy?"

William will probably be in subspace by now and I will make him beg me for the right to touch my body. Since this is professional Domination, no sexual contact can occur so I have to play the tease.

"Touching me is forbidden Billy, because you are too young. My, such dirty little thoughts coming from such a young mind. I am afraid I must spank you again to drive those impure thoughts out of you."

I will then pull him back across my lap for some more spanking. Men eat this up as they sigh with pleasure and purr with contentment as I role-play these Adult Female/young boy scenarios with them."

So how does this fantasy come into play as far as an actual FemDom relationship is concerned? One can imagine the many different directions such a role-playing scenario could venture if it were between a wife and her husband within the private walls of their bedroom. Wives who discover that their husbands have this particular fantasy might want to consider role-playing the Adult woman/male child fantasy. It can create an incredible bond of intimacy as well as being very fulfilling to the submissive man who has a desire for Age play. Besides adding some spice to the bedroom, such role-playing can actually be productive within the wife/husband relationship. The goal of these fantasies is not only to re-visit a man's childhood and thus explore the beginnings of his submissive nature, but it will also program the male psyche that the wife is also a female authority figure. This is important for such role-playing can help the male to make the connection that he need not fantasize about his childhood to be under the control of loving females, but by submitting to his spouse, he is living the reality of being under the control of a loving female.

By role-playing that she is the Babysitter, the Teacher, the Nurse, the Governess, the Mommy and other such Female Authority Figures, a woman can be instilling into her submissive husband that the Wife is also a Female Authority Figure who can administer both love and discipline. Besides being a lot of fun, this kind of role-playing can be healthy from an emotional standpoint.

Roxanne and Victoria primarily role-play with their clients the Adult Female/adolescent male scenario, as it is during this timeframe in a young man's life that he begins to feel sexual desires toward his Female Authority Figures. However, another form of Age Play is Infantilism. This involves the role-playing of a Mother and her infant son.

When a male enjoys playing the role of an infant (infantilism) he craves to be cuddled, cared for, and to regress back to the earliest stages of his childhood. A grown man playing the role of a submissive baby could be seen by some as being embarrassing or demeaning, but an adult male may have a need to play the role of a baby or little schoolboy. Infantilism is a way for a submissive man to express emotions that are normally forbidden to him. Given society's constant demands on men to be masculine, to take charge, and to succeed, it is no wonder that even the strongest and brightest male may seek contact with his hidden softer self in his relationship to a Mommy's firm but kindly rule.

Believe it or not, some women enjoy easing (or forcing) their husbands into an adorable role of being an infant. Women are by nature nurturing and even some vanilla wives enjoy babying their husbands to some degree. This is especially true if no actual children exist in their home. Within Female Domination, Infantilism is a chance for the Dominant Female to gain more control and power in her marriage by treating her husband more as her male child, thus he is no threat to ever be her equal. In most cases, Infantilism is primarily a form of role-playing. One benefit to getting the male to regress back to being an infant, the wife may be able to uncover the root of his submissive nature and thus be able to understand and thus utilize it to her advantage.

So what would make a man gladly submit to (or even crave) this kind of treatment? The reasons can be numerous. First, there is the joy of escaping into a fantasy world. Second, there is the sheer sensual delight of the emotional risk and the physical stimulation. Finally, there is the bliss of sharing the deepest possible intimacy and trust between two people. If the male will truly surrender and fall into the infant role, he will get to see and experience the loving and nurturing side of the female nature. As an adult male role-playing an infant, he will be able to truly appreciate the beauty and the love that the female ministers as a Mommy. This will bring him comfort and contentment and can even heal any wounds that were caused in his own childhood if he lacked that love and nurturing from his natural Mother. The babied male enjoys being "Mommied" because it feels good from an emotional and psychological standpoint. His reward is sexual and mental pleasure of an intense and prolonged nature. Some of the components of that pleasure may be the desire for discipline (like spankings or punitive enemas) but even the humiliation and the punishment is pleasurable because they promote a psychological surrender to the female.

Without trust, a Mommy/male baby relationship is impossible. Only trust allows the partners to discuss their fantasies in the first place, much less act them out in great detail. If the fantasy entails some humiliation or pain, the deepest possible trust is necessary to make the relationship work. In fact, one cannot imagine a truly satisfying Mommy/male baby relationship outside the bounds of marriage or a long-term commitment. By giving himself over to his Mommy, a male is saying, "I trust you completely."

Infantilism is not a common lifestyle but there are couples who enjoy this practice. Melissa and Patrick engage in Infantilism and for them it has gone from just role-playing to become an actual lifestyle. Melissa shares their story.

"When I first met Patrick, I was twenty years old, working as an exotic dancer in a cabaret, not far from the refinery where he was employed as an engineer, here in San Francisco. He was a small but intelligent man. My sheer physical size and strength assured my dominance of the

relationship from the beginning and he was mine from the first lap-dance. Within two weeks, I required him to move in with me and our love culminated in marriage six weeks subsequent. I then proceeded to take total control over the course of our honeymoon and he loved it. We have now been happily married for over twenty years.

Patrick recognized from the beginning that both my native intelligence and career ambitions were superior to his own and he willingly conceded to my preeminence as Head of Household. Although successful in his own right, both as an engineer and later as an engineering manager, he simply is not comfortable in a position of authority or leadership. Away from work, he has never shown any real skill or even interest in the exercise of power and authority, which to me has always seemed so perfectly natural and easy. It was thus with relative ease that our marriage soon settled into its essentially Matriarchal pattern that enabled me to launch my own career. I simply informed Patrick that I intended to go to college, attend law school and become an attorney at his expense. I required him to pay for my education, provide me with tutoring in several subjects, furnish me with a car for transportation and maintain an ample spending allowance for myself.

This career decision and the attendant financial arrangements also helped establish the First Rule of Our Relationship: We discuss; I decide; he obeys. In cases where my mind is already made up, or I feel strongly about a particular issue, the need for discussion is obviated and Patrick is simply informed. This eliminates the need for discussion in about seventy percent of all cases, allows Patrick to concentrate on his engineering career and leaves other issues in my far more capable hands. My decision to require that Patrick underwrite my education went very far in establishing my Authority and re-enforcing my complete control over him. At no time has he ever resented this arrangement and has always accepted it natural and logical. This pliability of character, his easy-going manner and child-like naivete are all very endearing to me, and through the years have steadily deepened the bonds between us. I do love him so much!

Upon graduation from law school with honors, I obtained a position as an associate attorney with a prominent firm here in San Francisco, at which I became a junior partner in less than two years. Thus I began to eclipse Patrick professionally and financially, as his engineering career had already passed its zenith. It was thus inevitable that I should take complete control of our finances, as my law practice was now the principal source of income. I soon realized that control of our income and assets meant much more than just financial freedom -- it meant complete freedom! Professional and intellectual freedom assured me continued success in my already burgeoning law practice. Financial freedom awarded me the power of investment to secure my future and my now rapidly rising standard of living. More importantly, it meant the freedom to determine and to live my own lifestyle. To enjoy such complete social freedom and such complete moral freedom also secured its highest, final and ultimate expression -- My complete sexual freedom!

This too was a Defining Moment and, like its predecessor, it set forth the Second Rule of Our Relationship: We have Absolutes; I have absolute freedom; he accepts and lives under My absolute control; this applies to all aspects; there are no exceptions. From the beginning, my sexual needs, energy and performance levels far exceeded his own and these disparities have, of course, progressively increased over time. This was hardly surprising given the difference in our ages. Patrick was realistic enough, not only to accept this, but actively encouraged the exercise of my new-found sexual freedom.

Consistency with the exercise of my sexual freedom and my now-Maternal relationship with Patrick, of course, required the formalization of my marriage and, for him, a program of male chastity. I had already initiated a progressive reduction in his conjugal activity as early as my first year of law school, in favor of supervised masturbation privileges. These too, however, I was determined to eliminate as well, in favor of bi-weekly milkings. This, I explained, was necessary to move his love for me to a higher plane and to afford me closer control. You cannot imagine my happiness when, on hearing this, he simply broke down and cried. In his tearful acceptance, I now saw there would never be resistance to me or to My Authority.

This redefinition of my marriage took nearly a full year to implement, and required a considerable effort on both our parts, which ultimately proved very rewarding. Patrick's journey into total submission to me led us to Infantilism. We each have roles. I, Mother-Goddess, loving, but always strict; He, the small, adoring and obedient child. The redefinition of my marriage completed, I now pursued both my law career and my freedom with renewed vigor. During the next three years, I became a full partner, made numerous successful investments and completed My Doctorate of Legal Letters. I remodeled my home, adding numerous objet d'arte and expanded it to palatial proportions with the addition of two large wings. My name was added to the San Francisco Social Register, greatly increasing both the number and quality of my social contacts and commensurately widening my erotic opportunities.

I filled out and, with routine workouts, toned up my already voluptuous body. I now resembled a large, muscular version of Anita Ekberg or Melanie Griffith. This I set off with a complete new wardrobe complete with business attire, evening gowns, expensive jewelry and, of course, lingerie. My sexual rebirth was wonderfully gratifying to me both physically and psychologically. My lovers included professionals, businessmen, and other celebrities.

Patrick's infantilization is a logical derivative of this process. For several years now, my relationship with him has steadily evolved in a progressively maternal direction. Infantilism has enabled Patrick and I to enjoy a very special and close relationship."

The wife or woman who enacts the Mommy role enjoys the intoxicating sensation of complete power over her grown male baby. Few males are as readily dominated as the adult baby. Moreover, in this fantasy the Mommy and baby are unusually close and intimate. If the Dominant Female has never had children of her own, this sort of role-playing (and in some cases lifestyle) affords her the chance to release and develop more of her nurturing nature. Some women really enjoy this activity as it fulfills a part of them. One thing is for certain, Infantilism will definitely form a powerful and intimate bond between the Dominant Wife and her submissive husband. It will elevate the woman to an authority position and the man will look at his wife as not only his life partner, but as also his superior guardian. As Melissa has discovered, this can cause a real power exchange and give the woman a real advantage within the marriage.

Chapter Fifteen

Leather Sex: Fetishism and BDSM

One of these days these Boots are gonna walk all over you. (Nancy Sinatra, "These Boots Are Made For Walkin")

Sometimes love don't feel like it should, You make it hurt so good. (John Cougar Mellencamp and G.M. Green, "Hurts So Good")

A man is so visually image oriented, that the mere viewing of a woman in fetish clothing can bring out his submissive nature. There was some research done on this. Many years ago, I read an article in a Fetish publication about a research project done by professional dominant women where they measured the level of submission in men. What they did was they gave each client that visited them a scale ranging from 1 to 10, with 1 being a little submissive and 10 being extremely submissive. The submissive man would verbally tell the dominant woman what number he felt after she performed various D&S activities on him. What the dominant women found was that they could get a man to go from 1 to 6 or 7 simply by putting on a fetish outfit. The sight of a woman dressed in a sexy leather outfit or a sexy latex outfit caused these men to become weak. This makes sense from a psychological standpoint because men are so visually oriented. That is why pornography is more popular with men than with women. Men can become extremely aroused (or submissive) by mere sight. So if a woman wants to take her man to subspace so she can more easily have her way with him, she will get him there much faster if she dons a fetish outfit.

Another advantage of the fetish outfit is the effect it can have on the dominant woman. A woman who puts on a fetish outfit is basically putting on power. This is particularly true for beginners in this lifestyle. The nervous and unsure woman who knows little about D&S may begin to feel powerful when she dresses in a sexy, fetish outfit. As she views herself in the mirror, she will see that she radiates power and sexuality and this may give her more confidence. Attitude is the key when dominating a man and a woman who looks powerful will feel powerful and the woman who feels powerful will be powerful. No man can overcome a woman who looks dominant and gives off an aura of dominance. The fetish outfit can assist in these goals.

Female Domination is more about a woman's attitude than her outfit. A woman who knows who she is and what she is about will command attention and submission from a man, regardless of her attire. Nevertheless, men are visually oriented and the outfits and props can greatly assist a woman as she uses a man's fetish to stir his submissive nature. It is not so much the clothes but rather the energy a woman perceives coming from the man when he sees her in the fetish outfit. The attire gives the woman an edge and she can use that edge to her advantage during a D&S scene.

If the appearance of a woman in a fetish outfit causes a man to become overpowered with submission, it would be foolish not to use this weapon against him. Attitude is the key and a woman can dominate a man with her looks, her aura, her voice, and her sexuality. The tools and the toys are there to assist.

Once a couple becomes experienced in this lifestyle, the need for fetish outfits are not as necessary. Since attitude is the key, the woman who is secure in her dominance will learn how to take her man to subspace by getting inside of his head and stimulating his submissive triggers by using her voice or utilizing other more subtle methods. The experienced dominant woman develops an aura and her need to wear fetish outfits will become less. The experienced dominant woman wears fetish outfits for the purpose to exploit the fetish in her man or to merely dress up to add some fun and spice to the session. Each woman needs to learn what triggers will stir a man's submission and each woman needs to utilize those triggers to her benefit.

While I have been unable to find any official statistics, based on my research, the number one so-called fetish among submissive men is the fetish for boots. Submissive men love women in boots. Submissive men say that a woman wearing leather boots (especially those of the thigh-high variety) portrays dominance. Boots are a symbol of female power and superiority. Men have been known to become physically and mentally weak by just the sight of a woman wearing leather boots. Leather is a powerful fetish in itself and leather boots makes this fetish within submissive men an even stronger fetish.

Most men find the female leg to be quite sexual. Encase the female leg in leather boots with high heels which enhance the female buttocks, and most submissive men are overcome by the woman's sexuality. To the submissive and masochist male, the female boot is also a weapon. It is sexy in appearance but the spiked heels are dangerous weapons as "these boots are gonna walk all over you." The appearance of a woman in boots enslaves a man and then the heels of the boots can torture the captive man.

Some women develop a fetish for wearing boots. I know women who wear boots everywhere they go. Boots can be very sexy, erotic, and powerful. A woman wearing boots can sense the submissive energy and sexual arousal coming from men. This makes a woman feel desirable and powerful. I must confess that I have quite a collection of boots. Thigh-high, Knee-high, Ankle-high, and I even own a pair of Crotch-high boots. Boots make me feel powerful and sexy. Maybe it's due to how submissive some men become when they see me wearing a pair of boots. Men can't resist a dominant woman wearing leather and they really go nuts over a woman who wears boots. Sometimes it's fun to put on a pair of boots, rent a good movie, and have my submissive worship my boots while I watch the movie. Submissive men with a boot fetish love to lick boots, plant sweet kisses all over them and even suck the stiletto heels. That can be a real turn-on for a woman to watch a man be overcome with passion as he worships her boots. Boot worship makes for great foreplay prior to female body worship.

It has been said that a fetish is when one has erotic feelings for a non-sexual object. If that is the definition of a fetish, then it might be hard to classify boots as a fetish because the boot was designed to highlight the sexuality of the female foot and leg. Thigh-high, spiked heel boots were designed for one reason and one reason only, to arouse the sexual appetite and the submissive nature of man. Men created boots for the female to wear for his own sexual pleasure. As was the case with the corset, I find it ironic that so many men have been enslaved by their own creation. Boots make women look so sexual and dominant that a lot of men become frozen and helpless in their desire to submit. With boots, women have once again used a man's fetish against him as a woman uses her assets and her sexual power to render a man helpless.

The number one fetish material is leather. Leather is the hide of an animal made into a smooth and sexy material. When a woman is adorned in leather, it sends off psychological and subliminal messages to the submissive male. It contains an animalistic meaning, as the traditional hunter is now the hunted. When a woman wears leather and disciplines a man, it represents the female conquering and dominating the male. Other common fetish outfits are comprised of latex or PVC. Men love the look of a black and shiny material covering the sexy curves of the female form. Leather is also quite flattering to the female form that is not the perfect shape. A larger woman looks sexy and powerful when adorned in leather.

Leather Sex has come to be identified with those couples who enjoy a more physical and rougher form of Domination and submission. S&M and B&D are considered Leather Sex. Obviously a man can become submissive and a woman can enjoy wearing leather without participating in Leather Sex. A fetish does not dictate the totality of a person's nature or desires. However, for the purpose of this chapter, we will focus on those FemDom couples who enjoy the rough stuff and who can be identifiable to the BDSM lifestyle.

BDSM is a pansexual lifestyle and one only need attend a BDSM support group to see the many variations of lifestyles represented. Female Domination is only one of many lifestyles. Men dominate women, men dominate men and women dominate women, but the driving force of D&S, Fetish and BDSM groups are the many submissive men in search of a dominant woman.

A male masochist has been said to be the inspiration of the entire S&M movement. The German neurologist Richard von Krafft-Ebing coined the word "Masochist" in his "Psychopathia Sexualis" (1886) from the sexual desires of Leopold von Sacher-Masoch. The word "Sadist" was coined from the life and fantasies of Marquis de Sade, who lived one hundred years prior to Sacher-Masoch. It was understood in psychology that some gained pleasure in hurting others but until Krafft-Ebing, it was never classified that some might gain pleasure in pain. He defined Masochism as mostly imaginary pleasure in pain. Krafft-Ebing coined the words Sadism and Masochism from the names of Marquis de Sade and Sacher-Masoch. Krafft-Ebing connected them as two sides of the same coin, but were the desires of Leopold von Sacher-Masoch the opposite match of the fantasies of Marquis de Sade?

When one reads the works of Sacher-Masoch, it is apparent that he longed to be dominated by a woman. Sure, he wanted to be whipped by a sexy female as she was adorned in furs and he wanted her to humiliate him, but as we have examined throughout this book, such desires are rather common within man. Sacher-Masoch was a gifted writer who happened to express his fantasies through the written word, but how many men had similar submissive fantasies which remained hidden within their own souls? Krafft-Ebing recognized that such a form of sexuality was common enough that a word was needed to classify such sexual desires. However, Sacher-Masoch was not the Yang to the Ying of Marquis de Sade. Marquis de Sade wrote of rape, murder and torturing women for sexual pleasure. Sade chose to personify and identify the animal world with that of mankind. Sade's pessimism in humanity came from his own persecution and imprisonment at the hands of the elite aristocracy.

Sade's "Juliette" was one of his most ardent attempts to explore the depths of how far the limits of morality could be stretched. Her journey throughout the novel is begun as an investigation of the human body. Every inch of the flesh is defiled over and over again. In one particular disconcerting moment, the house of a Duc is visited where Juliette is flogged and molested to an inch of her life in a room where bodies are recklessly thrown around. Over blood pouring from Juliette's flayed buttocks, the Duc screams,

"By the guts of Almighty God, I have no great fondness for women; if God made them, why can't I exterminate them?... I see blood and I am happy... (Juliette, 197)."

Now contrast this to the works of Leopold von Sacher-Masoch. In "Venus in Furs", he wrote of a man who loved women so much, that he wanted to be the slave of a woman. He felt inadequate to be superior or even the equal of a woman because he esteemed women to be so beautiful and so mysterious, almost Goddess-like.

"Overcome by desire I fell at her feet and threw my arms about her. "Yes, you have brought my dearest dream to life!" I cried. "It has slept long enough."

"And that dream is -- ?" She laid her hand on my neck. The pressure of her warm hand, and the tender searching gaze she bent on me through half-closed eyes, filled me with a delicious vertigo.

"To be the slave of a woman, a beautiful woman whom I love, whom I worship!"

Sacher-Masoch lived at a time when men ruled women but he was not comfortable in that role. He wanted women to rule him. He wanted to be abused by a woman because he felt guilty about the sins of the patriarchy. He was in need of loving female authority.

It is a great injustice to link Sacher-Masoch to Marquis de Sade. The submissive male may desire a female sadist but his motivation and psychological need for abuse at the hand of a woman is rooted in man's longing for loving female authority. Sacher-Masoch saw women in the spiritual and saw their divinity, thus his fascination with the Goddess Venus. Sade saw mankind as animalistic and he wrote of man's lowest qualities, as the strong prey on the weak. Sacher-Masoch elevated women by degrading himself. Marquis de Sade degraded women as he sought to degrade both society and religion.

The term Sadomasochism (S&M) forever links the desires of a sadistic man with the desires of a masochistic man. Yet, the masochistic man wanted to be whipped and humiliated by a beautiful woman, whom he felt inferior although he lived during a time when men believed they were superior. The desires of Sacher-Masoch were spiritual in origin. The desires of Sade were animalistic. Thus these two men were worlds apart in their sexuality.

Since most people who engage in S&M in our society are eager to talk about the spiritual aspects of their lifestyle and how they practice a safe, sane and consensual form of sexuality, it is difficult to label such a sexuality with the desires and writings of Marquis de Sade. Although his life is held up as a celebration of sexual thought and freedom by those who practice S&M, his obvious disdain for women and his pessimistic view of the human condition only lends itself to the negative perception that most of society holds toward the term S&M. In stark contrast, the writings and desires of Sacher-Masoch are a better representation of what those involved in the BDSM community want to convey to society. Namely, a Dominant/submissive relationship based on mutual love and trust.

In reality, S&M started out as an underground group of purely dominant women and submissive men based on the writings of Sacher-Masoch. Over the years, S&M has changed to become pan-sexual where either a male or a female could be dominant and either a male or a female could be submissive. But S&M originally stood for a sadistic woman and a masochistic male based primarily on Sacher-Masoch's book "Venus in Furs".

In the early 1900's, there was an underground society in Europe called the SM Society. Little is known about this society but it is believed that a wealthy German man who had submissive and masochistic desires founded the SM Society. Domination was popular and prevalent in Germany prior to the reign of the repressive regime of Hitler's Third Reich. In the 1920's, one could walk down certain streets in Berlin and see whip wielding women standing in door ways or standing in open windows, inviting men inside for a session of professional female domination. It was during this time that German women gained a worldwide reputation as being tough, no-nonsense Dominantly Frauen (Dominant Women).

German men of high society would never frequent one of the flogging houses in Berlin for fear of being recognized, therefore the wealthy male who desired to be flogged by a woman would pay to have Dominantly Frauen come to him. According to the unofficial story about the SM Society, a wealthy German man had an affair with one of the Dominantly Frauen. Together, they started the SM Society where other Female Sadist/male masochist couples would join to share in their common sexual interests. The SM Society was a kind of a forerunner to the many BDSM groups that exist today. However, in the 1920's such an organization had to be totally underground and secretive. The popularity of the SM Society spread from Germany to Austria and eventually to other European countries like England. The oppression of Hitler's Nazi Party closed down the flogging houses of Germany, launched a World War across Europe and the SM Society was never heard from again. However, its influence continued as the couples of the SM Society no doubt secretly practiced female sadism and male masochism within the privacy of their homes.

Those who are familiar with Stanley Kubrick's 1999 film "Eyes Wide Shut" that starred Tom Cruise and Nicole Kidman might not know that Kubrick based his movie on the 1926 novel "Traumnovelle" (Dream Story) by the Austrian Arthur Schnitzler. Schnitzler was a close friend of fellow Viennese Dr. Sigmund Freud. Schnitzler and Freud were both aware of the stories about secret sex societies within the aristocratic society of Germany and Austria. The New York secret sex society featured in "Eyes Wide Shut" was taken from Schnitzler's book "Traumnovelle", which featured a secret sex society in 1920 Austria. Schnitzler's inspiration could have been a number of stories and rumors about aristocratic sex societies that supposedly existed in Germany and Austria. The SM Society was rumored to be one such secret society, which was comprised of wealthy men with masochistic desires and the sadistic women who would dominate them.

While it is impossible to prove, the name "SM Society" was more than likely derived from the name of the author who greatly influenced the wealthy German who founded this secret organization. That author would be none other than Sacher-Masoch and his book "Venus in Furs" no doubt was a major influence on those couples who became involved in the SM Society. While it is possible that the S in SM Society stood for Sadist since the female members of the SM Society did engage in sadistic practices with their masochist male partners, it is more probable that the S stood for Sacher and the M stood for Masoch.

Sacher-Masoch was Austrian and it is rumored that the SM Society was active in both Germany and Austria. Since Sacher-Masoch died in 1895, he obviously had no part in the secret society that bore his initials. However, I think it is safe to assume that his works and his life were the inspiration for this Society's name. It is interesting to note how popular the Dominatrix remains in Germany today. Perhaps only the United States has more practicing Professional Dominant women. The Dominantly Frauen is alive and well in Germany in the new millennium.

After World War II, the Female Domination lifestyle reemerged, particularly in England. Fetish and Female Domination publications became popular in Europe and by the late 1940's, Fetish publications began to surface in the United States. From the late 1940s through the 1960s, Irving Klaw did a brisk business selling photos and films of attractive women being both dominant and submissive, wearing bizarre leather, rubber and satin outfits. Klaw was a New York City cheesecake photographer and publisher who began his business (Movie Star News) in 1947. One of his chief models was the popular pinup girl Bettie Page. She often played the Dominatrix, wearing leather and high heels. In 1955 she won the title "Miss Pin-up Girl of the World." In January 1955, she was the centerfold in Playboy's January issue. She was nicknamed the "Girl with the Perfect Figure." It is estimated that Irving Klaw burned over 80% of his photos when the government went after him as a pornographer in the early 60's.

In the 1950's, Leonard Burtman created the fetish magazine "Exotique". Burtman presented the pin-up as a Femme Fatale and a Dominatrix. Illustration artists Eric Stanton and Gene Bilbrew created FemDom drawings and comics for Butman's "Exotique". It was men like Burtman, Klaw, Stanton and Bilbrew who introduced the American public to kinky sex and dominant women, which triggered the submissive desires within countless numbers of men.

In the 1960's, Leonard Burtman published the fetish magazine "Bizarre Life". Burtman formed a friendship with English fetish clothing designer John Sutcliffe who produced custom made leather outfits, boots, corsets, and cat-suits. Sutcliffe designed the sexy, leather outfits for Emma Peel in "The Avengers" television series. Sutcliffe provided many of the outfits worn by the American and English models in Burtman's "Bizarre Life". Burtman's publication featured not only FemDom photos but also FemDom stories and personal ads.

In my research, I discovered a number of small, intimate FemDom groups that existed in the United States as far back as the late 1950's.

While the origin of these groups cannot be traced with any certainty, it is my belief that their roots can be attributed to the SM Society of 1920 Germany. These groups primarily flourished within the more affluent circles of European and American societies during and after the war. Most FemDom groups were very small and very secretive. Some groups consisted of no more than two or three couples. New York and California were the breeding grounds for these groups in the United States and the introduction of Fetish and FemDom magazines provided for the first time a vehicle in which these underground groups could communicate and begin to form a community.

One of the earliest known BDSM groups was The Menlo Park School of Bondage founded in San Francisco in 1968. This group was founded by the owner of a fetish store called A Taste of Leather. This group later became known as Backdrop, which was the forerunner of The Society of Janus, which was founded in 1974 and still exists today. A man by the name of Bill Burns started the Bay area Female Dominant organization called the Service of Mankind Church in 1977, which was an off-spring of The Society of Janus.

In New York, The Eulenspiegel Society was founded by male masochists in the winter of 1971. Its name is a result of an excerpt from Theodore Reik's "Masochism in Modern Man" in which he quotes German Folklore about a masochist by the name of Till Eulenspiegel. The Eulenspiegel Society is the oldest and largest BDSM organization in the United States.

Throughout the 1970's and 1980's, S&M organizations began to appear across the United States. In 1986, Sex Educator Nancy Ava Miller founded an S&M support group in Albuquerque, New Mexico by the name of People Exchanging Power (PEP). The popularity of her group inspired Nancy to open up other chapters across the United States from metropolitan areas like Washington DC to more conservative cities like Buffalo, New York. The Washington DC Chapter of PEP was founded in 1989 and would later become the BDSM group The Black Rose. As was the case with The SM Society of 1920 Germany, the driving force that launched the majority of BDSM groups in the United States were males with submissive desires. Some men were indeed masochists but most were seeking loving female authority. Nancy Ava Miller understood this as she often sought females to head up her S&M support groups.

So just how did BDSM groups become pan-sexual organizations that cater to all expressions of the D&S lifestyle? A union between heterosexual people who practiced Female Domination and homosexual people who practiced S&M was formed in order to fight persecution. As homosexuality came out of the closet and many Gays and Lesbians fought for the legal right to practice their sexuality without persecution, the homosexual community developed into a mighty political and legal force in the free world. People who practiced S&M began to feel like more of an island. To protect themselves from legal persecution, many heterosexual D&Sers joined Gay and Lesbian S&Mers in order to have the legal protection to meet and practice their alternative lifestyle. Today, most BDSM organizations are big tents that welcome all expressions of sexuality where one partner is dominant and the other is submissive. Pan-sexual BDSM groups exist in almost every major US city, providing workshops and education to people who are interested in learning how to practice a safe, sane and consensual form of Sadomasochism (S&M), Bondage and Domination (B&D) and Dominance and submission (D&S).

The advantages of pan-sexual BDSM groups are the vast educational resources and hands on experience they make available to their membership as well as the sense of community they provide to those who feel as outcasts to the norm of society due to their sexual interests. Pan-sexual groups teach tolerance as interacting with people who share ones overall interests, yet live a different lifestyle, can help change harmful attitudes about misunderstood lifestyles and thus cause people to be non-judgmental and less critical of those who have a different sexual orientation. Pan-sexual BDSM groups form a tight-knit world-wide community that assists each other in their exploration of human sexuality as well as forming a strong defense against outside forces that would seek to limit their personal and sexual freedom. There is strength in numbers and the networking of different BDSM groups provide that sense of community and security.

The biggest negative of these pan-sexual BDSM groups, as far as Female Domination is concerned, is that when a woman is in the process of overcoming her sexual inhibitions and as her dominant nature is beginning to come alive, the shock of witnessing such a smorgasbord of sexuality can be overwhelming and can in fact de-motivate the curious novice to the point that she closes her mind to the entire FemDom lifestyle. As a woman is beginning to embrace the philosophy that women should be the dominant partner within a female/male relationship, the witnessing of men dominating women at a pan-sexual BDSM function can cause confusion and become a real turn-off to the budding dominant female.

While the education value of these groups and the wonderful sense of community they have provided to thousands of people (whom would otherwise feel helpless in their sexuality) cannot be overstated, there seems to be a common complaint from FemDom couples that such groups do not fit their personal philosophy. I can't begin to count the number of women who have remarked over the years how they feel uncomfortable in BDSM groups because they do not enjoy being around men who dominate women. While BDSM groups still provide legal protection and a vast source of education for FemDom couples when it comes to the safe practices of D&S and S&M, there does seem to be a desire among many FemDom couples to participate in an exclusively FemDom organization.

As we have noted, originally S&M was based on the lifestyle of a man submitting to a woman but somehow over the years the life of Marquis de Sade was given credit for this. Thus this justified men dominating women sexually as a recognized form of alternative sexuality. I must ask, what is alternative about that? Men had been dominating women for centuries. Nevertheless, it was men with masochist desires in search of a female sadist that launched what has become known as S&M and as women come into their natural dominance, I believe they will seek out exclusive FemDom organizations, which are beginning to appear across our society.

Sadomasochism takes on a whole different meaning when the female is the sadist. The image of a male sadist causes fear among the masses as sadistic serial killers, ruthless dictators like Adolph Hitler and violent sex offenders have plagued humankind throughout history and has taken hold on the psyche of society. That is why a large portion of the population freaks out at the mere mention of the term S&M. That is also why the majority of S&M organizations now refer to themselves as BDSM, Fetish or D&S groups. By putting the emphasis on the domination and submission and less on the sadism and masochism these groups sound less bizarre to the public.

However when the female is the sadist, the image is less intimidating and in fact, a large portion of the male population is not only not fearful but is in fact sexually aroused at the thought of a sadistic woman who sexually dominates a masochistic man. For the most part, sadistic tendencies are displayed differently in women than in men. Women tend to display sadistic tendencies through the imposing of disgusting tasks and moral humiliation.

Sadism within men is dangerous but some sadism within women can actually be beneficial. Men are naturally aggressive and are physically stronger than women. Strength and aggression are dangerous if not controlled. Add sadistic desires to a man who is strong and aggressive, and you have the formula for disaster. Maximum-security prisons and death row are full of males who could not suppress their sadistic desires and the pain they have caused on society is evident.

Society has been trying to develop a model where these men can be reached when they are children and thus re-programmed to be submissive and not aggressive. There are all kinds of pilot programs in schools (most developed my feminists) to teach young boys to be less aggressive. Most of these programs fail because being aggressive is a part of being a boy. But if these boys can be taught and encouraged to be submissive to the female gender and to view the female gender with respect and admiration, studies show they stand a great chance of growing up to be law abiding and less violent.

Boys left undisciplined, tend to gravitate to violent and sadistic desires. Pulling the wings off of butterflies or burning grasshoppers with the reflection of the sun off a piece of glass is common mischievous behavior from boys. Look at how many boys get in trouble in grade school for pulling the hair of a female classmate. This is common in every elementary school because boys are basically the same everywhere. Something is within the male to be violent and mischievous and that natural aggression must be fettered, harnessed and brought under control when he is a child or else society may be at risk when he becomes a two hundred pound young man.

Fortunately, nature also places within males the natural desire to be submissive to the female gender. This desire keeps the desire to be aggressive in check. I believe the natural sexuality and feminine power of women touches boys at a young age and tames the beast within. Show me a society where women are kept at home and under cover and I will show you a society of young boys who are easily recruited to be violent. There is a correlation between the two. Where women are respected and admired, the males of that society will grow up to be more submissive and less violent, if these boys have a strong woman in their lives to cultivate and nurture those submissive seeds within.

Women are different. Girls tend to gravitate to the lovelier things in life. Yet, women possess the inner strength and the desire to be both nurturing and dominant. The problem has been that women have been programmed and kept down for centuries and have only recently been liberated to the place where they can effectively use their natural dominance for the common good.

The key for women is for women to overcome past stereotypes and past societal expectations. One way to overcome is for women to experiment with their own aggressive and dominant traits. While not as strong in women as in men, the ability to be aggressive is within women. Women possess the intellect and the moral character to lead but where they fall short to the male gender, is women allow the more aggressive males to bully them and intimidate them. This is understandable because on the outside, men are physically stronger. However, women are now beginning to understand that they possess inner power through their sexuality and feminine ways. Men cannot resist this and in fact, men want to submit to this.

If the female gender will free and exercise her aggressive and out going tendencies, when combined with her intellect, moral character and sexual power, she will be able to assume positions of authority in our society and lead with success. Men cannot resist (and does not want to resist I might add) a powerful, confident and dominant woman. All that women need do is exert a little outward aggressiveness to free her previously dormant dominant nature.

That is where D&S comes into play. What a Godsend the D&S lifestyle has been for women because it allows the woman a safe and fun arena to practice releasing her aggressive side. It gives the woman an outlet to be aggressive and yes, in some cases, sadistic. It allows her to exercise her dominant nature and this will help her not to be intimidated by the male gender when she is out in the world. A woman who is accustomed to seeing a man on his knees before her at home in her bedroom, will come to be at ease with seeing men under her authority and dominance in society as a whole.

Since men are physically stronger and usually larger than women, this affords the female the opportunity to be a little sadistic with her man in a D&S session. When combined with the knowledge of how to be sadistic in a safe and sane manner through educating herself, a woman can draw out more of a man's submissive nature and thus the experience can be beneficial and fulfilling for both the dominant female and the submissive man. A mild form of female sadism can be a liberating thing for a female as it is an exercise that can help her to experiment with and develop the aggressive and dominant side of her persona.

Female sadism is usually expressed more psychologically than physically. This is because of two reasons. Outside of D&S, a woman has to practice mental domination and mental sadism on men because men are physically stronger. Women use their intellect to get inside of the man's head to torment him. Women are great at spotting a man's weakness and exploiting it for her advantage. This demonstrates the inner desire of women to be dominant over the male gender. Some call this "a woman knowing how to push a man's buttons" and it is a reality. Women have been referred to as manipulative and cunning as far back as the Garden of Eden. But the fact is that women know how to dominate a man from a psychological edge. It comes natural for women to do this.

Even within a D&S relationship, women seem to prefer mental and psychological domination to physical domination. I must admit that I gain a lot more satisfaction in dominating a man using my mind than I do using a whip. To me, the whip is merely a tool. What I am saying and how I am getting inside of a man's head during a scene of corporal punishment is far more important than the actual physical act. Yes, I enjoy being physical because I get to exercise my aggressiveness but my real enjoyment comes from the mind games and the control I get from the mental domination.

In the end, S&M is really played out in the arena of the minds. All power exchanges are completed in the mental realm long before they manifest in the physical realm. The same goes for female sadism. Extreme female sadism is as dangerous as male sadism if the motivation is anger and hate. But within a loving Female Domination relationship, a little female sadism can be a productive thing for both parties involved.

The desire to submit to women is expressed differently within men. The core nature is the same but the expression of that nature will manifest itself differently within men based on a number of factors and variables. It is the submissive male that has masochist fantasies and desires. They originate from within the psyche of the male, not the psyche of the female. Masochism is a part of submission with some men.

Probably the most visited Female Domination website is "The Other World Kingdom". The OWK claims to be an actual place in the Czech Republic where women rule and men are their slaves. The OWK site shows images of women being sadistic toward men and from these images one can ascertain that OWK is not about loving female authority but rather a place of hardcore female sadism. The OWK sells videos and magazines depicting men being beaten, abused and enslaved. Why is such a site so popular with men?

To the male psyche, there is something about seeing a beautiful woman torturing a man. There is that black widow spider aspect to the female nature that fascinates men. Eric is a man with strong masochistic desires. He told me, *"Women lure us into their web with their beauty and sexuality and get us to drop our guards and surrender to them. Then once they have our trust, they toy with us, control us and dominate us. Men may rule the world in an outward way but women really rule the world because they rule men."*

Men explore the female nature in secret, behind closed doors, through books, magazines, movies, and now the Internet. Men worship women in secret and crave to be tortured by them and to watch other men be tortured by them. Men are still trying to figure out the complex Female nature as well as the sexual power of the Female. Some men esteem women as being superior to them, almost Goddess like. Eric described it this way.

"Female domination is the ultimate male sex fantasy. We want to see and experience the outward expression that portrays that which happens internally when we try to have relations with a woman. Women are

beautiful, sexy and lovely but they know how to manipulate us and control us but we have no answer for it. We cannot do anything about it for we are helpless. Why do women win our hearts and than as the Billy Joel song proclaims, "She casually cuts you and laughs while your bleeding?"

Eric is not alone in his feelings, as other men have expressed similar thoughts to me about the excitement they feel and the allure of viewing a beautiful woman expressing her sadistic side. Men get excited seeing the feminine body adorned not in soft lingerie but in wicked looking black leather. Or seeing a sexy woman with a pretty face, wielding a whip while flashing a devious smile. Or hearing the soft and angelic voice of a woman barking out authoritative commands or even spewing profanity or verbal humiliations. Or watching a sophisticated and refined lady administering a severe whipping or punishment on a man. All of these images are a contrast in most men's minds and this contrast does captivate men. These images do touch the psyche of a man and unleashes his submissive desires to serve the female. When a woman comes into the knowledge that her man sees himself as a slave to her beauty and feminine nature, she will begin to see herself in a similarly positive light. To men, women are complex and mysterious and that will always be the woman's advantage as she seeks to gain control over the men in her life.

Is the OWK a real place or merely a male sexual fantasy? Some say it is nothing more than a website designed to cater to the male fantasy of Female Sadism. From doing my research, I can definitely say that OWK is indeed a real place and I have interviewed dominant women, submissive men and FemDom couples who have actually been there. Lady Anai is a frequent visitor to The Other World Kingdom who has been featured on their site. When I interviewed her about The Other World Kingdom, she told me the following:

"First of all, opposite of what the majority of people in the US believe, The Other World Kingdom is very real. What I have in common with these sadistic women is the mere fact that I have a very sadistic side to me. Lest people don't understand this behavior; they think we hate the male creature. A woman who is a true believer in FemDom and female superiority MUST love the male creature or we could not train them to be what we want them to be. We work very hard to mold and train them. At OWK, all male creatures are given a choice of programs to choose

from. If they do not like it they are allowed to leave. In advance of their arrivals they are asked what their limits are. Most say, " I want no safe words or limits". If they don't like what they experience, that's their own stupidity because they WILL get what they ask for. If they go there as a prisoner for punishment training and are fed only bread and water, they have no right to complain. They know WELL before they arrive all the details of what their stay will be like.

The pictures are true on the OWK site. I've looked on in horror at these young girls 22-24 beat the living daylights out of slaves. I've even seen a Frenchman who was beaten so severely that a staff member and I ran out of the pub from the screaming. He was beaten so badly that he literally moved the stock he was in and his screaming had all of us run out of the pub. Needless to say, he left the next day. Everyone MUST remember men do ask for this. This Frenchman had previously been to OWK as a punishment prisoner and later wrote that he felt like it was a holiday. So this time they made sure it was no Holiday. He ONLY got what he asked for.

I will never forget a time I beat my personal slave whom I attended with for a visit, who happened to break out of the Queen's prison underground of the Palace. He was shackled legs and arms, and when Myself and one of the Guardesses went to check on him, he was not only gone from the prison but out of a locked Palace and the prison cell he was in was locked behind him. I found him outside after we searched the Castle and I started screaming as all the Czech's were trying to figure out how he got out. He was sitting there on a bench outside, cocky and smoking a cigar. I beat the living daylights out of him, I was so very angry that I think I beat him into the next week. Sadistic? Yes, but he deserved it. His cuts and bruises didn't go away for weeks.

The pictures and videos you see from OWK are extremely REAL. I've done a film for them. (The film was never released but some photos were in their quarterly magazine.) The women of OWK are young, beautiful and sadistic. The pictures men see on the site are the real deal. The women are that beautiful, they look that fabulous in their fetish outfits and yes, they are that sadistic. However, there is more to OWK than just women beating the crap out of men. I love going to OWK. I adore each and everyone who works there and hold the Queen in very high regard. She has done miracles.

Once that gate is closed and locked, you breathe a sigh of relief because you can be who and what you want to be without being judged. And, when I have been there a number of times without any other visitors, I love it even more. It is one of the most peaceful places I have ever visited. We have a great time, staff, My slave and of course Myself. My last visit My slave and I threw all the staff a "Lobster party," No one had ever tasted it there, I cooked the entire meal, which I do a lot of times when I and my slave are there with no other visitors. The joy and fun we had watching them and I have pictures which show all those "sadistic ladies" having a great time. This is not acceptable behavior for a Sublime Lady Citizen, but the Queen knows I do this at almost every visit. I'm a good cook and they love to taste the things I surprise them with. I gain great joy in watching them. In other words, the Kingdom is absolutely what you want to make of it. I respect OWK so much that I can have my choice. I can sit back on My butt and have it waited on or I can give back what I have gotten so much of from the staff. Believe me, there were times I did sit back and was pampered to the absolute umpth degree."

So how did Lady Anai come to find the Other World Kingdom?

"I first discovered The Other World Kingdom almost 4 years ago. I was out in Seattle double Domming with a very good friend of mine and her husband said, "let me show you this website." He said the place is fake and that put me on a high horse and I decided to find out on my own. Many people in America think that OWK is a "hoax" or not a reality. When people tell me that something is not real, yet I have many conversations with the people there, then being the type of Dominant that I am, I found Myself compelled to explore it personally. And the very fact that I support what OWK is trying to do and accomplish was a real attraction to me. I can validate that it is very real and quite remarkable and an experience that I recommend.

I had been all over Europe but never to the Czech Republic. I was accompanied by one of my submissives. I advertised in the "travel together" section of the OWK's web page and received well over 30 responses. I therefore screened everyone very carefully, and met one gentleman that seemed compatible. He flew to my location in the US to meet and get to know me. I made my decision when I was assured that we were compatible. We arrived via Czech airlines the day after we departed the US due to the time difference. Our driver wasn't there when we arrived, so we rented a car and drove the 2.5 hours. There was no one there that I knew when we first arrived. A couple from Germany came later in the week that was extremely pleasant. At that time, I knew not one bit of the Czech language and they knew no English. One of the Guardesses was so cute as she blurted out "you are so American." That was due to my southern accent. Nothing substantial happened that visit except I gained peace and contentment. I had lost my Mom shortly before this trip and OWK provided me with the comfort and peace I needed. I have been there six other times. It is my safe haven. I love the peace and beauty of OWK, the staff, the Queen and the small villages which surround it. I feel it's a very healing place.

My next trip was to one of their celebrations. There are hundreds of Dominants who attend the Celebration. Dominant women from the Czech Republic, Austria, Germany, Belgium, Denmark, Spain, Holland, France, Greece, Sweden, England and the US attend these celebrations."

My own fascination with The Other World Kingdom made me inquire into their origin. Is it truly operated by women just as their website proclaims? Lady Anai set the record straight.

"One thing I want to make clearly understood is that OWK is totally owned and operated by Dominant women. This place was started by one extremely smart cookie, and that is Queen Patricia. She took the ruins of a Kingdom from when the Russians let it go to squander and made it into what it is today. She's sincere about her endeavors and she has done one hell of a job doing it. I'm far from dumb and certainly a good businesswoman, but I could never pull off what she has done. The Other World Kingdom is a gated kingdom, which is referred to by many there in the Czech Republic as the Black City or The Black Kingdom. It is a gated city within itself. Once you are in the gates, the world shuts down around you and you can be who or what you want to be. I simply breathe a great sigh of relief whenever I know those gates are shut. It is operated solely by the Queen and her staff. The Czech government DOES NOT interfere.

Most of the Queen's female staff are in their twenties and like I said, they are intelligent, beautiful and sadistic. Men go there from all over Europe and the US to experience being ruled by these women. Wives will also send their husbands to be trained by these women. A wife can send her husband there to be trained to be her housemaid, her personal maid, a house servant, a waiter and even a cook. The wife can set the terms of the training and establish her husband's limits. Her husband will be treated as severely by the OWK female staff as the wife wishes. A husband can also be trained to be a Pony boy or a piece of human furniture, including a sitting pillow. A wife can even send her husband to OWK to lose weight and to get in shape. A week of hard labor with only bread and water to eat will cause a man to lose weight. They even have a program to train a man to be a whipping post if a wife wants her husband to be trained to be able to take more severe discipline. A wife can send her husband there to be punished if he has been bad or in need of an attitude adjustment. A man sent to OWK will definitely be better trained after his visit.

I want to get the word out to American women. I recommend OWK 100%. They will truly feel dominant there. Wait, let me really be exact. I recommend OWK 117,000.00 %. The first time a woman visits, I recommend that she take her favorite slave or submissive. Don't go alone. Firstly, the slave should pay for the visit. I would suggest letting him loose and let the Guardesses take over for a day. It is awesome to watch these ladies work their magic on submissive men. Next, I would recommend the Queen's prison. While you are being pampered, your male submissive will be slaving away or being trained. Finally, I also recommend keeping your submissive in close proximity to you. Remember that it's YOUR choice. Experience it all if you can."

Of course one does not need to travel to the Czech Republic to experience Female Sadism or BDSM. Many women don fetish outfits and many couples practice BDSM in the privacy of their own home. One must wonder how many couples in our society have a secret chest full of BDSM toys and fetish outfits? From talking to the owners of a leather clothing and BDSM toy store, the demand for such items is at an all-time high.

Wild leather outfits for the female such as leather corsets, bustiers, cat-suits, gloves, pants, chaps, skirts, halter-tops, leather bras, panties, thongs, high-heel shoes and lots and lots of boots are flying off the shelves. Likewise bondage equipment like spreader bars, wrist and ankle cuffs, body harnesses, collars, shackles, restraints, straight-jackets, stocks, bondage tables, bondage chairs and spanking benches are selling faster than an inventory can be maintained. In addition, male cock and ball (C/B) bondage devices such as cock rings, chastity devices, and ball stretchers have never been more in demand. Then there are the toys such as whips, paddles, strap-on harnesses and dildos that are selling like crazy. So obviously, a lot of people are practicing D&S behind closed doors in our society. With the invention of the Internet, people are ordering fetish clothing and BDSM toys who would never don the storefront of such an establishment for fear of being recognized.

When one looks at what is being sold at these stores, it is obvious that Female Domination is alive and growing in our society and many of these FemDom couples are incorporating into their FemDom lifestyle some form of Leather Sex. Leather outfits and whips for the woman and C/B bondage devices for the man are leading the way in sales at most of these establishments. That signifies to me that couples who practice Female Domination are driving the Leather Sex industry.

Nicole and Felix like to incorporate Leather Sex into their FemDom marriage. Both are athletes and they enjoy being physical. Nicole is tall, slender and muscular. Felix is broad and powerful but Nicole rules the roost in their house. Nicole describes one of their sessions.

"We like the rough stuff. Felix converted out utility room into a mini-dungeon. I took our old massage table and converted it into a bondage table. I have hooks in the ceiling and the walls and I have hooks in the side of the massage table. I like to place Felix in tight, restrictive bondage and then I will do C/B torture on him. I might attach a parachute device to his balls, stretch them as far as I can, then tie the chain hanging from the parachute to one of the hooks in the wall or ceiling. Or if he is standing, I will hang weights from the parachute and stretch his balls that way. I might attach nipple clamps to his nipples and attach clothespins to his stretched ball sac. I will then take my riding crop and lightly slap his penis and balls until he is moaning and groaning from the combination of pain and pleasure.

Next, I might remove the nipple clamps and twist his sensitive nipples. I've seen tears in his eyes from the sensitivity and pain this can cause. I may sit on his face and have him pleasure me while I twist the clothespins and flick his penis and balls with my fingers. I might scratch his skin with my long fingernails or I will lightly caress his body with one of my sharp and prickly vampire gloves. I may light a candle and drip hot wax all over his nipples and his genitals. It sounds cruel but he loves it. We are members of a BDSM group and I have been educated on how to play rough in a safe way. I never injure him, maybe just hurt him a little, but he is a big guy and he can handle it."

Most couples who practice Leather Sex practice a safe, sane and consensual form of BDSM. Although there are couples who like to experiment with Female Sadism and male masochism, these couples usually incorporate the use of a safe word so the submissive can stop a session at any time if he is in any real pain.

"Felix has a safe word and he will use it if I go too far. That is rare because I have learned how to read his body language and I will usually stop before he asks me to stop. We also like to do Pony Play and I have a saddle specially made for him and I will ride him around our house while I slap him with my riding crop and even nudge him along with the spurs that attach to my leather boots. We play rough but we have a lot of fun."

Nicole will be the first to admit, even with all the outfits, props and toys, the majority of FemDom is practiced in the arena of the minds. All of the hardware is just the icing on the cake. One does not need to invest in thousands of dollars of stuff to practice Female Domination. The attitudes of those involved are the key to a successful and fulfilling FemDom relationship.

Lee has sadistic tendencies and she likes to incorporate a more intense form of discipline as she trains her husband in the ways of obedience.

"I have controlled my husband for all of our 7 married years. My husband confided that he had always had female domination fantasies and he showed me some of the literature he had collected on the subject. I enthusiastically embraced the concept. Before we were married, we agreed that he would obey me at all times no matter what, unless doing so would endanger his or my life, or cause some other dire consequences, and that he would submit to whatever discipline I imposed.

He was a bit surprised I guess to find out that reality is different from his fantasies. He found out that spankings really do hurt; in fact, that discipline really hurts. Sometimes I wonder what world some guys are living in. They see a picture of a caned ass and think it looks cool, never stopping to realize what it must feel like. Well, ask my husband, it hurts! A cage is also no fun to spend time in; did he really expect it would be? The reality is that the excitement of the cage wears off very quickly since it is very boring and very uncomfortable. However, I believe that pain is a very effective correction tool. While I have compassion for my husband's suffering, I understand that the pain itself is short-lived but, hopefully, the lesson learned will be long remembered.

My main advice to women is that they should understand, really understand and embrace the fact that the pain they inflict will fade very quickly so they shouldn't fear inflicting it. A man's not made of glass. Stubbing a toe hurts, right? But a minute later the pain is gone, almost forgotten, but you have learned to avoid that table leg, right? Women happily accept their own pain, terrible pain (examples: child birth, monthly cramps), but does that crush us beyond repair? Of course not! So why fear giving a man the discipline he needs when the pain itself is momentary?

Although we live this lifestyle, we keep it very private. To all who know us, and actually for the vast majority of the time, we are the everyday married couple. We do things and live just exactly as most people do. There are, of course, a few aspects of the marriage that are probably unique. For instance, whatever I say goes, no exceptions. Also, the door leading to the basement has a deadbolt lock (to prevent snoopers) and even though we have no pets, there is a large dog crate down there.

Occasionally he will require correction. Lately we have been using a technique called Riding the Horse and I learned about it on the Internet. The horse is basically a bench with a beam. The idea is that he is made to stand with his male sexual organs resting on a pointed, but not actually sharp, wooden board as he straddles the beam. The board is just a little too high, so that having both feet flat on the floor is just too painful. His hands are usually handcuffed behind him and attached to the ceiling by rope, forcing his body to lean slightly forward, which exposes primarily the perineum and his organs to the pointed beam. Time becomes the big enemy, since eventually his leg muscles tire and he must adjust positions to relieve the stress. But that just causes new stress and pressure, so there needs to be another shift, and so on. It creates a downward spiral where shifting becomes more and more frequent. All the while his organs are being raked across the pointed beam.

When he gets to the point where he is shifting continuously, he is now properly Riding the Horse. It usually requires just under an hour for him to get to that point and during that build up time we have some very productive discussions. Once he is fully Riding, it becomes impossible to have a coherent conversation since his mind is pretty much occupied. Sometimes I have him wear high heels, which both increases his discomfort, and makes a really great sound. The time he is made to ride depends upon the infraction being corrected. The pain level is obviously intense which is, of course, the point. A session on the Horse makes him very penitent.

By the way, I recently began introducing him to the idea of cuckolding. He put up a bit of fuss (for him) at first, but a session on the Horse can be very persuasive. The great thing about the Horse is that it requires hardly any effort from me. Time and weight, physics if you will, do all the work. In fact, the only effort required from me is to make it stop, and I have all the time it takes. We also use other punishments, but the Horse is fast becoming my preferred correction instrument.

I never understand why women are so resistant to considering dominating their marriage. I've read that some women think it is too much trouble or too weird; and it would be if you had to cater to someone else's unrealistic fantasies. But the reality of it is much different from that, at least the way we live it. I use the analogy of having an automatic dishwasher: set it up and let it do the work. If something is not working right, take corrective steps until it's fixed. Really, while life is never that simple, it doesn't have to be super complicated either. I fully endorse women making their men be useful, productive, labor-saving joys to love and cherish! If their men are predisposed that way, even better!"

Leather Sex and S&M are merely additional expressions of the male desire to submit to the female and the female desire to dominate her man. Some couples enjoy having intense BDSM scenes, as that is what draws out more of a man's submissive nature and more of a woman's dominant nature. While the majority of FemDom couples do not engage in extreme Sadomasochism activities, there are couples who like to explore and expand the limits of female sadism and male masochism. As long as these couples are educated about such practices and as long as they practice a safe, sane and consensual lifestyle, the potential is there for them to bond on a deep emotional level.

Lee makes an important observation when she mentioned how some men fantasize about being a masochist only to discover the reality is a far cry from the fantasy. In the first chapter of this book, Jeremy shared his story about how he was obsessed with female sadism and male masochism. Jeremy became sexually aroused when he read the "Kalmann Diaries" which was a series of fictional articles about female sadism that appeared in Club Magazine back in the early 1980's. As a result of these erotic articles, Jeremy became convinced that he needed to experience male masochism to a sadistic female. He became obsessed with his desire to such an extreme that he put his dreams and his life on hold for years while he sought sexual and submissive fulfillment. Then once he found the sadistic woman of his dreams, he quickly discovered that the reality of being severely whipped and abused was not pleasurable but instead was painful and unfulfilling. Jeremy discovered that he was not really a masochist after all. He only thought he was.

A couple of chapters ago we met Darren and he told of his real life experience of becoming his wife's 24/7 slave. Darren is of the sexual and emotional make-up that he finds fulfillment in such an advanced FemDom relationship. Yet, he is quick to point out how difficult and how challenging such a life can be in reality. Most men would not want such a life, no matter how aroused they may become when they read erotic stories of female sadism and male masochism. The fact of the matter is that while a lot of men want to be dominated and brought under the authority of a loving female, most men could not handle being a real masochist to a sadistic woman. They may think they want to be a masochist because they enjoy the fantasy but the reality is that most men would not enjoy being on the receiving end of severe D&S activities.

As Lee correctly points out, severe whippings do indeed hurt, being locked in a cage can be extremely uncomfortable, and having nasty things done to the genitals can be very painful. Lee is also correct by pointing out that when administered by an educated and skilled woman, these activities can be done in such a way as to cause no actual harm or injury. The couples that enjoy advanced S&M are usually educated and skilled so they can engage in intense and severe D&S activities in a safe and sane manner. Nicole and Felix and Lee and her husband are two such couples.

In my twenty plus years of practicing this lifestyle, I have met couples that were into female sadism and male masochism. Nevertheless, the majority of FemDom couples do not engage in severe activities. While their D&S sessions may be very intense and powerful, the main purpose of the D&S is not so much what occurs in the physical but rather the effect D&S activities have on the psyche. At the end of the day, the majority of S&M and D&S practices are a mind game and a power exchange that occurs in the arena of the mind. Female Domination is ultimately a sexuality that takes place within the creative world of the human psyche. Therefore, as FemDom couples experiment and explore each other's sexuality, it is vitally important that they remain rooted and grounded in reality.

Chapter Sixteen

Reality Check:
Staying Grounded with Female Domination

Can one desire too much of a good thing? (William Shakespeare, "As You Like It", Act IV, Scene I)

For what does it profit a man to gain the whole world, and forfeit his soul? (Mark 8:36 NASB)

As we have seen, Female Domination is a large umbrella with many forms, expressions and lifestyles. I have shared the personal and intimate experiences of forty different couples who have incorporated Female Domination into their relationships. Some like it soft and sensual, some like it hard and rough, some like it wild and trend setting, some like it romantic, some like it controversial, some like it primarily in the bedroom, and most like it both inside and outside the bedroom. Regardless of the flavor, most have claimed to have better marriages and relationship thanks in large part to the Female Domination lifestyle.

We have witnessed how Female Domination can build the bond of intimacy and trust between a couple. We have seen how FemDom can defuse arguments, relieve stress, transport sex to a higher level than just the physical, empower women in society, and inject excitement into the mundane tasks of life like household chores. We have seen how FemDom can satisfy the inner male child, build up a woman's self-esteem, add spice to the bedroom, re-ignite romance, and cause a power exchange within the female/male relationship. We have seen how society is evolving toward Female rule, one relationship at a time.

Female Domination is an exciting and fulfilling lifestyle choice. It has a way to dominate one's time and attention. This is especially true with men who have been seeking for loving female authority most of their lives. As men seduce the dominant natures of their female partners with their genuine submission, it is important that all parties stay rooted in reality. Men have a tendency to expect too much, too fast. Female Domination is an ever-present reality for many couples in our society. However, one's fantasies do not always translate over into reality. For the most part, Female Domination is not "The Kalmann Diaries" or "The Story of O". It is everyday people relating to each other with mutual love and respect. A woman needs more than a slave and a servant. She needs a life-partner who will make her life more enjoyable through FemDom.

A FemDom relationship needs to be looked at in two ways, the overall picture of the relationship and the segmented snapshots of the relationship that makes up the overall picture. The male need for loving female authority is the overall motivation and the big picture if you will. How this deep-rooted need within males is expressed and fulfilled requires the totality of the female character and nature.

On the surface, the submissive male is attracted to the outward expressions of the dominant female. The woman who acts like the Bitch, who is bossy, aggressive, opinionated and no-nonsense sends out the signal that she is indeed dominant and this outward expression attracts and excites the submissive male, especially in the sexual realm. Likewise, to some submissive males, the image or portrayal of a woman who is cruel and abusive to men attracts them because it represents dominance and authority. It excites theses males sexually because this exterior display of dominance signals that the interior of the female is one of dominance and power.

Terms like Female Domination, Female Supremacy, and Female Superiority were all coined by men, as they tried to explain their desires toward the female gender. So women are wise to capitalize by using those same terms. Words are merely verbal pictures. The right signal sent to the male mind will conjure up the programming that has gone into his subconscious since he was a child. Men create the majority of FemDom art, pictures and images to express how powerful women are in their eyes and how weak they feel in a woman's presence. These images represent what men are feeling inside. The poet and the songwriter use words and the artist uses pictures to express their inner feelings. So when a woman becomes that image by donning a fetish outfit or saying a term or using her voice in a certain manner, she touches the male submissive nature and triggers his feelings and desires, thus he becomes weak and helpless. Then the woman can interact with the man with all barriers and defense mechanisms down. Now she is free to interact with the man in a more meaningful way. Now true intimacy and bonding can take place between the woman and the man because she now can see herself as he does. She now sees that in his eyes, she is indeed a Goddess.

So I say to the ladies, please do not get offended by FemDom artwork, videos, or literature, no matter how graphic in nature some of these may be. Instead, look more closely at what is being expressed by the male gender. What are men trying to convey when they produce media that shows men collared and bound at the feet of a woman? Ask yourself, why are sites like The Other World Kingdom so popular with men? What do these pictures say about the male submissive nature?

If a woman will look closer, get over her prudish and self-righteous ways and examine the message more than the content, then she will gain an incredible insight into the male psyche. What is the underlying message to all of these expressions, regardless of the content? Is it not simply the male gender recognizing his need to submit to the female gender? Is it not the inner male child, crying out to be disciplined and trained by the female gender? Is it not the true nature of man breaking forth in his attempt to surrender himself to the female gender?

Love and nurturing is the flip side of the female authority coin. Men need love and nurturing for emotional health and social stability but these traits rarely touch the sexual and it is the sexual that is usually at the forefront of the male psyche. It is no different than the basic sexual attraction that men have toward women. A woman wearing a sexy outfit or showing some skin will attract and excite most males. Men will fall all over themselves to be with the sexual woman. At that moment of sexual arousal, men could care less about whether the woman is sweet or loving or nurturing. All they know is that they are under her power and are drawn to her because of her sexual power.

With the submissive male, a woman portraying a dominant personality has the same effect as the woman who portrays sexuality. The submissive male is attracted to both of these characteristics. If you were to have a room full of men, each at a different level in the development of their submissive nature and a dominant woman were to enter the room and interact with the men, how she would be perceived would vary based on the strength of each male's submissive desires.

If a woman would walk into this room wearing conservative business attire, the men would all notice her because she is a female but how they responded to her would be based on her outward portrayal and their inward nature. If she were to request something from these men (lets say something they did not want to do) in a meek and soft manner, some men would ignore her and some would respond favorably but reluctantly. But if this same woman were to enter this room radiating sexuality through her sexual attire that highlighted her female features, all the men would take notice and fall all over themselves to assist her. The sex drive would overpower the logical and reasoning side of the male mind and the men would respond to this woman by being controlled by their penis, as her sexual energy would be too much for these men to resist.

Now take this experiment a step further. If this same woman would walk into this room of males dressed in her non-sexual and conservative business attire but instead of making a difficult request in a soft and meek manner, she would instead bark out an order in a bitchy and aggressive tone, the submissive males in the room would become aroused and would respond to her sexually. The men who had weak submissive desires would be offended by her and refer to her as a Bitch in the negative. But the men who had strong submissive desires would be sexually aroused by her brazenness and they would view her as a Bitch in the positive.

Outwardly the submissive male wants to be dominated by the Bitch. Inwardly he wants both, the Bitch and the Nurturer. It's just that his sex drive and his submissive desires overpower him and he seeks the Bitch first. However, a woman is multi-dimensional with many sides to her nature. She can be the Bitch but she also can be the Angel. Men need both but to some men the sex drive and the desire to submit tends to want more of the Bitch.

Just as the marriage must be about more than sex, the FemDom relationship must be about more than just the Bitch. A healthy relationship must be built on friendship and compatibility. The submissive male must get to know and appreciate all the many moods and sides of the female. The male who only wants the Bitch is out of balance and does not truly understand the female. The submissive male needs to worship the female in all her glory. He needs to enjoy all of the characteristics of the female for only then will he be fit to be a valuable servant to the female. The submissive male must know the female to serve the female.

The submissive male needs the Bitch to discipline him and keep him in line but he also needs the Angel to love him and nurture him. It is the totality of the Female and her nature that fulfills the submissive male. Loving Female Authority is about both the Bitch and the Angel. The wise woman will use her sexuality and her outward dominance (aka The Bitch) to capture the submissive male via his sex drive and his submissive nature but for a lasting and meaningful relationship there must be that intellectual and social connection as well.

The female will most likely express both as that is her nature and this is good because the male needs both. If the proper motivation is there, it is all loving female authority and loving discipline. Being the Bitch might be the female expressing a more intense and aggressive side of her dominant nature but the submissive male needs that and is attracted to that. Thus, being the Bitch (no matter how severe) can indeed be an act of love as the woman is giving the man what he needs for submissive fulfillment.

A Female Domination lifestyle works best within marriage because of the level of commitment. There must be a deep level of trust, honesty, and commitment in order for a FemDom relationship (as well as any relationship for that matter) to thrive. A marriage is a covenant and neither partner should have the attitude that if things don't go their way, they can just up and leave. If they have this attitude, the marriage is doomed no matter if it is a FemDom marriage or not.

The vast majority of the time, it is the submissive male that introduces the Female Domination lifestyle to the wife. The male desires and longs to be dominated by his wife. In the beginning, his desire to submit to the woman is greater than the woman's desire to dominate and to be served. However, over time this changes and the woman's hunger to be in charge and in control will become as strong, if not stronger, than the man's desire to submit. Once this balance is achieved, the FemDom relationship becomes very fulfilling to both partners. It transcends any other kind of relationship as the bond of trust and love between the Dominant woman and the submissive man grows beyond what either ever thought possible.

Few women want a man to be a total doormat. The male needs to bring the proper balance to any relationship. Fantasies do not always translate to reality. The female is superior and the male should always treat her as such and should always strive to obey her and to serve her. But she also needs a friend and a life partner. A relationship must be about more than D&S. A man should not sacrifice the things that his wife or girlfriend loves about him at the altar of D&S. D&S will enhance the relationship but it cannot be the foundation of the relationship.

A woman needs a life partner whom she can share her goals and dreams with. She will need a friend that she can share her hobbies and interests with. Yes, the dominant woman calls the shots. Yes, some dominant women love to don leather and engage in D&S. Yes, the dominant woman needs to be worshipped and served by her man. However, she also needs stimulating conversation, a dinner partner, someone to have fun with, and someone to share life with. The man should be his Queen's friend, partner, lover, servant and slave. A woman needs all of this in a man.

One of the biggest misconceptions about this lifestyle is that a man must lose his masculinity when he submits to a woman. While some men want to be feminized and stripped of their masculinity, a majority of submissive men are still quite masculine. Many dominant women and dominant wives like to dominate a masculine male and they like to control a masculine male. What most dominant women dislike is a macho male, not a masculine male. There is a big difference. Dominant women like to strip a man of his macho ways and his male ego, not necessarily of his masculinity.

A man does not have to lose his masculinity to submit to a woman. He will have to humble himself and lose his male pride and his male ego. A Dominant woman will help him with this, as she will demand that his macho ways go by the way side. That is the good news. Once a man begins to submit to the woman in his life, she will help to develop his submission as his submission will feed off of her dominance and thus it will grow even stronger.

There are women out there that want their man to be feminine all of the time. They don't want to see any macho or manly ways coming from him, so they train him accordingly. There are also many women who like for their man to be manly in public. They may want their man to portray a manly image at times and a sissy and feminine image at times. Neither is right or wrong. It totally depends on what the woman wants and what the male submissive nature responds to favorably.

Few women want a man to be a doormat. Most women want a man that she can connect with on an intellectual level and every woman wants a man that she can share life with as her friend. The submissive man can fulfill this social need within a woman and still be in total submission to her. Women for centuries have fulfilled the social need within men and yet, were expected to be in submission to them at the same time.

Most women do not want a wimp outside the bedroom. What is a wimp? Being a wimp means being weak but women want that weakness confined in the relationship. It doesn't mean that they want their man to be weak in his interactions with others or in his ability to handle life's challenges. Dominant Women enjoy causing a man to surrender his will and his strength over to her by using her feminine power. It is a power exchange. He is humbling himself and consenting to the fact that she is the dominant gender and that she is in charge. Her feminine power and sexual energy causes him to become weak in her presence. Thus, he becomes a wimp in her presence. It has nothing to do with how big he is or how successful he is or how confident he is around others. It all has to do with how he relates to his Queen.

Life consists of decisions and fence sitting only leads to stress and uncertainty. Having a dual nature is known as being double minded and it is difficult to grow in life when you are double minded. The two minds will always be in conflict with each other and you will have many internal struggles. Double mindedness causes a person to make decisions only half way and thus goals and accomplishment are never fully achieved. If a man wants to experience true submission to a woman, then he must lay aside his male pride and humble himself by submitting to his Queen. Once she begins to take charge, the man must allow her. It is not always easy, even for a submissive male, to yield his will over to the will of his partner. This is especially true when the woman makes a decision that the man does not agree with. At such times, this is where a man's commitment to his Queen and this lifestyle comes into play. The submissive male still has a freewill and he is free to be difficult and macho toward his Queen but such an attitude will never bring him submissive fulfillment.

Submission is a desire but it is also a decision. The human will decides which force within him will win. The more a man submits to a woman, the stronger that desire to submit to women will grow and thus it will become easier to submit. The sooner a man can come to terms with his desires to submit to the female gender and the sooner he makes the quality decision to choose submission when he dislikes the choices the female makes for his life, the sooner he will experience true submissive fulfillment.

It is easy for a man to say that he loves his Queen and he wants to serve her but if he spends all of his time fantasizing about his Queen in leather and in D&S scenarios, then is he really focusing on her needs? Now it is Ok for him to visualize her in leather and to recall how sexy and dominant she was during his last D&S session with her. However, he should use that image and that sexual excitement as motivation to serve her outside of the bedroom. The reality is that the submissive male must learn to channel that sexual and submissive energy into doing things that are pleasing to her and much of that will be in non-sexual and practical life situations.

A man can motivate his Queen to have more D&S sessions within the bedroom by serving her outside the bedroom. Then when she comments on what a great job her male servant is doing around the house or being attentive to her needs, he can open up to tell her how their last D&S session (when she wore that wild leather outfit) is helping to motivate him. By telling his Queen that he feels so in love with her and so submissive toward her that he cannot help but to serve her, a man is demonstrating the kind of attitude that will stir his Queen's dominance and she will want to play with her man more frequently. But if the submissive male nags her about wearing leather and having a D&S session, she will become disheartened and she will be turned off. That is reality. True submission comes from serving a woman without the expectation of getting something in return. It is Ok for the man to be honest with her about what motivates him, but he needs to serve her regardless of her mood. That is true male submission.

The male within a FemDom relationship must motivate his Queen by showing her the benefits to a Female Domination relationship. The wife who has embraced FemDom obviously enjoys some aspects of this lifestyle but it is important that the male allow the female the room to grow. The worst course of action for a submissive male is to push his Queen too hard into the D&S aspects of the relationship. That will only result in turning her off. The male with submissive fantasies and desires needs to focus on serving his Queen on how she likes to be served and that will provide her with the motivation she needs to perhaps don some leather and to wield the whip. Give to her what she needs and the male will in return be given what he needs.

The woman disciplines, dominates, and humiliates a man in order to fulfill his desires and in order to train him for her service. This lifestyle should enhance romance, not take away from it. A woman needs romance and not all D&S need be wild. Here are some practical ways a man can romance his Queen within a D&S setting:

Write her poetry when she is not with you and allow your submissive feelings toward her to be channeled from your mind to your hand as you write (or type) your heart felt feelings for her. Then when she is in your presence, get on your knees and recite your poetry to her.

Buy her gifts, flowers, or balloons and present them to her. If she dominates you some night, you should be enthralled with her the next day and you should go out of your way to express your gratitude by surprising her with a gift.

Here is one of my favorites. Draw her a bubble bath, light candles around the tub, undress her and bathe her. Pour her a glass of wine and allow her to drink it as she soaks. Then bathe her, dry her off, carry her to her bed and orally service her. She is your Queen and you are her servant. She is still in control and you are pleasuring her with a worshipful and submissive attitude. This is very romantic but is still an exercise in FemDom.

Take her out for a night of romance. Take her to dinner at a nice restaurant then take her dancing or to see a show. You could add some D&S to the evening as she can be wearing sexy lingerie under her dress and you can be wearing a pair of her panties or a cock ring or a chastity device under your pants. Lavish her with kisses and affection throughout the evening and I guarantee you if she is not too tired, she will want you to worship her body when you two get home.

Romance is the expression of a man's love toward his Queen. Love is an act of submission in a man. A man should allow his submissive energy and desires to be channeled in the expression of his worshipful and subservient attitude toward her. A man should humble himself and write poetry or a song for her. He should humble himself and serve her in intimate and personal ways. A woman needs balance in her life so the submissive male must be willing to balance out the hardcore D&S with plenty of soft and romantic FemDom activities as well.

Many men make the mistake of expecting constant D&S from their life partners. What they risk is driving their wife out of FemDom with the demands for domination. A submissive needs to concentrate on serving his wife and seducing her dominance with his submission. The best way for a man to stir those dominant juices in a woman is by submitting to her in a humble fashion. The worst thing a man can do is to nag a woman to be dominant. This lifestyle is about the woman's needs being met by the man. It is not about him pressuring her into being what he wants.

Most FemDom marriages are no different than any other marriage when it comes to the need for openness and the ability to communicate. In fact, the FemDom marriage is usually stronger because of the level of trust and honesty that has been established. The male who has introduced this lifestyle to his wife has made himself vulnerable and this will forge a deeper level of trust and intimacy between them both.

Just because the woman has taken charge of the marriage, that does not mean she is no longer allowed to communicate her feelings and emotions to her husband. It has been my experience that the submissive husband is more open to listen to his wife, as he now exists to serve her. Compare the submissive husband to the so-called macho or traditional husband and I think one will find the submissive husband is more eager to make himself available to meet his wife's needs. The submissive husband is motivated to serve and the D&S causes that more intimate bond. The dominant wife still needs that life partner to be there to express her disappointment or frustration. The woman who had a horrific day at work and wants to be cuddled and comforted by her husband should discover that the submissive male is truly interested and is honored to be there for her. Comfort and support is not dominance but submission. For centuries the submissive wife has been there to comfort and support her husband. Society has expected this out of the woman so now that the tables are turned, the submissive husband needs to be there for his wife to provide emotional support. The D&S sessions and FemDom activities should keep the husband centered and focused on serving his Queen, be that service domestically, sexually, socially or emotionally.

Some FemDom couples have small children at home. The reality is this. It's important that FemDom couples protect their children's innocence and not expose them to any kind of sexual or dominance activities between the wife and her husband. Most FemDom couples do an excellent job in allowing their children to grow up as normal children. They protect them from seeing or experiencing anything that, due to their age and immaturity, they are not equipped to emotionally handle. Therefore, most FemDom couples only play and practice their D&S lifestyle when the children are away or when they go away without the kids. In other words, they steal away to play.

I always recommend that FemDom couples with children purchase a trunk that can be locked, to put all of their D&S materials, tools, and clothing in. They should make sure it is locked securely and that they keep the key hidden from their children. Then when the kids go to visit relatives or friends, it can be playtime. It's not much different than all couples with children encounter when they want to have sex. A FemDom couple with young children do not want to play if the kids are just next door and there's a chance they might walk in on the festivities. They should make sure that there is no way the kids are coming home for the night, before the Adults open up the trunk and play.

Most FemDom wives with kids will testify that her playtime with her husband is much more important, since it will be rarer than couples without kids. The wife has to make sure that she gets her husband's complete obedience during this playtime, so she can re-enforce to him how she wants him to behave around the children. Plus, assign him all of the necessary chores. If the wife uses her playtime wisely, she can guarantee that her husband will show her the proper respect around the children and that he is an excellent father to them. If he ever does anything in rearing the kids that she doesn't approve of, she can address this during the next playtime. This will mean less arguing around the kids, which in turn means the kids will grow up in a peaceful and harmonious home.

A Female Domination marriage should encourage harmony in the home and the wife should deal with her husband and his behavior behind closed doors. The husband must show respect to the wife and never argue with her. He is to obey the wife in a reverent manner that will ensure harmony in the home and allow for a healthy environment for the children to grow up in. If the wife diligently disciplines the husband during their playtime, this will ensure an obedient husband and a loving father. Children will witness their father loving their mother, being a responsible citizen, doing chores around the house, and spending quality time with them. This is an excellent male role model for boys and girls. The children will also notice that Mom is the head of the household and this will be a great help to a daughter as she will be less inclined to fall into society's stereotypes of male and female roles.

Neither parent should ever push their sexuality or their lifestyle on their children, even as the children mature. Each of us are individuals and we must explore and discover our sexuality in our own time. Parents are obligated to share the facts of life with children and encourage a strong code of morality. However, they must never discuss D&S or Female Domination. Their kids will discover all of this naturally at the right time. A submissive male need not have a parent explain this lifestyle to him. As we have seen, his desires will develop and his nature will eventually come forth in due time.

In closing, let me reiterate the following. Both men and women are created in the image of God and thus are very valuable. Female Domination is not about the treating of men like dirt or abusing men.

Submission and slavery in this lifestyle is a willing submission and a willing slavery. It is the man laying down himself for his Queen and Goddess. It is an act of devotion to the female gender and a revelation within the man that the female is superior to him. Nothing is forced nor can be. It is a condition of the heart. Female Domination is all about Loving Female Authority and the continuing societal evolution toward Female rule. This lifestyle has enhanced many marriages and many female/male relationships.

Some say that Female Domination is only about sex, as if sex was not important. Sex is much more than a bodily function and the female domination lifestyle is much more than sex. Sex builds intimacy. Sex is about relationships and about marriage. Sex is two people becoming one. Sex is about romance and love. Sex is about commitment and bonding together. Sex is fun and God created it to be fun. Sex is important and Female Domination is about more than just sex. Female domination is sexual, mental, emotional, social, and spiritual.

It takes so much more trust and openness to share with each other the most hidden secrets and desires within one's soul. Too many married couples must hide their desires from each other. How sad that people hide their true selves from the one that they have chosen to spend their lives with. Female Domination is all about the sharing and the fulfilling of both the submissive male's desires and the dominant female's desires. When done in love, it is simply beautiful.

Appendix A

For Couples Only:
The Psychoanalysis of the submissive male

Ladies, if you want to get started in the Female Domination lifestyle but do not know where to begin, perhaps this exercise can assist you. When I met a new client/patient, I first took on the role of Dominatrix to arouse his submissive nature and to break him of his inhibitions in order to get him to open up to me. I would recommend that you prepare for your mental examination by first getting your husband or submissive male in a state of total submission.

Dress in your most sexy, yet dominant outfit. Have him get totally naked before you. Then dominate him to get him into a submissive frame of mind. If you do not yet know which triggers will stimulate his submission, then perhaps you could start with an erotic spanking. If he responds to verbal humiliation, than by all means verbally humiliate him as you administer the spanking. You could humiliate him about being a lowly male or humiliate him for having too small of a penis. Don't be afraid to be tough, play the bitch.

Then once you have him to that magical place of submission, change your demeanor. Become soft, hold him, kiss him, and love him. Find a comfortable bed or couch and have him lay with his head on your lap as you begin to softly question him about his past. When he gets into some real deep, personal areas, I would recommend that you use your sexuality. Allow him to suck your breasts and allow him to touch you in your most intimate areas. Allow his most deep desires to submit to women as a gender, and more importantly his desire to submit to you, to overwhelm him.

Keep encouraging him to open up more. You will come to understand him more than you ever thought was possible. One final word of warning. If anything ever comes out that you don't think that you can handle (such as discovering that he was abused as a child or something similar), encourage him to see a professional psychologist.

Below are the questions that I use to dive into the submissive male's psyche. It is important that you ask them in the exact order that they are numbered. Do not add or subtract from them. If you are the wife, when a question asks him about his wife, do not change it. Ask it as is. You are not only the wife, but you represent women as a gender to him. If he says anything that you don't like, do not scold him about it. Be accepting. You can deal with things that you do not like at a latter time. Also, do not rush through the questions. Take your time and probe him as much as possible.

The Psychoanalysis of the submissive male:

1. Do you remember the first time that you ever had a sexual orgasm?
(As you ask this question, lightly stroke his penis)

1a) Please explain this experience in detail.

2. How old were you when you first realized that you wanted to be sexually dominated by a woman?
(Give his balls a firm squeeze)

2a) Explain where you were and what triggered these feelings?

2b) Why do you think that you had these feelings?

2c) Would you say that the desire to be sexually dominated by a woman has grown stronger or weaker as you have grown older?

3. What kind of relationship did you have with your Mother when you were a child?
(Stroke his face and hair)

3a) Was she the one who would discipline you when you misbehaved?

3b) Can you recall any intense experiences that you had with her when she was disciplining you? Like was she ever extra forceful or physical with you?

3c) How is your relationship with your Mother today?

3d) How do you feel about your Mother?

4. Do you have an older sister (or older sisters)?
(Continue with face and hair stroking)

4a) What kind of a relationship did you have with her (or with them) when you were growing up?

4b) Can you recall any experiences with her (them) that you would classify as female domination?

5. Can you recall having submissive feelings toward any other women when you were growing up?

5a) Grandmother?

5b) Aunt?

5c) Teacher?

5d) Babysitter?

5e) Other female authority figures?

6. How about dreams? Can you recall having any dreams about being dominated by a woman?
(Play with his nipples)

6a) Tell me about these dreams in detail, as best as you can remember them.

6b) How old were you when you had these dreams?

6c) Did you ever have any re-occuring ones?

6d) Do you still have dreams about female domination today?

7. How about dating? Did you date a lot before you got married? (or before your current relationship?)
(Caress his chest and stomach)

7a) What type of a girl were you attracted to? Aggressive? Shy? Any certain hair color or physical build? Nice girls or ones with a bit of a reputation?

7b) Were you sexually active as a teen or young adult?

8. Describe in detail the first time that you had sex with a girl? How old were you? Was it a pleasant experience?
(Continue to caress his body)

8a) Would you say that you were the aggressor or was she?

8b) What type of sex did you engage in? You performing oral sex on her? Her performing oral sex on you? Both? Intercourse with you on top? Intercourse with her on top? All of the above?

8c) Would you say you have had sexual relations with Many women, Few women or just an Average amount over your lifetime?

8d) Why do you think that you slept with that many (or few) women?

9. How about fetishes? Do you have any?
(Place an article of leather clothing next to his lips and nose and allow him to smell and lick the material as you ask these questions)

9a) Does seeing a woman wearing leather turn you on? Why do you think that is?

9b) How about boots? Do you get excited seeing a woman wearing leather boots? Why do you think that is?

9c) (If he answers yes to 9a or 9b). Can you recall the first time you got excited seeing a woman wear leather? Did it make her seem more powerful to you? Did you feel weak seeing her wear leather?

9d) Do you like my leather? Would you like to see me wear more of it?

9e) Do you have a fetish to rubber, PVC, Lace, or any other material?
(If yes, repeat 9a through 9d only replace leather with the material that he has a fetish for)

10. Have you read much on the subject of Female Domination? What books or magazines did you read?

10a) Describe a story or two that you remember reading that really excited you?
(As he describes any stories or articles, give his balls an occasional squeeze, his penis an occasional slap, and his nipples a pinch to re-enforce the woman's dominance.)

10b) Why do you think these stories excited you so?

11. Did you watch many Female Domination videos or main stream movies that had female domination themes or scenes in them?

11a) Describe a couple of scenes that you vividly remember that got you sexually excited.
(Do the same as in 10a)

11b) Why do you think that these scenes excited you so?

12. What was it specifically about your wife (or current girlfriend) that attracted you to her?
(Softly kiss him on his face and neck)

12a) Do you consider her to be dominant?

12b) Who was more of the aggressor when you started dating? You or Her?

12c) Is it possible that it was her potential to dominate you that attracted you to her?

13. Describe your relationship with her today?
(Continue to kiss him)

13a) Who would you say is in charge of your relationship? You, her, or neither?

13b) Have you ever confessed to her about your desires to be dominated by a woman?

13c) How do you think that she would respond?

13d) If she was willing, would you allow her to rule over you and would you be willing to surrender yourself to her?

13e) What parts of yourself would you be willing to surrender over to her? Your sex life? Your personal life? Your finances? Your free time? Every area of yourself?

13f) What area of yourself are you least likely to surrender over to her?

13g) What if she demanded that part of yourself? Would you give in? Is it possible that you would surrender that area over to her?

14. Do you believe in God?

14a) If so, do you think that God is male or female?

14b) Why do you believe the way that you do?

15.What are your feelings about Female Supremacy?
(Squeeze his penis and balls very firmly)

15a) Do you consider females to be superior to men, men to be superior to females, or do you think that both are equal?

15b) Why? What traits make one sex superior to the other, or why are they equal?

15c) Would you like to be ruled by women?

15d) Would you like to be ruled by your wife (current girlfriend)?

16. Knowing both the male makeup and the female makeup, I can tell you that the only way for a female to totally dominate a man is through tough and even extreme measures. Would you be willing to endure these tough and extreme measures?
(If he answers yes to any of the following questions, give his balls a firm squeeze and say "It will give me great pleasure to make you endure this for me".)

16a) Would you endure corporal punishment, including spankings, whippings, and other tough measures? Do you desire this and if so, Why?

16b) Would you endure being humiliated by the female, including being belittled, degraded, and verbally abused? Do you desire this and if so, Why?

16c) Would you endure being denied sexual orgasms for long periods of time, while being made to give the female as many orgasms as she demands? Do you desire this and if so, Why?

16d) Would you endure having your genitals punished and even tortured? Do you desire this and if so, Why?

16e) Would you endure having the woman turn the tables on you and having her use a strap-on dildo to put you in your proper place? Do you desire this and if so, Why?

16f) Would you endure the humiliating act of having a woman urinate on you? Do you desire this and if so, Why?

16g) Would you endure being forced to watch your woman take another lover in your presence? Do you desire this and if so, Why?

16h) Would you endure having her dominate you in front of other women? Do you desire this and if so, Why?

16i) Finally, would you endure being her total slave, having to do all chores that she assigns to you? Do you desire this and if so, Why?

17. Do you trust me with this kind of power over you?

17a) Then tell me your most hidden secrets. Confess to me something that you have never confessed to anyone. Something that you have hidden deep inside of you. You can trust me. Surrender all of your hidden secrets to me. Confess all to me.

***This is where he might confess anything. It might be earth shattering or it might be something that sounds insignificant. However, it will not be insignificant to him. If it is earth shattering, it is important that you respond with understanding and love. Again, if it's something that angers you, you can punish him later. This is where he is most likely to break down. If he does, this is a positive sign. He is losing control of his will over to you. He is surrendering. Either way, it is important that you seize the moment.

Comfort him. Then once you are done comforting him, get him aroused by touching his penis and kissing him. Then mount him and allow him to enter you. Hold still and let him feel the warmth and the pleasure of you. Tell him that you love him. Then before the pleasure gets too good for him, withdraw him from you. Give his penis and balls a firm squeeze, look him in the eyes, and say to him something like the following:

"My Dear, I know that you have searched your entire life to find your rightful place, which is to be in complete submission to a woman. Well, your search is over. I am here and I am here to stay. I want you to surrender all to me. Your mind, your body, your finances, your male ego, your all. I expect you to be my total slave. You will have to endure much for me and I will always be expanding your limits. However, you can just let go and submit to my female power.

I want you to realize that women are superior to men, and that it's OK. It's your rightful place to be in submission to me. Don't fight it, just give in and surrender. You have looked and searched your entire life, but now I am here and your search is over. Just surrender and do all that I command. Do you understand?"

After he agrees, which I am sure that he will, explain to him that you are taking total control of his genitals and that his orgasms will be few and rare. Tell him that women are the ones who are to receive pleasure and men are here to give them pleasure. Then order him to humble himself and to take his proper place between your legs and order him to orally please you, and for as long as you would like.

Build upon this intimate experience by putting your new knowledge to work for your advantage and his well-being. I would love to hear your feedback. My e-mail address is: elisesutton@yahoo.com

Appendix B - Resource List

Female Domination Websites:

Elise Sutton's Female Superiority Site – If you enjoyed the book, you'll enjoy the site.
www.femalesuperiority.com

Akasha's Web - FemDom Erotica Stories
www.akashaweb.com

Camille Paglia – For Intellectual stimulation and Political commentary
www.privat.ub.uib.no/bubsy/nomore.htm

Goddess Club - A site for men who worship Supreme Women and for Women who want to be treated like a Goddess. Practical advice articles for both Women and men.
www.goddessclub.com

Real Women Don't Do Housework - Lady Misato gives sound advice to wives on Female Domination, Erotic Power, and Matriarchy.
www.geocities.com/ladymisato

The Other World Kingdom - An actual Private State of Female Supremacy
www.owk.cz

Women Who Administer Punishment (WHAP) - Advocates women take charge of their relationships using the techniques of female domination and domestic discipline.
www.whapmag.com

Female Domination Support Groups:

ClubFEM (Females Enslaving Males) - Houston based FemDom group with other chapters nationwide.
www.clubfem.com

ClubFEM-Maryland/DC - My close friend Ms Kathleen is the Head Mistress of the Maryland/DC chapter of ClubFEM.
www.clubfem-maryland.com

Disciplinary Wives Club - An organization whose purpose is to encourage the application of "Good Old Fashioned" spanking and other very traditional methods of discipline by wives and committed partners.
www.disciplinarywivesclub.com

Alice Kerr-Sutherland Society International
Box 12, Hastings, East Sussex, England
http://easyweb.easynet.co.uk/~~sartopia/akssi.html

Pan-sexual BDSM and Leather Groups:

The Eulenspiegel Society
P.O. Box 2783
New York , NY 10163
212-388-7022
www.tes.org

The Black Rose
P.O. Box 11161
Arlington, Virginia 22210
703-715-6507
www.br.org

Pan-sexual BDSM and Leather Groups (cont):

Boston Dungeon Society
119 Drum Hill Rd #152
Chelmsford, MA 01824
617-783-1386
www.bostondungeon.org

Knot For Everyone
P.O. Box 45
Fanwood, NJ 07023
www.knot4every1.org

The Society of Janus
P.O. Box 411523
San Francisco, CA 94141-1523
415-292-3222
www.soj.org

The Threshold Society, Inc.
12828 Victory Blvd. #282
North Hollywood, CA 91606-3013
(818)782-1160
www.threshold.org

The Triskeli Guild
PO Box 111
Bellingham, WA 98227-0111
www.triskeli.org

Recommended Reading:

Venus in Furs
Leopold Von Sacher-Masoch
Penguin Classics

Sexual Personae:
Art and Decadence From Nefertiti To Emily Dickinson
Camille Paglia
Vintage Books, Random House

The Mistress Manual
Mistress Lorelei
Greenery Press

The Art of Sensual Female Dominance
Claudia Varrin
Citadel Press
Kensington Publishing

The Sexually Dominant Woman
Lady Green
Greenery Press

Some Women
Laura Antoniou
Rhinoeros

Charm School for Sissy Maids
Mistress Lorelei
Greenery Press

Different Loving
Gloria and William Brame
Villard Books

Recommended Reading (cont):

The Governess Compendiums Vol I, II and III

The Governess Compendiums contain the very best of the twelve issues of "The Governess", republished in single volumes. Dozens of letters, essays, articles, poems, reviews, and intriguing archive material about the disciplining of young men at the hands of Female Guardians. Hard to find but available over the Internet. Try: www.januslondon.co.uk
(The Governess is listed under paperbacks – Loads of other FemDom literature as well)

The Natural Superiority of Women (Fifth Edition)
Dr. Ashley Montagu
Altamira Press

Zondervan Amplified Bible or The NIV Bible and The NIV Exhaustive Concordance
Available at your local Christian Book store

Finding a Professional Dominant Woman (Dominatrix):

Dominant Directory International (DDI) Magazine
www.ddimag.com
Strictly Speaking Pub. Co.
P.O. Box 8006
Palm Springs, CA 92263

Max Fisch Domina Guide - Best Source on the Internet to find a Professional Dominant Woman!
www.maxfisch.net

Quality and Professional Phone Domination/Counseling:

Ms Kathleen
By appointment only
Contact at domkathleen@yahoo.com

Ms Roxanne
(509) 324-3666
roxannesden@yahoo.com

Kink Friendly Psychologists and Counselors:

Kink Aware Professionals
www.bannon.com/kap/psycho.htm

Dorothy C. Hayden, CSW
209 East 10th Street, Suite 14
New York, NY
www.sextreatment.com

Fetish Clothing and BDSM Toy Stores:

JT's Stock Room
2140 Hyperion Avenue,
Los Angeles, CA 90027
www.stockroom.com

Stormy Leather
1158 Howard St.,
San Francisco, CA 94103
www.stormyleather.com

Versatile Fashions
535 W. Walnut Ave.
Orange, California 92868
(714) 538-0337
www.versatile-fashions.com

The Outer Skin (Pittsburgh, PA)
416 East 8th Street
Munhall, PA 15120
www.xtc2hot.com/outerskin.html

Fetishes Boutique
704 S. 5th Street in Philadelphia
(215) 829-4986
www.fetishesboutique.com

Purple Passion
211 West 20th Street
New York, NY 10011
Between 7th & 8th Avenues
www.purplepassion.com

Fetish Clothing and BDSM Toy Stores (cont):

Dream Dresser
1042 Wisconsin Avenue, N.W.
Georgetown, Washington, DC 20007
202.625.0373
or
Dream Dresser
8444-50 Santa Monica Boulevard
West Hollywood, CA 90069
323.848.3480
www.dreamdresser.com

Male Chastity Devices:

Neosteel Chastity Devices
http://www.neosteel.de
Neosteel GmbH
Bornstraße 8
D-57629 Malberg
Germany
Tel./Fax 0049-2747-912376

CB-2000
www.cb-2000.com
A.L. Enterprises, Inc.
141 Industrial Park Rd Suite 301 - 302
Henderson, NV 89015 (1-800-331-8005)

The Male Chastity Tube (or Remy Tube)
www.chastytube.com

The Carrara's Belt
www.chastity-belts.com

Male Chastity Devices (cont):

Tollyboy Belts
www.tollyboy.com
PO Box 27
Dronfield
Derbyshire
S18 8DN
England
+44.(0)114.237.5232

Mistress Lori's Chastity Devices – For those interested in advanced male chastity. Most designed to fit with a Prince Albert Piercing or a Frenum Piercing. Permanent Chastity Devices available complete with break-off screws.
www.chastitytube.com/device.html

Vanilla and Spice - So its Chastity you are interested in? Well lots to find here from which belt to choose to stories regarding chastity, reviews, etc.
http://yourkey.sufferware.com/chastconts.htm

Female Domination Art and Illustrations

Sartopia – The FemDom art of Sardax (who designed the cover for this book).
www.sardax.com

Eric Stanton Bibliography - Contains samples of Stanton's early work
www.geocities.com/elvis_paris/stanton/index.html

The art of Gene Bilbrew – Bio and samples of his work, including the covers for Exotique Magazine (1951-1957).
www.dushi.com/bdsm_art/work/bilbrew

Printed in the United States
25339LVS00001B/322-324

9 781411 603257